Accountability in the EU

Accountability in the EU

The Role of the European Ombudsman

Edited by

Herwig C.H. Hofmann

Professor of European and Transnational Public Law, University of Luxembourg, Luxembourg

Jacques Ziller

Professor of European Union Law, University of Pavia, Italy and formerly of the European University Institute, Florence, Italy and the Université de Paris 1 – Panthéon-Sorbonne, France

Edward Elgar PUBLISHING

Cheltenham, UK • Northampton, MA, USA

This book is a publication in the framework of PRIN project 2012 (2012SAM3KM) on Codification of EU Administrative Procedures, financed by the Ministero dell'Istruzione, dell'Università e della Ricerca, Italy.

Published by
Edward Elgar Publishing Limited
The Lypiatts
15 Lansdown Road
Cheltenham
Glos GL50 2JA
UK

Edward Elgar Publishing, Inc.
William Pratt House
9 Dewey Court
Northampton
Massachusetts 01060
USA

A catalogue record for this book
is available from the British Library

Library of Congress Control Number: 2016962573

This book is available electronically in the **Elgar**online
Law subject collection
DOI 10.4337/9781785367311

MIX
Paper from responsible sources
FSC® C013604

ISBN 978 1 78536 730 4 (cased)
ISBN 978 1 78536 731 1 (eBook)

Typeset by Servis Filmsetting Ltd, Stockport, Cheshire
Printed and bound by CPI Group (UK) Ltd, Croydon, CR0 4YY

Contents

Contributors

P. Nikiforos Diamandouros, PhD Columbia University, 1972, is an Emeritus Professor of Political Science and Public Administration at the University of Athens. He has served as European Ombudsman (2003–2013) and as founding Ombudsman of Greece (1998–2003). He is also a member of the Academy of Athens. His recent published work focuses on democracy, the rule of law, and the ombudsman in comparative perspective, as well as on the relationship between politics and culture.

Dacian C. Dragos is Jean Monnet Professor of Administrative and European Law and Vice President of the Research Council of the Babes Bolyai University, Cluj Napoca, Romania. He was EU Legal Expert for Albanian Civil Service reform; former Vice Dean and then Acting Dean of the Faculty of Political, Administrative and Communication Sciences (2008–2012); Marie Curie Fellow at Michigan State University (2005–2006); Visiting Scholar at Rockefeller College of Public Administration and Policy, SUNNY at Albany, USA (2002); Romanian Writers Association National Prize for legal research (2003); Scientific Coordinator of the Commission for drafting the Administrative Procedure Code of Romania (2006–2008) and Expert in the Commission for drafting the Administrative Code (2010–2011); Member of the Presidential Commission for Analysing the Constitutional System of Romania (2008–2009); Chair of the 'Law and Administration' Panel of the European Group of Public Administration (since 2010).

Ian Harden is Honorary Professor at the University of Sheffield, United Kingdom. From 1976 to 1996, he pursued an academic career, becoming a professor of law in 1995 and publishing extensively in the fields of public law, including the UK and EU constitutions, institutions and structures of accountability in the public sector and European economic and monetary union. Between 1996 and 2015 he worked for the European Ombudsman's Office, successively holding the positions of Principal Legal Adviser, Head of the Legal Department and Secretary-General.

Herwig C.H. Hofmann is Professor of European and Transnational Public Law and founding Director of the Robert Schuman Institute of European Affairs at the University of Luxembourg. He is author of numerous books and articles on EU public law and is on the board of several law journals.

Before joining the University of Luxembourg, he was lecturer in law at Trinity College Law School in Dublin. He has held visiting positions at many European, US and Asian universities including Sciences Po in Paris and Columbia in New York. He has advised EU institutions and national governments in various functions.

Roberto Mastroianni is Full Professor of European Union Law at the University Federico II in Naples, Italy. He graduated in Law at the University of Florence, and holds a PhD in European Law from the University of Bologna as well as a LLM from the Penn State/ Dickinson School of Law in Carlisle, Pennsylvania. Former Researcher of International Law at the University of Florence, he served as Référendaire at the European Court of Justice in Luxembourg in the Cabinets of Advocate General Giuseppe Tesauro and Antonio Saggio. Since December 2015 he has led the legislative office of the Italian Department of European Affairs in Rome.

Joana Mendes is Professor of Comparative Administrative Law at the University of Luxembourg. Until 2016 she was affiliated with the Amsterdam Centre of European Law and Governance (University of Amsterdam). She obtained her doctoral degree in law in 2009 at the European University Institute (Florence), with a thesis on participation rights in EU administrative law (*Participation in EU Rule-making. A Rights-based Approach*, Oxford University Press, 2011) and her masters degree in Public Law in 2002 at the University of Coimbra. More recently, she has been conducting research titled 'Unveiling EU Administrative Discretion: The Role of Law and Good Administration', a project funded by the Netherlands Organization for Scientific Research (NWO).

Bogdana Neamtu is Associate Professor in public administration and chair of the Public Administration and Management Department at Babes-Bolyai University, Romania. Together with Professor Dacian Dragos, she also co-directs the Center for Good Governance Studies, a unique research entity focused on advancing interdisciplinary research in areas such as administrative transparency, Europeanization of Romanian administrative law, sustainable public procurement, corruption, etc. She holds a PhD in sociology and has been interested in advancing empirical research in the framework of legal topics. She has published extensively on topics such as sustainable development, corruption and administrative transparency in the context of the former communist countries.

Christine Neuhold is professor within the Department of Political Science, Faculty of Arts and Social Sciences (FASoS), Maastricht University. Since May 2013 she has held the Special Chair of EU Democratic Governance.

Since September 2013 she has been the Director of the Graduate School of FASoS, Maastricht University. She is a political scientist by training and holds her doctoral degree from the University of Vienna (awarded in 2000). Before joining Maastricht University she held positions at the European Institute of Public Administration (EIPA) in Maastricht (1997–2000) and at the Institute of Advanced Studies in Vienna (2000–2002).

George Tridimas is Professor of Political Economy at the University of Ulster. He obtained a Bachelor of Arts in Economics (First class) from the University of Athens and a Master's and a Doctorate in Economics from the University of Oxford. Before joining the University of Ulster, he held positions at the University of the Witwatersrand in South Africa, and the University of Reading in England. His research interests are in political economy, public economics, and law and economics. His work combines theory, analysis of policy and applied econometrics and has a strong interdisciplinary element borrowing from history, political science and law. He has held various visiting fellowships in Canada, the Czech Republic, Romania and the USA. He is a member of the editorial boards of a number of academic journals. He has wide experience in teaching microeconomics-related course and has served on various university committees.

Takis Tridimas is Professor of European Union Law at Dickson Poon School of Law, King's College London, having joined King's College in September 2013. Before then, he was the Sir John Lubbock Professor of Banking Law at Queen Mary College, University of London (2004–2013). He also served as Référendaire (law clerk) to Advocate General Sir Francis Jacobs at the European Court of Justice (1992–1995). He was senior legal adviser to the EU Presidency (2003) and Chairman of the Committee set up by the EU Council of Ministers to draft the Treaty of Accession of 2003. He has acted as advisor or counsel to many public and private organizations, including the European Central Bank, the European Parliament, the European Commission and the EU Court of Auditors.

Jarle Trondal is Professor in Public Administration at University of Agder and at the ARENA Centre for European Studies, Oslo. He is also Honorary Professor at the University of Copenhagen. He has a doctoral degree from the University of Oslo, ARENA (2001) and his fields of expertise include the study of the European executive order and the nascent EU multilevel administrative system. The research focuses particularly on the European Commission, agency-like institutions such as EU agencies, governance by committees, and the multi-hatted role of national agencies. The research also focuses more generally on governance in turbulent times, such as how European government institutions tackle evolving and ambiguous internal and external constraints. Jarle Trondal has initiated and coordinated several research projects.

Anchrit Wille is Associate Professor in Public Administration at Leiden University's Faculty of Governance and Global Affairs. Her research focuses on executive politics, accountability, political-administrative relationships, institutional dynamics, democratic governance, citizen participation and political equality. She has (co)-authored several articles and books. In 2013 she published *The Normalization of the European Commission: Politics and Bureaucracy in the EU Executive* (Oxford University Press).

Jacques Ziller has been Full Professor of European Union Law at the University of Pavia, Italy since 2007. He holds a PhD (*doctorat d'Etat*) in law of Paris 2 Panthéon-Assas University and graduate and post-graduate degrees in law (Paris 2), political science (Sciences Po, Paris and Paris 2) and German language and literature (Paris IV). He has been Full Professor of Public, Comparative and European Law at Paris 1 Panthéon-Sorbonne University and at the European University Institute of Florence. He is a past President of the European Group for Public Administration (EGPA, 1995–1996) and President of the Societas Iuris Publici Europaei since July 2016.

Foreword

I am delighted to write the Foreword to this collection of chapters written to mark the twentieth anniversary of the Office of European Ombudsman.

The fact that such a wide variety of insights into the work of the European Ombudsman's office can be brought together in one publication is itself a tribute to the breadth and depth of activity of the office in its first 20 years. The different perspectives of academics from different disciplines, the former Ombudsman, and the former Secretary-General not only demonstrate the impact that the office has had on transparency, accountability and good administration in the EU, but also provide a glimpse of how that has been achieved by those responsible for leading the development of the office and its practices from its inception until recent times.

It is right that a work that marks an anniversary is primarily retrospective in its focus. The achievements of the office and its emergence as a key player in the EU administrative landscape of dispute resolution are significant. However, as I write this, I am conscious of the fact that the landscape of the EU itself is changing in a way which was not envisaged 12 months ago, let alone 20 years ago. The office cannot and does not rest on its past achievements. My strategy of ensuring the European Ombudsman's continuing relevance, visibility and impact requires flexibility and resilience to meet the new challenges which face us on a daily basis.

Since taking office, I have moved to insert the office even more strategically and dynamically into the life of the institutions and to see how I can use all the powers and tools available to me to deal with matters of significant citizen interest. The Maastricht Treaty, which created this office, encourages me to take the widest possible view of the role and that includes not just passively waiting for citizens to approach it but also proactively reaching out to them, or on their behalf, through strategic investigations and other appropriate interventions.

Having said that, each Ombudsman can build only on the foundations laid by her or his predecessor. In that regard, Jacob Söderman, as the first European Ombudsman, arguably had the most difficult task of establishing the office from scratch. I have the privilege of building not only on his initial achievements, but also on the great contribution of Professor Nikiforos Diamandouros, in whose time a comparable volume to this was published to mark the institution's tenth anniversary.

I am grateful to him, as I am to all the authors of the chapters in this work, for their continuing interest in the work of the European Ombudsman and for their thoughtful and thought-provoking contributions to this collection. I should also like to thank in particular Professors Jacques Ziller and Herwig Hofmann, for their editorial oversight.

Emily O'Reilly
European Ombudsman
Strasbourg, October 2016

1. The developing role of the European Ombudsman

Herwig C.H. Hofmann

THE EUROPEAN OMBUDSMAN – BACKGROUND

The European Ombudsman (EO) as established by the Treaty of Maastricht is entrusted with the objective of combatting maladministration by the executive branch of the European Union (EU).[1] The EO's mandate and powers are Union-specific but were developed against the development of ombuds-review in various jurisdictions since the early 19th century.

The European concept of an ombudsman was first developed in Sweden. Swedish constitutional legislation of 1809[2] created an ombudsman as representative of citizens' interests, who, in the absence of direct remedies against the Swedish crown, was authorized to take cases against public authorities to court on behalf of individuals.[3] In the twentieth century the idea of an independent ombudsman spread to many other jurisdictions. The concept of ombuds-review has since been adapted to a variety of different situations, such as public bodies adjudicating conflicts between individuals and certain sectors of public-interest industries, like insurance, or between minorities and the central government.[4] But today's EO is

---

[1] The EO now has its legal basis in Article 228 of the Treaty on the Functioning of the European Union (TFEU).

[2] The *års regeringsform* of 1809. See further: Hans Gammeltoft-Hansen, 'The Establishment of the European Ombudsman', in European Ombudsman (ed.), *The European Ombudsman, Origins, Establishment, Evolution*, Office for Official Publications of the European Communities (Luxembourg: 2005) 13–26 at p. 14.

[3] Address of Jacob Söderman given to the conference organized at the occasion of the 20th anniversary of the Ombudsman Office in Brussels, 22 June 2015.

[4] See for many such institutions the Finnish Ombudsman for Minorities (an institution established in 2001 by The Finnish Anti-Discrimination Act, www.ofm.fi); the Belgian Insurance Ombudsman ('Ombudsman pour les services des assurances Belge' set up under Article 302 of the Loi relative aux assurances of 4 April 2014, Moniteur Belge of 30 April 2014 or the Canadian Public Procurement Ombudsman (http://opo-boa.gc.ca/lrpa-rarp-eng.html).

probably most closely modelled on the Danish ombudsman. In Denmark, the office of the public ombudsman was established in the second half of the twentieth century as a body mainly empowered to fight against maladministration in the public sector and searching together with the administration to setting things right and settle the reason for complaint from the complainant's point of view. The key characteristic is thus a 'problem-solving function' with the objective of finding amicable solutions to problems between the administration and the citizenry.[5]

Already in the 1970s, proposals for the establishment of a European ombudsman were made.[6] These were taken up in the run-up to the Treaty of Maastricht by the Spanish government, who made the first attempt to introduce a 'European Ombudsman' as an accessible body helping to overcome the perceived distance and potential alienation felt by EU citizens from the complex administrative procedures needed for implementation of EU law.[7] This ombudsperson would be in charge of reviewing all implementing activities of EU law by both EU bodies and institutions as well as Member States.[8] When it appeared that the Spanish version was too broad for some Member States, the Danish government then proposed limiting the ombudsman's powers to review of EU institutions only. This was the proposition which gained majority support and subsequently entered into force with the Treaty of Maastricht.

Not by coincidence, the creation of the EO took place simultaneously with the creation of the concept of Union citizenship in the Treaty of Maastricht. In fact, the right to turn to the EO with a complaint about an instance of maladministration is quite explicitly linked to the concept

---

[5] Address of Jacob Söderman given to the conference organized at the occasion of the 20th anniversary of the Ombudsman Office in Brussels, 22 June 2015.

[6] For the history of the idea of establishing a European Ombudsman and a general overview over the office, see, e.g., Saverio Baviera, 'Les pétitions au Parlement européen et le Médiateur européen', *RMC* 445 (2001) 129–36; Simone Cadeddu, 'The proceedings of the European Ombudsman', *L & Contemp. Probs* 68 (2004) 161–80; Jacob Söderman, 'A thousand and one complaints: the European Ombudsman en route', *EPL* 3 (1997) 351–61; Alexandros Tsadiras, 'The Ombudsman', in Paul Craig (ed.), *European Administrative Law* (Oxford University Press 2006) 829–32.

[7] Anne Peters, 'The European Ombudsman and the European Constitution', *CMLRev*. 42 (2005) 697–743 at 699–700.

[8] Carlos Moreiro González, 'The Spanish Proposal to the Intergovernmental Conference on Political Union', in The European Ombudsman (ed.), *The European Ombudsman, Origins, Establishment, Evolution*, Office for Official Publications of the European Communities (Luxembourg: 2005) 27–37; speech by Jacob Söderman given to the conference organized at the occasion of the 20th anniversary of the Ombudsman Office in Brussels, 22 June 2015.

of EU citizenship, in such rules as Articles 20(2)(d) and 24 (third paragraph) TFEU, pursuant to which '[e]very citizen of the Union may apply to the Ombudsman established in accordance with Article 228' TFEU. This is also explicitly protected as a fundamental right in Article 43 of the Charter of Fundamental Rights of the European Union ('Charter'), which gives citizens and persons residing in the Member States the right to refer to the 'Ombudsman cases of maladministration in the activities of the institutions, bodies, offices or agencies of the Union'.

The Approach Taken by the First Three Holders of the Office of the European Ombudsman

For the first twenty years of its existence, three individuals have held the role of the EO and each has interpreted the role's mandate a bit differently. The approach taken by the individual office holder, particularly in such a personalized body as the EO, can be – and has been – quite decisive.

The first holder of the office was the former Finish Ombudsman, Jacob Söderman. He approached the office's mandate to review EU administration activities by first finding that the EO should deal with the concerns expressed by citizens about the Commission's role as the 'Guardian of the Treaty'. However, he also interpreted the mandate of the EO broadly to include also the growing number of European agencies. This approach was officially vindicated with entry into force of the Treaty of Lisbon. Article 228 TFEU now explicitly recognises the EO's mandate to supervise actions of institutions, bodies, offices and agencies of the Union. An explicit exception exists only for the Court of Justice of the European Union (CJEU) when acting in its judicial capacity.[9]

Söderman's approach was further to indirectly include Member State activity by requiring the Commission to provide information to individual complainants about a Member State's violation of EU law. One of Söderman's central contributions was ensuring that the institutions respected their obligations through a careful-but-forceful review of complaints. By mostly handling individuals' complaints, he embodied the EU-legitimizing role of the defender of citizens' rights and interests in the good administration of the Union. In this context, he defined maladministration through a soft-law guidance document entitled 'The

---

9 Article 228(1) TFEU and Nikiforos Diamandouros, 'The European Ombudsman and the Application of EU Law by the Member States', *Review of European Administrative Law* 2 (2008) 5–37 at p. 7.

European Code of Good Administrative Behaviour'.[10] Despite efforts to convince the institutions to adopt the soft-law code as a binding act of the Union, no EU administrative procedure act has entered into force. Nevertheless, EO Söderman successfully lobbied for the inclusion of Article 41, entitled 'Right to Good Administration', in the Charter. On yet another front, in order to overcome the shortcomings of a mandate limited to just the institutions and bodies of the Union, EO Söderman initiated a network of ombudsmen, including national ombudsmen and similar bodies throughout the Member States, which was designed to address complaints about implementation of EU law by Member State bodies.

The second EO, the former Greek ombudsman, Nikiforos Diamandouros, placed particular emphasis on the fact that the maladministration the EO should be expected to address is a far-wider and more encompassing concept than just illegal activity on the part of EU institutions and bodies. Rather, he added to the EO's already accepted role as defender of citizens' rights and interests the additional role of 'enhancer' of the Union's integrity, which required all ombuds-review to also focus on the manner and effect of EU administrative activity.[11]

Twenty years after the Treaty of Maastricht entered into force, the European Parliament (hereafter, the 'Parliament') elected a third person to hold the EO office, Emily O'Reilly, a former ombudsman of Ireland. She has taken what she describes as a more 'political' approach to her role; according to her, the EO's mission should be understood as reaching well beyond a simple adjudicatory role since 'a narrow description of this institution as a complaint handling [*sic*] body fails . . . to give adequate expression to its deeper role as an embedder of democracy, as a driver of change in a culture that still lacks the requisite levels of accountability and transparency appropriate to institutions crafted from the finest European ideals'.[12]

This politicization of the role of EO is an attempt to ensure more public visibility for the EO. Ombudsman O'Reilly seeks to use her office's resolution of individual complaints not only as a problem-solving tool for the individual complainants, but also as a 'driver of change'

---

[10] See www.ombudsman.europa.eu/en/resources/code.faces#/page/1, accessed 4 January 2017.

[11] See with further explanations Nikiforos Diamandouros, Chapter 9 in this book.

[12] Speech by Ombudsman Emily O'Reilly at the Conference at the occasion of the 20 years of the European Ombudsman, 22 June 2015, Brussels.

and a 'vehicle' by which to 'tackle wider systemic problems' within the EU.[13]

Challenges Arising from Defining the Future Role of the European Ombudsman

The ambitious tasks formulated by O'Reilly raises the question of whether the EO's Treaty mandate allows the EO to act as a 'driver of change' and to take the initiative to actively tackle some of the EU's 'wider systemic problems' as autonomously identified by the EO.[14] Is such politicization of the role of the EO and of the instrument of ombuds-review compatible with the Treaty's design and, if so, to what extent? How should the balance be struck between, on one hand, a reactive approach based on investigations of individual complaints, and, on the other, a more proactive approach based on own-initiative investigations? This chapter looks at these questions, first, by analysing the legal framework of EO activities, second, a look at the current nature of ombuds-review in the EU and, third, by an analysis of the accountability mechanism the EO faces in an attempt to answer the time-honoured question: '*quis custodiet ipsos custodes*'.[15]

THE LEGAL FRAMEWORK: THE OMBUDSMAN AS AN INDEPENDENT SUPERVISORY BODY OF THE PARLIAMENT

The role and possibilities of ombuds-review are defined by the constitutional mandate in the Treaty provisions. These influence the notions of the EO's independence and investigatory powers and the concept of maladministration and the consequences of finding it. Although interrelated, these elements will be addressed separately in the following pages.

---

[13] Speech by Ombudsman Emily O'Reilly given to the conference organized at the occasion of the 20th anniversary of the Ombudsman Office in Brussels, 22 June 2015.

[14] Speech by Ombudsman Emily O'Reilly given to the conference organized at the occasion of the 20th anniversary of the Ombudsman Office in Brussels, 22 June 2015.

[15] D. IVNI IVVENALIS SATVRA VI, at www.thelatinlibrary.com/juvenal/6.shtml, accessed 4 January 2017, line 347.

Independence and Relation to the Parliament

The EO is a position designed to both require and protect the independence of the office holder. The nature, extent and potential of this independence define the areas in which development of the EO's activities is possible, that is to say, the potential to develop specific approaches to the office. To look for such independence, one must start with the office holder's nomination and election. Each EO must be elected by the Parliament[16] 'after each election' for the duration of that particular Parliament's term of office, such that the terms of office for both the Parliament and the EO coincide. Thus, the appointment and reappointment of any particular individual to the office of EO is, to a certain degree, dependent on the political majorities in the electing Parliament.

Once elected by the Parliament, the elected individual must give his or her solemn oath, before the CJEU, to maintain his or her independence and impartiality throughout his or her term of office. Impartiality is a key term; the law requires the EO to 'be completely independent in the performance of his [or her] duties' and to 'neither seek nor take instructions from any government, institution, body, office or entity' in the performance of his or her duties.[17] Consequently, to ensure the EO independence, he or she can only be dismissed by the CJEU at the request of the Parliament. Nevertheless, if an incumbent would like to be re-elected for an additional mandate, he or she might well keep an eye on the likely majorities in the next Parliament.

Post-election, the formal relationship between the EO and the Parliament consists of the EO forwarding reports to the Parliament after receiving the investigated body's or institution's response to his or her initial finding of maladministration, and presenting an annual report to the Parliament on the outcomes of his or her enquiries.[18] These reports allow the Parliament, which is formally in charge of supervising the executive branch of the EU, to stay informed about maladministration and use those certain limited powers it has to force a recalcitrant administration to rectify a problem identified by the EO.

The Parliament also has a particularly strong role in designing the

[16] Article 228(1) TFEU.

[17] Article 228 (3) TFEU and Articles 6(2) and 9 of the Decision of the European Parliament on the regulations and general conditions governing the performance of the Ombudsman's duties, originally of 9 March 1994; (OJ 1994 L 113/15, as amended by Decisions of 14 March 2002 (deleting Articles 12 and 16) (OJ 2002 L 92/13) and 18 June 2008 (OJ 2008 L 189/25)) (hereafter, the 'Ombudsman Statute').

[18] Article 228(1) TFEU.

role and powers of the EO: Article 228(4) TFEU gives it the power to enact regulations and general conditions governing performance of the EO's duties, commonly referred to as the EO's 'Statute'.[19] The procedure applicable to this power is unique, in that it is one of the rare occasions in which the Parliament has been given the authority to legislate on its own initiative 'after seeking an opinion from the Commission and with the approval of the Council'.[20]

Reactions to Complaints and Own-Initiative Investigations – the Ombudsman as 'Inspector of the Executive'

The independence of the EO from executive bodies (and its link to the Parliament) is designed to permit his or her impartiality when addressing complaints about executive maladministration. Reflecting that independence, the EO is entitled to initiate an investigation either upon receipt of a complaint or on his or her own initiative.

For the former, the EO exercises his or her duties by seeking solutions to disputes between citizens, on the one hand, and EU institutions, bodies, offices, and agencies, on the other. Harden finds that '[a]lthough the focus is on the question of whether there is maladministration or not, the EO works in dispute-resolution mode, associated with the search for consensual solutions'.[21]

Therefore, ombuds-review contains both a review function and a redress function. This allows the EO to act, in many instances, as a cost-effective alternative to judicial redress.[22] In other instances, a complaint to the EO could be the only possible redress for an individual (e.g., where

---

19 The Parliament exercised that power, adopting the Ombudsman Statute.

20 The legislation in force at the time this chapter was written pre-dated the Treaty of Lisbon and was adopted in the form of the Ombudsman Statute with its implementing provisions (Decision of the European Ombudsman adopting implementing provisions, 8 July 2002 as amended by decision of the Ombudsman of 5 April 2004 (hereafter, the 'Implementing Provisions')). The European Parliament is the seat of the Ombudsman (Article 13 Ombudsman Statute) which is also the seat of the Ombudsman Secretariat (Article 11 Ombudsman Statute).

21 Ian Harden, 'Article 43 Ombudsman', in S. Peers, T. Hervey, J. Kenner and A. Ward (eds.) *The EU Charter of Fundamental Rights* (Hart 2014) 1121–50 at 1128; see also N. Diamandouros, 'The Relationship between the Principle of Good Administration and Legal Obligations', in C. Baudenbacher, C. Gulman, K. Lenaerts, E. Coulon, E. Barbier (eds.) *Liber Amicorum Bo Vesterdorf* (Bruylant 2007) 315–41.

22 Milan Remac, *Coordinating Ombudsmen and the Judiciary* (Intersentia 2014) 234–5.

procedural errors are challenged that result in non-binding acts which are not subject to judicial review under Article 263 TFEU). More generally, ombuds-review is always subordinate to judicial review, because the EO has no power to investigate facts that 'are or have been the subject of legal proceedings' at the level of either the Union or the Member States.[23]

The Treaty of Lisbon introduced, in the first paragraph of Article 228(1) TFEU, a formal obligation on the part of the EO to examine complaints by individuals. After first empowering the EO to receive complaints concerning maladministration, the paragraph goes on to say that '[h]e or she shall examine such complaints and report on them'. This last sentence leaves the EO no discretion as to whether or not to report on a complaint. Nevertheless, notwithstanding this obligation to assess a complaint, a complaint to the EO must still be admissible; the rules on the admissibility of such a complaint are outlined in the Statute, which provides, in relevant part, 'a complaint shall be made within two years of the date on which the facts on which it is based came to the attention of the person lodging the complaint'.[24] The assistance of the EO is subordinate to seeking 'the appropriate administrative approaches to the institutions and bodies concerned'.[25] Moreover, the EO may not receive complaints that concern 'work relationships between the Community institutions and bodies and their officials and other servants unless all the possibilities for the submission of internal administrative requests and complaints, have been exhausted'.[26]

The right to make a complaint rests with any citizen of the Union or any natural or legal person residing or having its registered office in a Member State.[27] To date, the EO has so far interpreted the Treaty's pre-conditions for access broadly: a complaint is only rejected as inadmissible if the complainant is not an EU citizen, is not physically present in the EU, or is not registered as a legal person in the EU. Questions regarding a legal person's place of registration or the existence of legal personality have been widely interpreted to include both private and public entities active in the Union. Moreover, even if a particular complainant cannot meet the strict requirements of the TFEU, the EO may, in its discretion, undertake its own investigation pursuant to Article 228(1) TFEU, as implemented

---

23 Article 228(2) TFEU.

24 Article 228(1) TFEU.

25 See Article 2(4) Ombudsman Statute. Moreover, complaints submitted to the Ombudsman do not affect time limits for appeals in administrative or judicial proceedings.

26 See Article 2(6) and (8) Ombudsman Statute.

27 Article 228(1) TFEU; see also Article 43 Charter, which uses the same terms.

by Article 3(1) of the Statute,[28] which permits the EO to review administrative activity for which an admissible complaint has not yet been, and may never be, submitted, and which may, or may not, involve European citizens. The EO's power to investigate without having received an admissible complaint[29] means that the institutional scope of ombuds-review is very broad. That fact may well explain the current disconnect in the general public's perception of the EO; people do not connect the EO with European citizenship – that is to say, they have decoupled the two concepts.

Second, the EO's task is to provide supervisory oversight over the administration in general, in order to enhance its accountability and to help to improve its quality, and is thus not restricted to responding to complaints but can act on its own initiative.[30] Harlow and Rawlings qualify the powers granted in Article 2 of the EO Statute to enter into own-initiative investigations as 'something of the quality of a "government inspector", standing halfway in-between administration and adjudication'.[31] The EO's own-initiative investigations are not only valuable in situations where there is a public interest in clarifying and improving a situation, but also in cases where individuals are unlikely to be in a position to launch a complaint.[32] His or her initiatives are a powerful tool, especially in cases where many complaints point to a more systemic problem, or in cases where individuals will generally not have the means or the know-how to complain, for example in the policy areas of immigration and asylum. The use of own-initiative investigations to overcome these specific problems, endemic in the EU system of executive governance and its multilevel administrative cooperation, appears sensible, particularly in view of the lack of other types of review available under EU law.

An own-initiative inquiry may also be launched by the EO on the basis of information provided by a so-called whistle-blower. Article

---

[28] For an overview of the decision-making practice of the Ombudsman's office with further references, see Alexandros Tsadiras, 'The Ombudsman', in Paul Craig (ed.), *European Administrative Law* (Oxford University Press 2006) 833–88.

[29] For example, the Ombudsman may decide to start his or her own investigation after having received an inadmissible complaint or having obtained information alleging maladministration in a form that did not qualify as a complaint.

[30] Anne Peters, 'The European Ombudsman and the European Constitution', *CMLRev.* 42 (2005) 697–743 at 711–12.

[31] Carol Harlow and Richard Rawlings, *Process and Procedure in EU Administration* (Bloomsbury Publishing 2014) 7.

[32] One such example is the Ombudsman's own-initiative enquiry OI/9/2014/MHZ regarding types of maladministration in the context of how FRONTEX ensures, in combination with national authorities, that joint return operations are conducted with full respect for the fundamental rights of individuals.

22a of the EU Staff Regulation,[33] for example, states that officials need to report possible cases of fraud, corruption, other illegal activity, or professional conduct that constitutes a serious failure to comply with obligations, and Article 22b permits, under certain conditions, those officials to provide that information to the EO.[34] Even before the Treaty of Lisbon introduced a broader definition of EU administration than the one contained in the Treaty of Maastricht, the EO undertook enquiries not only into the EU institutions, but also into all 'bodies established by the Treaties. This includes the Economic and Social Committee and the European Central Bank, as well as bodies set up by legislation under the Treaties, including agencies such as the European Environment Agency and the European Agency for the Management of Operational Co-operation at the External Borders (FRONTEX).'[35] The EO's oversight responsibility also extends to entities that have been established jointly by the EU and one or more Member States with the aim of furthering the Union's interest (e.g., the European University Institute in Florence).[36]

Investigative Powers of the Ombudsman

When investigating a complaint, the EO Statute grants the EO special powers; he or she enjoys access to information and documents held by European and national administrations and may require the institutions to supply any documents within a reasonable time, conduct on-the-spot investigations, and take copies of any relevant documents found.[37] Union

---

[33] Regulation No. 1023/2013 of the European Parliament and of the Council of 22 October 2013 amending the Staff Regulations of Officials of the European Union and the Conditions of Employment of Other Servants of the European Union, OJ 2013 L 287/15-62 (hereafter the 'EU Staff Regulation'). Any such information must be provided in writing and directed to either the individual's superior, his Director-General, the Secretary General of the institution (or persons in equivalent positions), or the OLAF (Article 22a EU Staff Regulation).

[34] Article 22b of the EU Staff Regulation further provides that, after a certain interval has passed, the official may also provide the relevant information to, *inter alia*, the Ombudsman. In practice, the Ombudsman either treats the receipt of such information as a complaint or opens an own-initiative investigation on the basis of that information. For a more expansive discussion, see Ian Harden, 'Article 43 Ombudsman', in S. Peers, T. Hervey, J. Kenner and A. Ward (eds.) *The EU Charter of Fundamental Rights* (Hart 2014) 1121–50 at 1139.

[35] European Ombudsman, Annual Report 2006, 36.

[36] For example, Decision of the European Ombudsman on Complaint 659/2000/GG of 24 November 2000.

[37] Article 3 Ombudsman Statute.

institutions and bodies are obliged to supply the EO with any information he or she requests, and to provide access to files (subject to certain exceptions for classified or sensitive documents).[38] At the EO's request, documents originating in a Member State are also to be provided after having informed the Member State concerned. Moreover, the EO has the power to compel Union officials and servants to testify as part of his or her investigation.

Recourse to the EO is also authorized for failure to publish information that must be published.[39] The Public Access Regulation is binding on the Member States, except where national laws on secrecy or other matters prevent disclosure, and the required information is to be provided via the Member State's permanent representation.[40] Where such information is not given as required, the EO is to inform the Parliament, which can then intervene itself. In addition, the EO may commission studies and hear testimony from experts external to the institutions and bodies.[41] These investigatory powers, when twinned with the EO's own-initiative investigatory power, make for a particularly powerful combination. Any politically-minded EO can use these tools beyond simple reaction to complaints. Temptation might be strong to act as a supervisory agency of its own making.

The Concept of Maladministration

EO activity can, according to Article 228 TFEU,[42] be undertaken 'concerning instances of maladministration in the activities of the Union institutions, bodies, offices or agencies'.[43] The EO has the functions of uncovering examples of 'maladministration' and 'mak[ing] recommendations to put an end to it'. The only other mention of 'maladministration' in the Treaties is in the first paragraph of Article 226 TFEU, which authorizes the Parliament to establish, without prejudice to the powers of other

---

38 Article 3(2) Ombudsman Statute.

39 Article 8 Regulation (EC) No. 1049/2001 of the European Parliament and of the Council of 30 May 2001 regarding public access to European Parliament, Council and Commission documents (hereinafter, the 'Public Access Regulation').

40 Article 3(3) Ombudsman Statute.

41 Article 3(2) Ombudsman Statute and Article 5(1), (2), and (4) Implementing Provisions (www.ombudsman.europa.eu/lbasis/en/provis.htm, accessed 19 February 2010).

42 See also Article 43 Charter.

43 Importantly, both Article 228 TFEU and Article 43 Charter make an exception relating to 'the Court of Justice of the European Union acting in its judicial role'.

institutions or bodies, temporary Committees of Inquiry to investigate contravention or maladministration of Union law. Such Committees of Inquiry also have far reaching investigatory powers.

The concept of maladministration, although mentioned in Treaty provisions, is not defined therein. It is however, decisive to identify the EO's mandate. It is decisive for identifying the types of misconduct the EO may investigate to which the EO may offer suggestions for improvement; thus determining the term's breadth and scope is an important undertaking. According to the first EO, Jacob Söderman, the essential quality of maladministration was defined in a legal manner aligned with the Finnish and wider-Nordic traditions of ombuds-review. During his tenure, at least, maladministration was said to occur whenever an EU authority, when acting in their administrative capacity, 'fail[ed] to act in accordance with the Treaties' or with European law in general. EO Söderman believed that maladministration could equally arise out of the case law of the European courts, including the so-called General Principles of EU law expressed by the CJEU and implemented throughout the Union by national courts.[44]

Today, however, the EO generally looks at two main criteria to determine if an act qualifies as maladministration. The first criteria is the institution's or body's compliance with the rule of law: does the act in question respect all procedural and substantive rights of individuals including, without limitation, the individual's fundamental rights?[45] In other words, the EO asks if the act or decision is legal. But, the EO's review in relation to this criteria does not extend to a review of the result of an exercise of discretionary authority undertaken within the limits of that institution's or body's specific legal authority: the EO can review the act or decision's legality but not the discretionary policy choices made by the administrative actors.[46]

Nonetheless, as Joana Mendes (Chapter 6 in this book) discusses, the broad nature of the EO's mandate should not, in principle, distinguish between instances of review where the administration enjoyed discre-

---

[44] European Ombudsman, Annual Report 1997, 2.2.1. See also Peter Gjerloeff Bonnor, 'The European Ombudsman: a novel source of soft law in the European Union', *ELRev.* 25 (2000) 39–56 at 42–3. Jon Marcus Meese, *Das Petitionsrecht beim Europäischen Parlament und das Beschwerderecht beim Bürgerbeauftragten der Europäischen Union* (Lang 2000) 190.

[45] See the definition of maladministration given in European Ombudsman, Annual Report 1997, 17 and 23 respectively. See generally also Paul Magnette, 'Entre contrôle parlementaire et "état de droit": le rôle politique du médiateur dans l'Union européenne', *Revue Français ScPol* 51 (2001) 933–48.

[46] So this covers cases of what might be referred to as *Rechtsaufsicht* and not *Fachaufsicht*.

tionary powers or not.[47] Maladministration can occur in all exercise of public powers. In this view, illegality implies maladministration but is not limited to it. Focusing solely on illegality would not sufficiently distinguish the EO from an (administrative) court[48] which might be regarded in violation of the *effet utile* of the Treaty provisions on the EO. Maladministration as a critiera takes into account the legality but not the expediency of a decision – a formal limitation of ombuds-review that should be taken into account, especially when the EO reviews discretionary decisions.

The second criteria the EO applies to determine if maladministration derives from a reflection on the very purpose of public administration: to perform administrative duties for the benefit of citizens and to enable citizens to exercise their rights.[49] For example, Article 12 of the Code of Good Administrative Behaviour expressly contemplates courtesy and responsiveness by EU officials towards individuals:

> The official shall be service-minded, correct, courteous and accessible in relations with the public. When answering correspondence, telephone calls and e-mails, the official shall try to be as helpful as possible and shall reply as completely and accurately as possible to questions which are asked. If the official is not responsible for the matter concerned, he shall direct the citizen to the appropriate official. If an error occurs which negatively affects the rights or interests of a member of the public, the official shall apologise for it and endeavour to correct the negative effects resulting from his or her error in the most expedient way and inform the member of the public of any rights of appeal in accordance with Article 19 of the Code.[50]

---

[47] See Joana Mendes, Chapter 6 in this book. See also Gregorio Garzón Clariana, 'Holding the Administration Accountable in Respect of its Discretionary Powers', in The European Ombudsman (ed.), *The European Ombudsman, Origins, Establishment, Evolution*, Office for Official Publications of the European Communities (Luxembourg: 2005) 191–209.

[48] For a more detailed discussion of this point, see Damien Chalmers, Christos Hadjiemmanuil, Giorgo Monto, and Adam Tomkins, *European Union Law* (Cambridge University Press 2006) 338.

[49] In the report of the first European Ombudsman, Jacob Söderman, 'The Citizen, the Administration and Community Law' at the XVIII Congress of FIDE (Fédération internationale de droit européen), Stockholm, 3–6 June 1998 (www.ombudsman.europa.eu/fide/en/default.htm, accessed 4 January 2017) this is described in the following terms: 'At the level of national systems of administration, the principle is formulated and expressed in different ways including, for example: service-mindedness, citizen-friendliness, the citizen as "customer" and the concept of public service. The basic idea which underlies all these notions is that the administration exists to serve citizens, not vice versa.'

[50] Article 12 of the Code of Good Administrative Behaviour.

While failure to abide by these requirements does not rise to the level of illegality, it may certainly qualify as maladministration. Thus, it is a perfect example of how 'illegality necessarily implies maladministration, maladministration does not automatically entail illegality'.[51] Therefore, maladministration cannot automatically be viewed as merely the opposite of 'good administration' as narrowly identified in Article 41 Charter but recognized more broadly as a General Principle of EU law.[52] Although the 'good' vs. 'bad' juxtaposition sounds intuitively compelling, it does not, in fact, hold up across all language versions of the Treaty.[53]

The limits of the concept of maladministration are thus extremely important in identifying the EO's mandate. They arise, generally speaking, from the distinction between the processes involving legislative and judiciary functions, on one hand, and administrative action by the executive branch, on the other. This limitation indicates that the EO does not have the right to intervene when a legislative act of the Union or a court judgement requires certain action from administrations. Action taken to comply with the law is not maladministration, even though it might be understood by the complaining party – and the EO – to be 'wrongful'.[54]

Overall, the purpose behind the EO's mandate appears to provide some potential recourse for those actions that, while in strict compliance with the law, still result in maladministration. As courts may only sanction actions taken outside the law, the EO's role is more nuanced. It can look at the manner in which compliance occurred, and find that, while the

---

[51] Nikiforos Diamandouros, 'The European Ombudsman and the application of EU Law by the Member States', *Review of European Administrative Law* 2 (2008) 5–37.

[52] See Herwig C.H. Hofmann and Bucura Mihaescu, 'The relation between the Charter's fundamental rights and the unwritten general principles of EU law – good administration as the test-case', *European Constitutional Law Review* 9 (2013) 73–101.

[53] Some language versions of Articles 226 and 228 TFEU, such as the English and French language versions, speak of 'maladministration' and '*mauvaise administration*', as opposed to 'good administration' and '*bonne administration*', respectively. However, in other language versions (e.g., the German version), this link is less compelling, with the wording in the TFEU referring with a more limited '*Missstände bei der Anwendung [des Unionsrechts]*' (Article 226 TFEU) and '*Missstände bei der Tätigkeit der Organe, Einrichtungen und sonstigen Stellen*' (Article 228 TFEU), which translate more to finding a 'wrong' or 'deplorable' state of affairs rather than the notion of good administration (*gute Verwaltung*) in Article 41 Charter.

[54] See, with further examples, Ian Harden, 'Article 43 Ombudsman' in S. Peers, T. Hervey, J. Kenner and A. Ward (eds.) *The EU Charter of Fundamental Rights* (Hart 2014) 1121–50 at 1133.

result was legal, it still constituted maladministration and thus the EO's mandate goes beyond what is sanctionable through judicial review.[55] But, the fact that the EO can review illegality as an instance of maladministration implies that the EO has the power to interpret the law and to classify the action accordingly. This power exists independently of judicial review, which suggests that positions taken by the EO do not have to comply with those of other Union institutions. It is possible that activity categorized by the EO as illegal will not be seen as such by the CJEU, or the inverse.

Such power to interpret the law, obviously, does not change the fact that an EO recommendation is not binding. Accordingly, the aim of EO investigations can go beyond an *ex post* review of grievances. The EO can also draft special reports on specific concerns of maladministration and focus on specific issues in the EO's annual reports to the Parliament. This *ex post* review is aimed towards proactively improving administrative procedures for the future, avoiding further instances of what the EO has classified as maladministration.[56] Maladministration therefore can imply unlawful conduct by an EU institution or body but maladministration can also occur where no illegality is found.[57] Due to the limitations of the EO's mandate, illegality in implementation of EU law by Member State administrations can only be sanctioned by a national ombudsman, court, tribunal or equivalent.[58]

The nature of investigations into maladministration – with a view towards ensuring the integrity of executive action when implementing EU law – explains why the various holders of the position of the EO have consistently developed their role in a strikingly similar approach to that of the manner in which the Court of Auditors expanded the concept of auditing and, thereby, expanded its role as an oversight body. Both EU bodies see themselves as being tasked with a duty to maintain the 'integrity' of administrative decision-making and implementation of EU procedures.

---

[55] See, e.g., T-294/03 *Gibrault v Commission* [2005] ECR II-635, para. 45 with clarifying reference to (Spanish language publication only); Joined Case T-219/02 and T-337/02 *Herrera v Commission* [2004] ECR-SC II-1407, ECLI:EU:T:2004:318, para. 101; and European Ombudsman, Annual Report 2006, 35 with references to the judgments of the CFI of 28 October 2004 in Joined Cases T-219 and 337/02 *Herrera v Commission* [2004] ECR-SC IA-319 and II-1407, para. 101, and of 4 October 2006 in Case T-193/04 R *Hans-Martin Tillack v Commission* [2006] ECR II-3995, para. 128.

[56] European Ombudsman, Annual Report 2004, 9.

[57] Case T-193/04 *Tillack v Commission* [2006] ECR II-3995, paras. 116 and 128.

[58] I.G. Dimitrakopoulos, 'Is an illegal Community act necessarily an instance of maladministration, in the sense of Article 195 EC?' *Review of European Administrative Law* (2009) 45–55.

Both the Court of Auditors and the EO have adopted approaches that exercise a broad contextual – and, to a certain degree, political – review of EU administrative activity. For the Court of Auditors, it started with a more encompassing standard of review, moving away from a purely financial audit towards a broader 'performance' audit. The current EO would also like to push for greater visibility and impact through high profile cases and more political activism, but the EO can only do so in the context of the EO's authority to examine instances of maladministration.

Consequences of Findings of Maladministration

If, as a result of ombuds-review, the EO finds an instance of maladministration, a number of possible steps can be taken. The effects of a finding of maladministration to a certain degree has an influence on the degree of review which the EO can, and possibly should, undertake. Once the EO finds maladministration, the next steps to be taken, and ultimate consequences, are provided for in Article 228 TFEU, Article 3(6) of the EO Statute, and Article 6 *et seq.* of the Implementing Provisions.[59] Article 228(1) TFEU provides:

> Where the Ombudsman establishes an instance of maladministration, he shall refer the matter to the institution, body, office or agency concerned, which shall have a period of three months in which to inform him of its views. The Ombudsman shall then forward a report to the European Parliament and the institution, body, office or agency concerned. The person lodging the complaint shall be informed of the outcome of such inquiries.

The Implementing Provisions go on to provide a more detailed and structured way of handling the matter. They obligate the EO, once he or she has found maladministration, to cooperate, as far as possible, with the institution or body concerned to find a 'friendly solution' to eliminate the maladministration and to satisfy the complainant.[60] Friendly solution proposals typically identify shortcomings in institutional behaviour, which are often remedied in accordance with solutions proposed by the institution itself and may take the form of a sincere apology or some type of compensatory action offered to the complainant by the institution.[61] In

---

[59] See, generally, Simone Cadeddu, 'The proceedings of the European Ombudsman', *L & Contemp. Probs* 68 (2004) 161–80.

[60] See Article 3(5) Ombudsman Statute and Article 6(1) Implementing Provisions.

[61] European Ombudsman, 'Putting it right? How the EU institutions responded to the Ombudsman in 2013' (2014) at www.ombudsman.europa.eu/en/cases/followup.faces/en/58401/html.bookmark, accessed 4 January 2017, at 5.

principle, the idea is that the EO facilitates finding such a friendly solution. But the fact remains that the measures available to the EO have no legally binding effect vis-à-vis the institutions and bodies concerned and do not generate subjectively enforceable rights in individuals.[62]

Where a friendly solution is not possible or the search for such a solution did not bear fruit,[63] or, in current practice, where the EO believes that such a solution would not be an effective instrument to achieve a systemic change in the public interest, the EO 'either closes the case with a reasoned decision that may include a critical remark or makes a report with draft recommendations'[64] to the institution concerned as to how the maladministration can be eliminated.[65] Within three months of receiving that decision or report with recommendations, the institution or body must submit its detailed opinion in response thereto[66] (e.g., the institution or body may accept the EO's recommendations and describe the measures it will take (or has taken) to implement them).[67] If there is no response, or the EO considers the response unsatisfactory, the EO may, but is not obligated to, draw up a special report to the Parliament, which may include recommendations; any such report must also be sent to the institution concerned and to the complainant.[68] The responsibility and competence of the EO is, thus, purely recommendatory; he or she has no power to order the offending institution or body to take rectifying action in the face of a finding of maladministration and his or her decisions do not bind any other EU actors (e.g., the Parliament or the CJEU).

Despite this, levels of complaints are steady. According to the EO's annual reports, the majority of complaints received by the EO are brought by individual citizens (87 per cent of all complaints in 2014).[69] This contrasts with the CJEU, before which the majority of plaintiffs in direct

---

[62] Order of the CFI in Case T-103/99 *Associazione delle cantine sociali venete v European Ombudsman and European Parliament* (ACSV) [2000] ECR II-4165, paras. 47–50; Andreas Hamers, *Der Petitionsausschuss des Europäischen Parlaments und der Europäische Bürgerbeauftragte – zu den außergerichtlichen Beschwerdeeinrichtungen der Europäischen Gemeinschaft* (Pfaffenweiler: Centaurus 1999) 174–5.

[63] Article 6(3) Implementing Provisions.

[64] Article 6(3) Implementing Provisions; see also Article 3(6)–(7) Ombudsman Statute.

[65] Critical remarks may only be included in accordance with Article 7 Implementing Provisions.

[66] Article 8(2) Implementing Provisions.

[67] Article 8(3) Implementing Provisions.

[68] Article 8(4) Implementing Provisions.

[69] European Ombudsman, Annual Report 2014, 17.

actions are legal persons. The overall number of new complaints, which were higher immediately after Union enlargement in 2004, has stabilized and now remains relatively steady. The first few years after Union enlargement in 2004 saw the highest number of complaints.[70] Since then the number of new complaints has consistently hovered around 2,100.[71] Moreover, consistently year over year, the percentage of admissible new complaints has remained at about 33 per cent. In 2014, for example, the EO launched 325 complaint-based investigations; the remaining 17 were own-initiative investigations. According to the EO, roughly one-third of the admissible cases have been settled by what the EO refers to as 'friendly' solution, i.e. without a formal report drafted by the EO.[72] Overall, however, the number of complaints to the EO appears rather low, considering a Union of over 500 million citizens and countless legal persons engaged in business therein.

An important difference between the EO's investigation (followed by a finding of maladministration) and judicial review offered by EU courts is that the EO has the power to, and regularly does, investigate the relevant institution's or body's follow-up compliance with her or his recommendations. The power to do so arises from the power to investigate complaints and make recommendations as well as produce reports to Parliament. Part of the complaint handling mandate is to see the solution of the issue through to its end. In fact, the EO tracks such compliance on a case-by-case basis and keeps statistical records thereof.[73] Where the EO finds cases of maladministration these are in fact regularly closed with some form of 'critical' or 'further' remarks by the EO .[74] According to a report commissioned by the EO in 2013 on the follow-up of the institutions and bodies of the Union to EO findings, the rate of what the report calls 'satisfactory follow-up' by the Union bodies and institutions 'critical' and 'further' remarks was above 80 per cent: 'The follow up to *further* remarks was

[70] There were 3,920 new complaints in 2005 and 3,830 in 2006 (European Ombudsman, Annual Report 2006, 40); 3,406 in 2008 (European Ombudsman, Annual Report 2008, 37); and 3,098 in 2009 (European Ombudsman, Overview Report 2010, 5). In 2010, the number of complaints dropped to 2,667 (ibid.).

[71] European Ombudsman, Annual Report 2014, 17.

[72] European Ombudsman, Annual Report 2014, 17.

[73] European Ombudsman, 'Putting it right? How the EU institutions responded to the Ombudsman in 2013' (2014) at www.ombudsman.europa.eu/en/cases/followup.faces/en/58401/html.bookmark, accessed 4 January 2017, at 5.

[74] European Ombudsman, 'Putting it right? How the EU institutions responded to the Ombudsman in 2013' (2014) at www.ombudsman.europa.eu/en/cases/followup.faces/en/58401/html.bookmark, accessed 4 January 2017, at 5.

satisfactory in 83 per cent of cases, whilst the rate of satisfactory follow up of *critical* remarks was 78 per cent.'[75]

The EO does not always limit his or her recommendations to those necessary to rectify the individual case. Rather, when he or she deems it appropriate, the EO may include recommendations for procedural changes, and even legislative changes, to prevent similar complaints in the future. For example, he or she might recommend that the institution should provide awareness or other staff training; redesign its internal procedures; or seek legislative changes to allow it to function better.

Distinguishing Ombuds-review from Judicial Review and Other Forms of Oversight

The definition of maladministration can result in overlaps between ombuds-review, administrative review, and judicial review. Some forms of specific administrative oversight with which potentially the mandate of the EO can collide include the European Data Protection Supervisor (EDPS) overseeing privacy and data protection by EU institutions and bodies and the European Commission anti-fraud office, OLAF, which has a broad, general supervisory mandate, which in the context of investigations of wrongdoing within the EU's administration can also cover instances of maladministration.[76] In fact, if the EO considers that certain facts have criminal law implications, he or she is obliged to inform the competent national authorities and, if appropriate, the OLAF.[77]

Overlapping responsibilities can cause duplication, inefficiency, confusion, and even divergent approaches to identical or similar issues. For example, the case *Commission v Bavarian Lager*[78] led to a Memorandum of Understanding (MoU) between the EDPS and the EO that establishes and coordinates their approaches to data protection and access-to-document rights.[79] Nevertheless, the EU's independent supervisory bodies, including

---

[75] European Ombudsman, 'Putting it right? How the EU institutions responded to the Ombudsman in 2013' (2014) at www.ombudsman.europa.eu/en/cases/followup.faces/en/58401/html.bookmark, accessed 4 January 2017, at 7.

[76] Regulation (EU, Euratom) No. 883/2013 of the European Parliament and of the Council of 11 September 2013 concerning investigations conducted by the European Anti-Fraud Office (OLAF) and repealing Regulation (EC) No. 1073/1999, OJ 2013 L 248/1.

[77] Article 4(2) Ombudsman Statute.

[78] Case C-28/08 P *Commission v Bavarian Lager* [2010] ECR I-6055, ECLI:EU:C:2010:378.

[79] European Ombudsman/European Data Protection Supervisor, Memorandum of Understanding between the European Ombudsman and the

the EO, are typically subject to a statutory prohibition against taking instructions from anyone in connection with their duties. Thus, the MoU between the EDPS and the EO, in which the latter 'envisages' taking the views of the EDPS concerning the correct interpretation and application of data-protection laws into account, probably reflects the outer boundary of self-limitation for the EO and all similarly situated bodies.

Regardless of the existence of agreements like the MoU, pre-existing arrangements will generally not be able to provide a complete solution to jurisdictional overlap, especially in situations in which multiple enquiries are simultaneously under way.[80] There are, thus, good arguments for having a central registry for recording all complaints currently or previously subject to investigation and all own-initiative investigations by all supervisory bodies. This would allow parties as well as institutions to be able to discover parallel concerns and coordinate efforts. Therefore, any such registry should be made available for inspection by all relevant authorities, subject to appropriate safeguards.[81]

Moreover, some argue that, despite the potentially counter-productive lack of consistency in their respective decision, duplicative or overlapping enquiries by different independent bodies may not be all bad.[82] Ultimately, the different enquiries may lead to an overall higher level of protection against maladministration and other administrative improprieties and to the achievement of the EU's goal of good administration, as different constituencies will be served. The type of complaints received by the EO differ from complaints made to other supervisory bodies and the courts. Not all matters subject to complaint before the EO are also eligible for judicial review before the CJEU.

European Data Protection Supervisor (2007/C 27/07), OJ 2007 C 27/21, illustrates the dangers involving the interaction of various supervisory bodies. *Commission v Bavarian Lager* dealt with the Commission's attempt to balance the right of one person to have access to information held by the Commission against the rights of other persons to protection of their personal privacy and data.

80 See particularly, Anne Peters, 'The European Ombudsman and the European Constitution', *CMLRev.* 42 (2005) 697–743 at 713–14.

81 The mere fact that parallel investigatory procedures are underway before different bodies need not lead to the termination or suspension of any given enquiry. It could, however, provide an opportunity for this, but only if that is consistent with the statutory obligations of the body concerned. Given that sensitive matters and information are likely to be recorded in any such registry, management thereof is probably best left to a small inter-authority committee, which is itself subject to strict confidentiality obligations.

82 Andreas Hamers, *Der Petitionsausschuss des Europäischen Parlaments und der Europäische Bürgerbeauftragte – zu den außergerichtlichen Beschwerdeeinrichtungen der Europäischen Gemeinschaft* (Pfaffenweiler: Centaurus 1999) 268.

The Ombudsman and the Integrated European Administration

One central problem to ombuds-review in the EU was already on the policy making agenda at the time of the creation of the EO: the problems of integrated multilevel administration in the EU. Although final decisions are either adopted by an EU body or by a body under national law, Member States authorities are in various cases authorized to apply EU law (e.g., in the field of competition law under Articles 101 and 102 TFEU). In fact, it is rare that the implementation of EU policy areas is organised in a way which does not involve some form of composite decision-making procedures. These are procedures in which EU and Member State administrations cooperate in preparation of the formal adoption of a final decision either on the national or the European level. With regard to allocating powers to address maladministration, this distinction of supervisory levels in the face of integrated administrative procedures is highly problematic.

As discussed earlier, when the Spanish government made its proposal in the drafting of the Treaty of Maastricht it was already acutely aware of this set of problems and had, as one of several alternative approaches, provided for the possibility of the EO to review action of Member State administrations acting in the scope of EU law.[83] But the mandate of the EO as introduced by the Treaty of Maastricht, now embodied in Article 228 TFEU, is more narrow: it only refers to the activities of 'Union institutions, bodies, offices or agencies'.[84]

EO Söderman, at the very outset of his term, recognized the lacunae created by his limited mandate; thus, he called for the organization of a network of national and regional ombudsmen (including the EO) to provide mutual support and the exchanges of views among its members. The resulting network (now known as the European Network of Ombudsmen, or just the 'Network'), improves the overall ability to supervise administrative activity concerning EU law throughout the Union.[85] For example, the Network provides the EO with the

---

[83] Carlos Moreiro González, 'The Spanish Proposal to the Intergovernmental Conference on Political Union', in The European Ombudsman (ed.), *The European Ombudsman, Origins, Establishment, Evolution*, Office for Official Publications of the European Communities (Luxembourg: 2005) 27–37, at p. 34 and Annex II at p. 249.

[84] As previously mentioned, Article 228 TFEU's mandate specifically excludes the CJEU when acting in its judicial capacity.

[85] For a more detailed discussion, see Carol Harlow and Richard Rawlings, 'Promoting Accountability in Multi-Level Governance: A Network Approach',

opportunity to transfer inadmissible complaints he or she receives to the relevant national or regional ombudsmen (and vice versa), so that those complaints can be handled by the ombudsman that actually oversees the administrative body responsible for the alleged maladministration. According to the EO's office:

> The European Network of Ombudsmen consists of over 95 offices in 36 European countries. The Network includes the national and regional ombudsmen and similar bodies of the Member States of the European Union, the candidate countries for EU membership, and other European Economic Area countries, as well as the European Ombudsman and the Committee on Petitions of the European Parliament. The national ombudsmen and similar bodies in the Network have each appointed a liaison officer to act as a point of contact for other members of the Network.[86]

In addition to transferring cases, Network members seek and offer advice, exchange information, and coordinate activities and investigations. Nonetheless, and notwithstanding such cooperation, the strict, organic distinction of every ombudsman's competence can still lead to difficult situations, particularly when complaints emerge from what are commonly known as 'composite administrative procedures' (i.e., forms of highly integrated, administrative-procedural activities in which national and EU actors cooperate to implement EU policies).[87] The use of such composite administrative procedures across a number of policy areas underscores the existing gaps or divergences among functionally different aspects of administrative organization. Unlike administrative decision-making network structures, supervisory and accountability mechanisms still mostly follow the traditional bifurcated system comprised of separate and distinct national and European levels.

The EO's oversight (i.e., limited to activities by EU-level entities) uses a traditionally organized supervisory structure that has difficulty allocating responsibility for procedural errors and finding adequate remedies for maladministration within such cooperative networks. The structure also has difficulty coping with the fact that the typical substantive cooperation in composite administrative procedures is the joint gathering and subsequent sharing of information. Thus, due to the EO's limited mandate and the

---

European Governance Papers No. C-06–02, 19–27 (www.connex-network.org/eurogov/pdf/egp-connex-C-06–02.pdf, accessed 19 February 2010).

[86] See www.ombudsman.europa.eu/en/atyourservice/enointroduction.faces, accessed 16 March 2016.

[87] Herwig C.H. Hofmann, Gerard C. Rowe and Alexander Türk, *Administrative Law and Policy of the EU* (Oxford University Press 2011) 928–36.

bifurcated nature of the supervisory system it contemplates, the EO's can only informally rely on the activities of national and regional ombudsmen throughout the Member States.

To address these problems, the Network devised a procedure through which national and regional ombudsmen can ask the EO to provide written answers to queries about European law, its interpretation, and its application to special cases. The EO either answers the questions him- or herself or, if appropriate, transmits the queries to the appropriate EU institution.[88] This so-called query procedure allows national ombudsmen to obtain information and clarification about how the EO understands and interprets EU law generally or in relation to particular complaints.[89] The latter can be important because national ombudsmen from Member States typically have a duty to review administrative activity in the implementation of EU law, which includes to ensure that substantive and procedural rights arising under EU law are fully respected within their national legal systems. The speed of the EO's response will, of course, be of the essence whenever such queries are received, which might not be feasible if the EO must frequently seek expert input by EU institutions (e.g., the Commission) and agencies.

Another manner to overcome problems arising from the EO's limited mandate is to participate in joint or parallel investigations. An example of this approach can be found in the EO's own-initiative investigation, OI/9/2014/MHZ, undertaken in cooperation with her national counterparts. The investigation concerned alleged types of maladministration in the context of the conduct of 'joint return operations' of immigrants to countries outside of the EU by the European agency in charge of border protection, FRONTEX, together with national authorities.

In her 2016 note entitled 'Reforming the European Network of Ombudsmen' the EO recently highlighted the benefits of parallel investigations seeing them as a key tool for advancing ombuds-review in an integrated European legal system with exchanges of information about pending allegations of maladministration, coordinated investigations into such allegations, and exchanges of investigative results, as well as coordinated procedural steps are indispensable in this context. Nonetheless, there appears to still be quite a bit of room for improvement in systematizing and formalizing cooperation mechanisms within the Network. If this cooperative Network approach were expanded, at least

---

88 The European Ombudsman, Annual Report 2006, 129.

89 Nikiforos Diamandouros, 'The European Ombudsman and the application of EU law by the Member States', *Review of European Administrative Law* 2 (2008) 5–37, at 26–7.

in policy areas with composite administrative procedures, the resulting coordinated ombuds-review would become a much more relevant form of citizenry protection than recourse to the CJEU. As everyone knows, its judicial review only has a one-way reference procedure[90] and certainly no possibility for coordinated action by the EU and national courts.

The Accountability and Supervision of the European Ombudsman

Supervisory authorities must, themselves, be subject to a certain amount of oversight and control to ensure their own accountability; they cannot, under the principles of democracy and the rule of law, be accountable to no one. Not surprisingly, the EO is primarily accountable to the Parliament, who exercises control through parliamentary supervision; ultimately, like every other EU institution or body, the EO can be held accountable by the CJEU. The CJEU's General Court has already exercised such judicial oversight, ruling on actions for damages brought against the EO pursuant to Article 340 TFEU. It has awarded damages for violation of procedural standards in cases of manifest error in the performance of the EO's duties when such error had a causal link to harm suffered by an individual that was subject to review under the criteria of Article 340, second paragraph TFEU (Article 288, second paragraph EC) in respect of an action for damages.[91] The type of unlawful acts that the Court has reviewed includes matters such as distortion of facts, failure to exercise diligence in duties of inquiry, and a violation of the obligation to act within reasonable time.[92] It is fitting that a body in charge of reviewing those same criteria in connection with others has been held to the exact same standards in the exercise of its functions. In that case, the Court ordered the EO to pay non-pecuniary damages for its violation of those principles.[93] Additionally, although initially pre-Lisbon, an action for failure to act was dismissed by that Court because it found that the EO was not an institution,[94] under

[90] Article 267 TFEU.

[91] Case C-234/02 P *European Ombudsman v Lamberts* [2004] ECR I-2803, paras. 31–70; Case T-209/00 *Lamberts v European Ombudsman* [2002] ECR II-2203, paras. 45–60. For further reading, see Peter Gjerloeff Bonnor, 'The European Ombudsman: a novel source of soft law in the European Union', *ELRev*. 25 (2000) 39–56.

[92] T-217/11 *Claire Staelen v European Ombudsman* of 29 April 2015, para. 336.

[93] T-217/11 *Claire Staelen v European Ombudsman* of 29 April 2015, para. 336 establishing the damages *ex aequo et bono*.

[94] On the basis of former Article 232 EC; see, e.g., Case T-103/99 *Associazione delle cantine sociali venete v European Ombudsman and European Parliament* (ACSV) [2000] ECR II-4165.

Article 265 TFEU the review now extends to omissions to all 'bodies, offices and agencies of the Union' including the EO. Actions against the EO for annulment under Article 263 TFEU or failure to act under Article 265 TFEU are, subject to the limitations otherwise stated in the TFEU, admissible.[95] The Court might also be called on to rule on the limits of ombuds-review and, thus, have an opportunity to provide its definitive, judicial interpretation of the concept of maladministration.

ASSESSMENT: THE OMBUDSMAN AS 'INTEGRITY'-BODY

This chapter outlined the constitutional mandate and legal framework of the EO with a view towards assessing future possibilities of ombuds-review within the EU. The EO is an alternative to judicial review ensuring that EU citizens and others residing in the Union can enjoy, to the fullest, their rights arising from the Treaties and Union law whilst being served by, as Article 298 TFEU now expresses, an 'open, efficient and independent European administration'.[96] By contrast to judicial review, ombuds-review commands no binding authority. Rather, the EO must rely on his or her powers of persuasion, in the form of publicized investigations of, and critical remarks or recommendations directed at, recalcitrant EU institutions, bodies, offices, and agencies, which are intended to 'name and shame' them because such critical remarks and recommendations are, to the extent permitted by law, made public. Also, to undertake his or her investigatory functions, the EO must often depend, at least to some extent, on the cooperation of the very Union institutions or bodies it is investigating. If the institution or body refuses to address any maladministration the EO finds, the EO must depend on the Parliament to take heed of his or her reports and actually follow up on unremediated maladministration.

The EO expands possible avenues of individual redress and stimulates systematic redress of administrative (mal)practice, but does so from a position of relative weakness. Independence and impartiality can thus be counted as amongst the EO's most powerful attributes. Arguably, it is the EO's ultimate lack of hard power – from a legal, rather than a moral or political point of view – that supplies his or her capacity to achieve positive results in a relatively simple and efficient way, even though the EO can never guarantee success. Maintaining what can be broadly referred to as

---

95 See, e.g., C-535/12 P *Olatra v European Ombudsman* of 6 June 2013.

96 Article 298 TFEU.

systemic 'integrity', as opposed to a purely legal review, is characteristic of bodies that are neither directly linked to any of the three 'classic' branches of power such as the EO. The EO's contribution to maintaining the 'integrity' of decision-making through their persuasive powers and their ability to raise public exposure and awareness through their reports and decisions. It is in these contexts that the EO occupies a unique position.

By handling individual complaints and basing proposals on real life cases, the the EO gains legitimacy, public standing and respect from the EU's institutions. The EO's mediation role in resolving complaint based cases in which the wrong becomes evident in an individual situation, leads increased compliance by EU institutions with the suggestions made by the EO. A high rate of compliance, if visibly achieved, can give credibility to the EO way of solving problems even in the absence of legally binding solutions and potential payments of damages. The decisive weakness of the complaint-based system of initiating ombuds-review, however, is that it is dependent on a high level of awareness among the European citizenry. Only if the citizens which can be affected of maladministration know of the existence, accessibility, and potential power of the EO as an institution, will they enter complaints. In that regard, more effort might be made by all EU institutions, bodies, offices, and agencies to promote the role of the EO. It might be unrealistic to expect the EU administration to embrace that task with great enthusiasm.

This is where the use of own-initiative investigations by the EO might have a place to raise awareness of the EO. They do however most good in cases where the individuals most affected by maladministration have no realistic chance of lodging a complaint, such as occurred in the case of refugees facing joint return operation administered by FRONTEX.[97] The EO's own-initiative investigations can also be a very helpful tool when the number of individual complaints indicates the existence of systemic problems in a certain field.

However, a systematic use of own-initiative investigations into fields the EO identifies as problematic (based on his or her own convictions rather than the volume of individual complaints) would require further scrutiny as to whether the advantages of such an approach outweigh the potential disadvantages. Potential constraints have to be weighed when devising techniques that would allow the EO to reach the highly ambitious goal of ensuring integrity and accountability within the Union's executive branch. Here, the EO would face a significant risk of being accused of

[97] See the Ombudsman's own-initiative inquiry OI/9/2014/MHZ regarding types of maladministration in the context of FRONTEX.

being politically motivated and acting indiscriminately, based on his or her own political agenda. The EO might even run the risk of being pulled into existing inter-institutional conflicts, which would be highly detrimental to his or her independence (or just the perception of his or her independence) and, thus, his or her impartiality. The risks of engaging in investigations that could result in a loss of status as an independent mediator between citizens and the EU administration must, therefore, be very carefully evaluated.

The big question, then, is whether taking on a decidedly political role limits, in effect, the EO's ability to conduct impartial enquiries, which is the basis of the EO's independence. Does taking on a more political role actually endanger the EO or risk accusations that the EO is just another policy 'entrepreneur'? If one accepts that the basis for the respect and legitimacy offered to the EO is his or her impartial mediating role and problem-solving capacity, the risks of undertaking a more political role are quite real. If, on the other hand, the EO's central problem is the public's lack of awareness of the existence of the EO, then headline-grabbing, politically sensitive investigations, which no other actors are able to undertake, may be an important tool in the EO's repertoire.[98]

---

98 See, e.g., European Ombudsman, Case OI/6/2016/AB opened on 26 May 2016.

2. The European Ombudsman: a resilient institution in a turbulent, evolving administrative order[1]

Jarle Trondal and Anchrit Wille

INTRODUCTION

One relatively unstudied development in the evolving order of the European Union's multilayered administrative system is the development of the ombudsman as a core institution of governance. At the national level, nearly all European Union (EU) Member States have introduced an ombudsman. World-wide, hybrid watchdog institutions have been created as 'satellites' of Parliaments[2] as 'review agencies',[3] and as 'integrity agencies'.[4] An ombudsman has certain characteristics, such as some formal independence; an ombudsman's main task is to assist with parliamentary control of the executive as well as to act as a guardian of citizens' rights. An ombudsman's powers are non-binding on the executive.[5] At the EU level, there has been a European Ombudsman (EO) since 1995. The multilevel nature of the EU system, we argue, is turbulent, and this makes accountability challenging, particularly since existing accountability mechanisms are imperfectly adapted to such multilevel turbulence. The

[1] This chapter was prepared for the European Ombudsman 20th Anniversary Colloquium, 22 June 2015, Radisson Blue EU Hotel, Brussels. We thank Nynke Kuperus for her research assistance.

[2] P. Wilkins (2015) 'Watchdogs as satellites of Parliament', *Australian Journal of Public Administration*, 75(1): 18–27.

[3] J. McMillan (2013) 'Commonwealth oversight arrangements – successes and challenges', paper to the Australasian Study of Parliament Group Annual Conference 2013.

[4] R. Wettenhall (2012) 'Integrity agencies: the significance of the Parliamentary relationship', *Policy Studies* 33(1): 65–78.

[5] A.E. Stie (2013) *Democratic Decision-making in the EU*. London: Routledge; P. Magnette (2003) 'Between parliamentary control and the rule of law: the political role of the Ombudsman in the European Union', *Journal of European Public Policy* 10(5): 677–94.

questions addressed in this chapter are how and why the EO has successfully developed its institutional capacity in the institutional landscape of the EU. What is the impact of the uncertainty and turbulence in the EU context facing the EO, in the way its accountability tasks are carried out? And, how can accountability be safeguarded through the EO when the EU administration is 'embedded in networks across levels of government'?[6] It is argued that the EO's turbulent nature and environment has contributed to – not hampered – the resilience of the institution.

Building successful public institutions is a continuing and long-term goal for the EU, especially in the uncertain conditions found in its turbulent, multilevel administrative settings. The EO has managed to take root and to be reasonably effective in delivering results, earning legitimacy, and developing resilience despite the existence of that multilevel, turbulent politico-administrative system. As an accountability institution, it serves as part of a wider accountability landscape, as we will show, that safeguards accountability as part of a wider political order.[7]

The EO was created by the Maastricht Treaty as part of the provisions on EU citizenship and became operational in 1995. The first EO, Jacob Söderman, was succeeded by Nikiforos Diamandouros in 2003. The third, and current EO, Emily O'Reilly, took office in 2013. Elected by the European Parliament (EP), the EO investigates complaints of maladministration of EU institutions, bodies and agencies, but also benefits from the power to initiate its own inquiries when appropriate. With the widening role of the executive branch of government in the EU system, it was felt that a separate institution was needed to deal with citizen grievances to ensure proper safeguards against mistake, negligence and direct abuse of power by EU authorities.[8]

This chapter sheds light on the strategies with which the EO is able to build its capacity and successfully adjust its institution to meet the changing political-administrative context. Drawing on an analysis of documents and a secondary analysis of existing empirical data, this chapter examines the institutional development of the EO over the past two decades. It describes the turbulent expansion of the European administrative system

[6] J.P. Olsen (2015) 'Democratic order, autonomy and accountability', *Governance* 28(4): 425–40, 434.

[7] J.P. Olsen (2015) 'Democratic order, autonomy and accountability', *Governance* 28(4): 425–40; A. Wille (2016) 'The accountability landscape: moving to an ever denser union', *International Review of Administrative Sciences* 82(4): 694–717.

[8] A.E. Stie (2013) *Democratic Decision-making in the EU*. London: Routledge: 149.

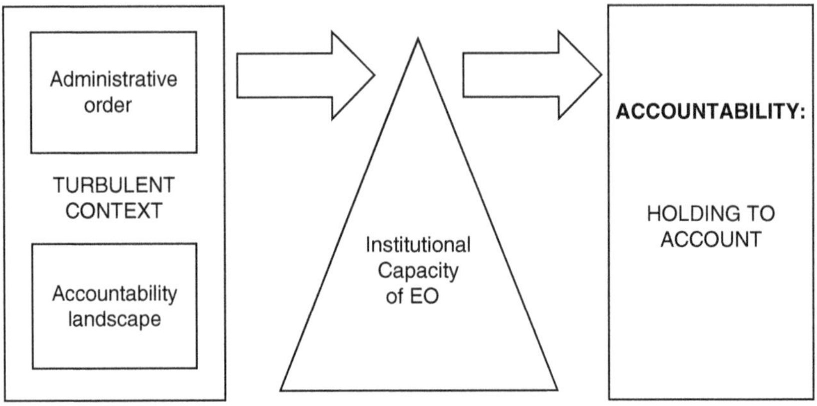

Figure 2.1 Theoretical framework

in terms of administrative and accountability institutions. It then focuses on the institutional development of the EO by examining three elements of its institutional capacity, along with the turbulent external environment and political context in which it exists. We will explain how environmental turbulence is an important driver for the EO's institutional development (see Figure 2.1). This turbulence may be seen in both the way the system is set up (administrative order and accountability landscape) and the way it works (practices). This chapter concludes by asking to what extent the multilevel nature of the EU political-administrative system is captured by the EO. Whereas the EU political-administrative order is a multilevel system, the EO may capture maladministration and misconduct mostly by EU-level institutions. A key challenge for the EO is, arguably, the EU politico-administrative order that produces turbulence of a scale (see below) that is difficult to manage by either regulators or account holders.

Figure 2.1 offers an overview of the turbulent context of accountability and the institutional capacity of the EO to address citizen grievances. Focus of this chapter is on the left and centre part of this model.

BUILDING ADMINISTRATIVE AND ACCOUNTABILITY INSTITUTIONS IN A TURBULENT CONTEXT

Operating in the present-day EU requires acting within broad and turbulent government networks with multilevel politico-administrative capacities that allow the EU-level institutions to act relatively independently from pre-existing administrative orders and to govern closely with government institutions at the national level. The continuous change of institutionalized practices in the EU implies a situation of great uncertainty for many actors. Actors possessing differing goals and, potentially, conflicting interests make the networks intrinsically heterogeneous. Moreover, the turbulent context of political conflicts (i.e., the politically, economically, and socially fluctuating developments due to both external and internal changes) adds to the difficulty of building stable institutional practices and capacity.

On Turbulence

Following recent theorizing regarding turbulence[9] the concept of turbulence refers to four properties related to the interaction of demands for action: variability, consistency, expectation, and unpredictability. Turbulence occurs where the interaction of demands is experienced as highly variable, inconsistent, unexpected, and/or unpredictable. Secondly, turbulence is not just one property; it must be unpacked at three levels, all of which are relevant when discussing the EO:

- *Environmental turbulence*: Turbulence may be brought upon organizations by external factors – such as external actors, expectations, belief structures, shocks, etc.;
- *Turbulent organizations*: Turbulence may be embedded in organizations and institutions through shifting rules, reform of formal structures, staff overhauls, etc.;
- *Turbulence of scale*: Turbulence may arise at the interface between organizations and their environments, which is of particular interest in this chapter: when incongruences appear between regulatory structures and accountability structures. Turbulence of scale appears when governance solutions at one level cause challenges at another level. In effect, 'bad' solutions could be 'good' solutions, and vice versa: there may be unreliable parts in a system that make the system, as a whole, reliable. What is often not realized, for example, is the impossibility of combining tightly integrated governance solutions at one level of government with tightly-integrated governance solutions across levels.[10] The tension between, on the one hand, central

---

[9] C. Ansell, J. Trondal and M. Ogard (eds.) (2017) *Governance in Turbulent Times*. Oxford: Oxford University Press.

[10] M. Egeberg and J. Trondal (2016) 'Why strong coordination at one level of government is incompatible with strong coordination across levels (and how to live with it). The case of the European Union' *Public Administration* 94(3): 579–92.

> steering and policy coordination across levels of government and, on the other, regional/local autonomy and coordination, is a well-known topic in research on federal states and central-local relations within unitary states.[11]

Turbulence, thus, is not only periodic and temporary exogenous phases that organizations encounter, but also, notably, it is an enduring feature embedded in organizations as well as at the interface between organizations. While implicit recognition of turbulence within organizations has a long historic path, the idea has rarely been explicitly theorized. Turbulence in organizations arises from enduring tensions within and across organizations, which produce ambiguity about what problems, solutions, and consequences to attend to at any time, as well as what actors are deemed legitimate and efficient. As suggested above, organizations and organized systems tend to live with turbulence of various kinds – some of these features are subject to design while others are subject to organizational evolution. Notably, *political organizations* are different than private organizations in this regard. Political organizations are 'created in order to handle conflicts'[12] and are, thereby, turbulent by design. Organized democracies have an embedded partisan responsiveness to a host of different, cleavages of conflict[13] that private organizations clearly do not have. Cyert and March suggest three mechanisms for how a private organization may resolve conflicts of these kinds: through local rationalities, through acceptable-level decision rules, and through sequential attention to goals.[14] Political organizations, arguably, can never solve such problems, but merely cope with them through organizational design. This is materialized in the organizational fabric of central administrations through the vertical and horizontal specialization of ministerial departments, through procedures for the recruitment of staff, and through accountability mechanisms, etc. From 1952 onwards, the EU system has faced shifting hostile and uncertain environments, as well as more or less

---

[11] See, e.g. J. Pierre and B.G. Peters (2005) *Governing Complex Societies*. Basingstoke: Palgrave; A. Fenna (2012) 'Federalism and intergovernmental coordination', in B.G. Peters and J. Pierre (eds.) *The Sage Handbook of Public Administration*. London: Sage.

[12] B. Jacobsson, J. Pierre and G. Sundstrom (2015) *Governing the Embedded State*. Oxford: Oxford University Press: 35.

[13] S. Rokkan (1999) *State Formation, Nation-building and Mass Politics in Europe*. Oxford: Oxford University Press.

[14] R.M. Cyert and J.G. March (1963) *A Behavioral Theory of the Firm*. Englewood Cliffs, NJ: Prentice-Hall.

hostile Member States, and responded by erecting turbulent organizational solutions of various kinds.[15] This chapter advocates that studying turbulence opens opportunities to rethink the institutional capacity of the EO when faced with a turbulent EU system.

Linking Turbulence and Resilience

Turbulent organizations may be resilient due to the creation of organizational capacities. Turbulence, thus, is not a deficit that damages organizations,[16] but a possible avenue for resilience.

Organizational capacities may, for instance, combine components from various organizational forms, making them compound and composite in nature. Such structures typically take the form of 'layering', whereby new forms are laid over existing forms rather than replacing such forms.[17] Organizational capacities are observed within nation-states as organizational devices to accommodate administrative dilemmas.[18] So-called post-New Public Management (NPM) reforms are 'seen as supplementary adjustments producing increased complexity in public-sector organizations'.[19] Notable examples are organizational duplication, redundancy and overlap, coordination committees, political advisors, and organizational de-coupling. These 'hybrids' can be seen as compensatory measures and organizational capacity-building in practice. For example, building organizational capacity within ministerial departments that partly overlaps agency staff ('duplication') may strengthen political steering of agencies without integrating agencies into ministries.[20] Another hybrid

---

[15] H. Wallace (1993) 'European governance in turbulent times', *Journal of Common Market Studies* 31(3): 293–304.

[16] L. Metcalfe (2000) 'Reforming the Commission: Will organizational efficiency produce effective governance?', *Journal of Common Market Studies* 38(5): 817–41.

[17] K. Thelen (2003) 'How institutions evolve. Insights from comparative historical analysis', in J. Mahoney and D. Rueschemeyer (eds.) *Comparative Historical Analysis in the Social Sciences*. Cambridge: Cambridge University Press.

[18] See P. Laegreid, T. Randma-Liiv, L.H. Rykkja and K. Sarapuu (2014) 'Introduction: Emerging coordination practices in European public administration', in P. Laegreid, T. Randma-Liiv, L.H. Rykkja and K. Sarapuu (eds.) *Organizing for Coordination in the Public Sector*. Houndmills: Palgrave Macmillan: 4.

[19] P. Laegreid and K. Verhoest (eds.) (2010) *Governance of Public Sector Organizations*. Houndmills: Palgrave Macmillan: 290.

[20] M. Egeberg (2012) 'How bureaucratic structure matters: an organizational perspective', in B.G. Peters and J. Pierre (eds.) *The Sage Handbook of Public Administration*. London: Sage.

solution is organizational de-coupling. Loose coupling may create high order sustainability, as a failure at one place does not necessarily travel across all parts of the organizations. 'Bad' solutions may be implemented in parts of organizations but not, thereby, 'ruin it all'. De-coupling of talk, decision, and action[21] may be seen as a tool for governments to satisfy multiple audiences at different levels. This approach also carefully introduces agency into the analysis. Means-end calculating reformists may carefully de-couple organizations into parts in order to seek legitimacy from multiple institutional fields and thereby secure long-term organizational sustainability.

In practice, the institutional form of public-sector organizations can vary in their pursuit of specific functions and in the way they cope with the complexity and uncertainty of their turbulent environments.[22] Three core outcomes define an institution's adaptive capacity to a turbulent context: results, legitimacy, and resilience.[23] These three dimensions are deeply intertwined and interdependent. An institution's legitimacy depends not only on rules and on law, but also – at least partly – on its results or its proficiency at achieving important objectives. Likewise, an institution that is seen as legitimate is more likely to be resilient, and similarly, a more resilient institution has a greater opportunity to earn legitimacy and achieve results.

Turbulence in the Evolving European Order

A vast part of the literature on the EU's administrative system has centred on the emergence of a *multilevel* administrative system,[24] which has since subdivided into a two-discipline debate. First, there is a political science debate that tries theoretically and more broadly to conceptualize multi-

---

[21] N. Brunsson (1989) *The Organization of Hypocrisy: Talk, Decisions and Actions in Organizations*. Chichester: Wiley.

[22] E. Ostrom (1990) *Governing the Commons: The Evolution of Institutions for Collective Action*. New York: Cambridge University Press; M. Welsh (2014) 'Resilience and responsibility: governing uncertainty in a complex world', *The Geographical Journal* 180(1): 15–26.

[23] N.H. Barma, E. Huybens and L. Viñuela (eds.) (2014) *Institutions Taking Root: Building State Capacity in Challenging Contexts*. World Bank Publications: 6.

[24] M.W. Bauer and J. Trondal (2015) 'The administrative system of the European Union', in M.W. Bauer and J. Trondal (eds.) *The Palgrave Handbook of the European Administrative System*. Houndmills: Palgrave Macmillan; J. Trondal and B.G. Peters (2013) 'The rise of European administrative space: lessons learned'. *Journal of European Public Policy* 20(2): 295–307.

level governance (MLG);[25] and, second, a more recent public administration debate has arisen, which tries to understand the EU as a multilevel administrative system (MLA).[26] Following the MLA track, Hofmann and Turk[27] have conceived of the multilevel nature of the EU system as a nested network-administration, in which institutions at different levels of government 'are linked together in the performance of tasks'.[28]

The MLA literature makes an important observation: the EU is a turbulent, multilevel administrative system coined by slightly hierarchized EU regulatory networks in which national agencies are 'double-hatted'. In addition to serving their respective parent ministries, such national agencies also find themselves being part of a multilevel EU administration in charge of practising EU policies and, to some extent, preparing it. National agencies usually deal with the Commission and EU agencies *directly* and not via their parent ministry.[29] The strengthening, and partial hierarchizing, of EU regulatory networks have been shown to affect the national ministry–agency relationship in significant ways: by taking part in such networks, national agencies become more autonomous and empowered in relation to their respective parent ministries, even in the policy-formulation phase. This even happens in well-resourced national

---

[25] A. Benz (2012) 'The European Union as a loosely coupled multi-level system', in H. Enderlein, S. Wälti and M. Zürn (eds.) *Handbook on Multi-level Governance.* Cheltenham: Edward Elgar Publishing; L. Hooghe and G. Marks (2001) *Multi-level Governance and European Integration.* New York: Rowman & Littlefield Publishers; G. Marks (1993) 'Structural policy and multilevel governance in the EC', in A.W. Cafruny and G.G. Rosenthal (eds.) *The State of the European Community.* Colorado: Lynne Rienner.

[26] M.W. Bauer, and J. Trondal (2015) 'The administrative system of the European Union', in M.W. Bauer and J. Trondal (eds.) *The Palgrave Handbook on the European Administrative System.* Houndmills: Palgrave Macmillan; M. Egeberg (ed.) (2006) *Multilevel Union Administration.* Houndmills: Palgrave Macmillan; J. Trondal (2007) 'The public administration turn in integration research', *Journal of European Public Policy* 14: 960–72; A. Benz (2015) 'European public administration as a multilevel system administration: a conceptual framework', in M.W. Bauer and J. Trondal (eds.) *The Palgrave Handbook on the European Administrative System.* Houndmills: Palgrave Macmillan.

[27] H.C.H. Hofmann and A.H. Turk (eds.) (2006) *EU Administrative Governance.* Cheltenham: Edward Elgar Publishing.

[28] H.C.H. Hofmann and A.H. Turk (eds.) (2006) *EU Administrative Governance.* Cheltenham: Edward Elgar Publishing: 583.

[29] M. Egeberg (ed.) (2006) *Multilevel Union Administration.* Houndmills: Palgrave Macmillan; J. Trondal (2007) 'The public administration turn in integration research', *Journal of European Public Policy* 14: 960–72; T. Bach and E. Ruffing (2013) 'Networking for autonomy? National agencies in European networks', *Public Administration* 91(3): 712–26.

administrations such as the Dutch and German ones.[30] By being part of a multilevel EU administration in charge of transposing EU policies, studies show that the respective ministries usually take the lead, although the relevant agencies are involved to a considerable degree. In the *application phase*, on the other hand, ministries tend to be more detached.[31] The latter seems to be particularly true in situations where the Commission harbours superior capacity and expertise relative to the Member State's administration, which may often be the case as regards *new* Member States.[32] However, at least in well-resourced administrations, the parent ministry seems to take the lead at the application stage, too, if dossiers become highly *politicized* and contested. The parent ministry also strengthens its role the more its organizational units *duplicate* those of the agency.[33]

Since delegation from the Member States to EU agencies has been more common than delegation from the Commission to such agencies,[34] we are witnessing supra-nationalization of regulatory networks in which EU agencies constitute important nodes. One vital factor indicating a high level of governmental control over EU agencies is the numerical dominance of national government representatives on agencies' management

---

[30] K. Yesilkagit (2011) 'Institutional compliance, European networks of regulation and the bureaucratic autonomy of national regulatory authorities', *Journal of European Public Policy* 18(7): 962–79; O.A. Danielsen and K. Yesilkagit (2014) 'The effects of European regulatory networks on the bureaucratic autonomy of national regulatory authorities', *Public Organization Review* 14: 353–71; T. Bach and E. Ruffing (2013) 'Networking for autonomy? National agencies in European networks', *Public Administration* 91(3): 712–26; T. Bach, E. Ruffing and K. Yesilkagit (2014) 'The differential empowering effects of Europeanization on the autonomy of national agencies', *Governance* 28(3): 285–304. DOI: 10.1111/gove.12087; M. Maggetti (2014) 'The rewards of cooperation: the effects of membership in European regulatory networks', *European Journal of Political Research* 53(3): 480–99.

[31] M. Egeberg (ed.) (2006) *Multilevel Union Administration*. Houndmills: Palgrave Macmillan.

[32] M. Martens (2008) 'Administrative integration through the back door? The role and influence of the European Commission in transgovernmental networks within the environmental policy field', *Journal of European Integration* 30(5): 635–51.

[33] M. Egeberg and J. Trondal (2009) 'National agencies in the European administrative space: government driven, commission driven, or networked?', *Public Administration* 87(4): 779–90; H. Wockelberg (2014) 'Political servants or independent experts? A comparative study of bureaucratic role perceptions and the implementation of EU law in Denmark and Sweden', *Journal of European Integration* 36(7): 731–47.

[34] R. Dehousse (2008) 'Delegation of powers in the European Union: the need for a multi-principals model', *West European Politics* 31(4): 789–805.

boards.[35] However, studies have revealed that management boards have weaknesses that might undermine such a control function: for example, they meet relatively seldom, they have too many members, and government representatives seem, on average, to be less prepared for the meetings than Commission representatives.[36] In addition, government representatives are typically coming from corresponding national agencies, rather than from ministries[37] and are subsequently sheltered from political steering signals.[38] Concomitantly, government representatives are not typically provided instruction from back home.[39] Other studies have shown that EU agencies have become closely linked to particular Commission departments, which usually see themselves as 'parent' directorates-general.[40] EU agency managers attach more weight to the concerns of the Commission than to those of any other institution and they perceive the Commission as the most influential actor in their task environment.[41]

In organizational terms, the underlying principle of specialization for this MLA is *purpose* or *sector*; that is, governance is expected to take place via sectorally limited sub-units. This organizational format is likely to trigger sectoral cleavages while simultaneously fostering standardization and uniformity *within* a particular policy field across territorial units.

---

35 R.D. Kelemen (2002) 'The politics of "Eurocratic" structure and the new European agencies', *West European Politics* 25(4): 93–118; R.D. Kelemen and A.D Tarrant (2011) 'The political foundations of the Eurocracy', *West European Politics* 34(5): 922–47.

36 M. Busuioc (2012) 'European agencies and their boards: promises and pitfalls of accountability beyond design', *Journal of European Public Policy* 19(5): 719–36; M. Busuioc and M. Groenleer (2012) 'Wielders of supranational power? The administrative behaviour of the heads of European Union agencies', in M. Busuioc, M. Groenleer and J. Trondal (eds.) *The Agency Phenomenon in the European Union.* Manchester: Manchester University Press: 128–51.

37 S. Suvarierol, M. Busuioc and M. Groenleer (2013) 'Working for Europe? Socialization in the European Commission and agencies of the European Union', *Public Administration* 91(4): 908–27.

38 M. Egeberg (2012) 'How bureaucratic structure matters: an organizational perspective' in B.G. Peters and J. Pierre (eds.) *The Sage Handbook of Public Administration*. London: Sage.

39 M. Buess (2015) 'European union agencies and their management boards: an assessment of accountability and democratic legitimacy', *Journal of European Public Policy* 22(1): 94–111.

40 M. Egeberg and J. Trondal (2016) 'Why strong coordination at one level of government is incompatible with strong coordination across levels (and how to live with it). The case of the European Union', *Public Administration* 94(3): 579–92.

41 M. Egeberg and J. Trondal (2011) 'EU-level agencies: new executive centre formation or vehicles for national control?', *Journal of European Public Policy* 18(6): 868–87.

Moreover, a multilevel structure of this kind seems to rest on two institutional conditions:[42]

- First, vertical specialization of administrative systems: national agencies that are organized at arm's length from their respective parent ministries ('vertical specialization'), make them available for direct coupling to supranational bodies; and
- Second, capacity-building at the EU level: 'adequate' administrative capacity at the supranational level (notably within the European Commission) gives supranational executive capacity that may influence the policy-formulation and implementation behaviour of national agencies.[43]

The Evolving EU Accountability Landscape: Moving Towards an Ever Denser Union

'Effective oversight relies increasingly on mutually supportive networks of accountability.'[44] The EU's accountability landscape evolved significantly

---

[42] See M. Egeberg (ed.) (2006) *Multilevel Union Administration.* Houndmills: Palgrave Macmillan.

[43] A growing body of literature on EU implementation at the application stage indicates that regulatory networks ('sectoral specialization') contribute to harmonizing guidelines and practices across countries (B. Eberlein and E. Grande (2005) 'Beyond delegation: transnational regulatory regimes and the EU Regulatory state', *Journal of European Public Policy* 12(1): 89–112; M. Egeberg and J. Trondal (2009) 'National agencies in the European administrative space: government driven, Commission driven, or networked?', *Public Administration* 87(4): 779–90; M. Groenleer, M. Kaeding and E. Versluis (2010) 'Regulatory governance through EU agencies? The role of the European Agencies for Maritime and Aviation Safety in the Implementation of European Transport Legislation', *Journal of European Public Policy* 17(8): 1212–30; M. Maggetti and F. Gilardi (2011) 'The policy-making structure of European regulatory networks and the domestic adoption of standards', *Journal of European Public Policy* 18(6): 830–47; C. Gulbrandsen (2011) 'The EU and the implementation of international law: the case of "sea-level bureaucrats"', *Journal of European Public Policy* 18(7): 1034–51; M. Maggetti (2014) 'The rewards of cooperation: the effects of membership in European regulatory networks', *European Journal of Political Research* 53(3): 480–99; E. Versluis and E. Tarr (2013) 'Improving compliance with European Union law via agencies: the case of the European Railway Agency', *Journal of Common Market Studies* 51(2): 316–33). Such a move is particularly relevant for understanding what happens in the application phase since the national political leadership is partly circumvented in the sectorally based structure.

[44] A. Wille (2016) 'The accountability landscape: moving to an ever denser union', *International Review of Administrative Sciences* 82(4): 694–717.

over the past two decades and included the establishment of several new actors. The accountability landscape is not a static structure; it is slowly changing.[45] Accountability is defined by Bovens as 'a relationship between an actor and a forum, in which the actor has an obligation to explain and to justify his or her conduct, the forum can pose questions and pass judgement, and the actor may face consequences'.[46] An accountability forum, can be a specific person, such as a superior, a minister or a journalist, or it can be an agency, such as parliament, a court or the audit office.[47] Building the EU into a polity that appeals to democratic standards of legitimacy implies the institutionalization of a variety of established systems, forums, procedures, and mechanisms prescribing who is accountable to whom for what.[48] Alongside the allocation of more power and financial resources within the EU, and the transfer of functions from national to supranational institutions, the political debate about democracy and legitimacy in the EU grew more intense in the late 1990s, raising questions about the accountability of the EU's executive bodies. Developing the institutional landscape of accountability is, thus, part of the struggle to achieve 'good' government at the EU level and the process of legitimization through accountability.[49]

Some of the most important actors who make up the landscape are the Court of Justice of the European Union (CJEU), the EP, the European Court of Auditors (ECA), the EO, the European Anti-Fraud Office (OLAF), and the national parliaments. The demand on these institutions is increasing. Some indicative figures in this regard are presented by Wille[50] and show that between 2006 and 2014, parliamentary questions practically doubled; while special reports from the ECA rose from 11 to 24, its specific annual reports grew from 23 to 51, and its opinions from 8 to 14. At the same time, the number of cases commenced, completed or pending

---

45 A. Wille (2016) 'The accountability landscape: moving to an ever denser union', *International Review of Administrative Sciences* 82(4): 694–717; J.P. Olsen (2015) 'Democratic order, autonomy and accountability', *Governance* 28(4): 425–40.

46 M. Bovens (2007) 'Analysing and assessing accountability: a conceptual framework', *European Law Journal* 13(4): 447–68, 450.

47 M. Bovens (2007) 'Analysing and assessing accountability: a conceptual framework', *European Law Journal* 13(4): 450.

48 J.P. Olsen (2013) 'The institutional basis of democratic accountability', *West European Politics* 36(3): 447–73, 450.

49 Cf. B. Laffan, (2003) 'Auditing and accountability in the European Union', *Journal of European Public Policy* 10: 777.

50 A. Wille (2016) 'The accountability landscape: moving to an ever denser union', *International Review of Administrative Sciences* 82(4): 694–717.

before the CJEU is more or less stable. The EP, being directly elected by European citizens, enjoys direct democratic legitimacy and its empowerment left a mark on the entire landscape of accountability. Furthermore, it is to be noted that the accountability landscape physically expanded and individual institutions are not only working more and more together among themselves, but also with the political forums at the supranational level as well as administrative and political forums at the national level. This networking trend deepens the influence of the accountability landscape on the democratic nature of the EU.

THE EVOLVING ACCOUNTABILITY CAPACITY OF THE EO

One of the major ways for ombudsman institutions to deal with uncertainty and environmental turbulence, is to develop its institutional capacity along three fronts (see Figure 2.2):[51]

1. *Results*: The institution must exhibit sustained improvements in key outputs and outcomes; it has to achieve measurable and gradually improving results with respect to a sizeable portion of its core mandate.
2. *Resilience*: The institution must be durable, sustaining, and enhancing results over time, and able to adapt to changing circumstances, anticipate new challenges, and cope with exogenous turbulence.

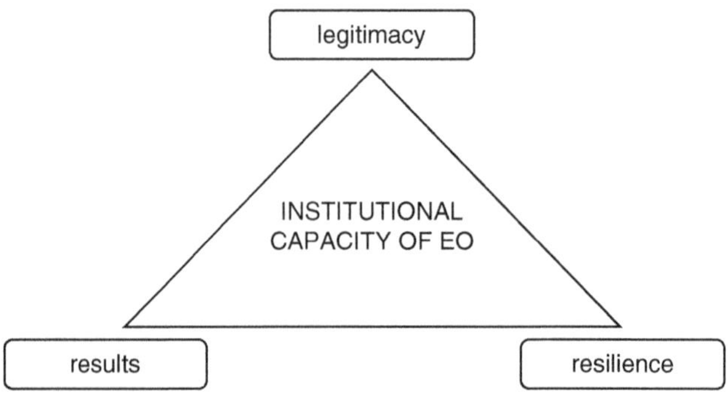

Figure 2.2 Core elements shaping the accountability capacity of the EO

[51] Cf. N.H. Barma, E. Huybens and L. Viñuela (eds.) (2014). *Institutions Taking Root: Building State Capacity in Challenging Contexts*. World Bank Publications: 6.

3. *Legitimacy*: The institution must derive authority from the political order, actors, and institutions with which it holds meaningful relationships.

The next sections describe the development of the EO's institutional capacity in terms of its results, resilience, and legitimacy and we consider the impact of the turbulent context.

Results: Shaping the Standards and Safeguarding Good Administration and Transparency

Over the years, the EO has dealt with an increasing number of complaints.[52] The EO had a record number of inquiries opened (465) and closed (390) in 2012. The 465 inquiries opened constituted an 18 per cent increase when compared to 2011, and 390 inquiries closed (then a new record) increased by 23 per cent compared to 2011. Although not displayed in the figure, most inquiries opened by the EO in 2012 concerned the European Commission (245 inquiries or 53 per cent of the total).

The large number of inquiries allows the Office of the EO to detect systemic failures. The key to its success, according to Magnette, is the hybrid nature of the EO: '[t]he powers of the [European] Ombudsman, limited as they are, give him the opportunity to combine the instruments of parliamentary scrutiny and judicial control [*sic*: review] in an original way'.[53] On the one hand, acting like a court, the EO addresses individual complainants by defining and applying 'general principles' to solve the inquiries it receives (and, through its interpretations, by building a body of examples of 'good administration'). The EO is *safeguarding* certain principles or standards. On the other hand, acting as a parliamentary organ, with the strong support of the EP, the EO uses its powers of inquiry and proposition to suggest wide-ranging reforms of EU governance (and, in doing so, promotes the principles of transparency, participation and explanation). It is, thereby, *shaping* the standards.

The Treaty that established the European Economic Community (now, the Treaty on the Functioning of the European Union, TFEU) empowered the EO to act upon 'instances of maladministration in the activities of the community institution and bodies', but it did not define

---

[52] A. Wille (2016) 'The accountability landscape: moving to an ever denser union', *International Review of Administrative Sciences* 82(4): 694–717.

[53] P. Magnette (2003) 'Between parliamentary control and the rule of law: the political role of the Ombudsman in the European Union', *Journal of European Public Policy* 10(5): 677–94.

what maladministration actually entailed.[54] The EO then worked hard to get the broadest possible definition adopted,[55] given that 'the open ended [*sic*] nature of the term is one of the things that distinguishes the role of the Ombudsman from that of a judge'.[56] Two years later, the EO wrote that 'maladministration occurs when a public body fails to act in accordance with a rule or principle which is binding upon it'. [57] This is the definition most cited in subsequent EO reports and elsewhere.[58]

General patterns of neglect can be addressed through the development of standards. If, for instance, the EO feels that the reactions to the issues the EO raises can improve, the EO may consider developing standards. From early on, the EO took the role of promoter for the principles of transparency and accountability that it considers inherent to the concept of 'good administrative practices'.[59] With that, it was clear that the very first EO would go beyond the mere handling of cases of maladministration.[60] The years following his tenure also carry marks of the same principles, and in recent years the EO has provided several examples of 'standard-setting', by developing the Public Service Principles (2012) and the new Code of Good Administrative Behaviour (2013).

From the very early years of the office's inception, the EO particularly stressed the value of transparency in the EU. Ombudsman Jacob Söderman gained a reputation for promoting norms for openness in the EU. With the strong support of the EP, the EO uses its power to investigate and to suggest wide-ranging reforms in European governance. The Office of the EO has successfully promoted principles of transparency, participation, and explanation. One example is its work regarding the accessibility of documents from the Community/EU institutions and bodies. Such accessibility has been the subject of intense lobbying by the EO. Several

---

[54] N. Vogiatzis (2014) 'Communicating the European Ombudsman's mandate: an overview of the annual reports', *Journal of Contemporary European Research* 10(1): 106–23.

[55] N. Vogiatzis (2014) 'Communicating the European Ombudsman's mandate: an overview of the annual reports', *Journal of Contemporary European Research* 10(1): 106–23.

[56] European Ombudsman, Annual Report (EOAR) 1995.

[57] European Ombudsman, Annual Report 1997: 23.

[58] N. Vogiatzis (2014) 'Communicating the European Ombudsman's mandate: an overview of the annual reports', *Journal of Contemporary European Research* 10(1): 106–23.

[59] European Ombudsman, Annual Report 1995: 5.

[60] P. Magnette (2003) 'Between parliamentary control and the rule of law: the political role of the Ombudsman in the European Union', *Journal of European Public Policy* 10(5): 677–94, 681.

inquiries initiated by the EO, itself, and EO Special Reports have been dedicated to this subject.

Results, standard-setting and safeguarding have contributed to the generic adaptive capacity of the EO to change its operating environment. The influence of the EO, to a large extent, is based on soft (non-regulatory) power that is fed by a solid track record handling complaints, with the knowledge that not only do such complaints form the basis for detecting systemic failure, but also the basis for thoroughly substantiated recommendations.

Resilience – Network Integration

If the EO has moved, over time, towards establishing networks for its continuing operation, that arguably contributes to its resilience. The search for enhanced accountability in the EU has contributed to the emergence of links to, and forms of, social organization among the EO and different forums in the EU accountability landscape. These networks are emerging horizontally between the political and administrative forums at the supranational level and, vertically, ombudsmen cut across the different levels of governance.

Horizontal relationships are those that are between political and administrative forums at the supranational level.[61] The growing cooperation of the ECA, the EO and the EP can be perceived as part of a wider attempt to enhance the democratic fabric of the EU. The strategy called 'Towards 2019' explicitly states that the mission of the EO is to serve democracy by working with the EU institutions to create more effective, accountable, transparent and ethical administration.[62] To be more effective, institutions addressing legal, political, financial, or administrative accountability are increasingly working closer together and closer together with the political forums. An example is the collaboration between the EO, the EP and the ECA. Another example is the collaboration between the EO and the CJEU with a view to interpret, influence and apply law and principles. While the exchanges with the CJEU may somehow be more indirect, the interpretation of law and principles is a subject on which both institutions wish to exchange thoughts.[63]

---

[61] A. Wille (2016) 'The accountability landscape: moving to an ever denser union', *International Review of Administrative Sciences* 82(4): 694–717.

[62] European Ombudsman, Annual Report 2014.

[63] P.N. Diamandouros (2005) 'Reflections on the future role of the Ombudsman in a changing Europe', in The European Ombudsman (ed.) *The European Ombudsman: Origins, Establishment, Evolution*, Luxembourg: OPOCE: 236.

One aspect of the environmental turbulence of the EO is the 'parliamentarization' of the EU,[64] from which emerged mechanisms that guard democratic accountability in the EU. This has made the horizontal networks relevant. The strongest ally of the EO, horizontally, is the EP. The EO, a formal parliamentary body, maintains strong relations with the EP that, over the years, has been significantly empowered. This empowerment of the EP and the EO are perceived to be signs that the accountability landscape is firming up more and more around the institutions and bodies that make up the EU.[65] In a sense, the increased weight of the EP has also positively reflected on the work of the EO.

Vertically, there is a multilevel network called the European Network of Ombudsmen (the 'Network'), this Network was also mentioned in the EO's strategy as a priority under the visibility objective.[66] The implementation of EU law falls, in many instances, within the mandate of national authorities and alleged infringements cannot, therefore, be addressed by the EO. Instead, complaints from EU citizens regarding a possible breach of EU law, as implemented by national authorities, have to be referred to the relevant national ombudsmen. It is in the EO's interest, because it frequently receives complaints that should be addressed to national ombudsmen, to further develop 'an effective and close system of cooperation to safeguard the rights of European citizens'.[67]

The first step was to set up the Network: by the end of 2000, the online version of the network, called the EUOMB, was launched. Since 2002, the membership of the EUOMB Summit has included the national ombudsmen in countries applying for EU membership.[68] The EUOMB was replaced by a new forum, called Extranet, in 2011.[69]

Ten years after inception, the EO reported to the EP that '[t]he network has steadily developed into a powerful collaboration tool for ombudsmen and their staff and serves as an effective mechanism for cooperation on case handling. Experiences and best practices are shared via seminars and meetings, a regular newsletter, an electronic discussion forum and a daily electronic news service.'[70] In terms of case handling, the numbers illustrate

---

[64] A. Wille (2016) 'The accountability landscape: moving to an ever denser union', *International Review of Administrative Sciences* 82(4): 694–717.

[65] A. Wille (2016) 'The accountability landscape: moving to an ever denser union', *International Review of Administrative Sciences* 82(4): 694–717.

[66] European Ombudsman, Annual Report 2014.

[67] European Ombudsman, Annual Report 1996.

[68] European Ombudsman, Annual Report 2002.

[69] European Ombudsman, Annual Report 2011.

[70] European Ombudsman, Annual Report 2013: 117.

the developments described above. In 1997, a year after the launch of the Network, the EO aided two national ombudsmen with queries related to the national implementation of EU law. Similarly, the EO referred, with the consent of the complainants, three complaints concerning issues with national authorities to the respective national or regional ombudsmen or similar bodies.[71] In 2005, 91 cases were directly referred to national or regional ombudsmen, whereas another 945 complainants were advised to take up the matter with their national or regional ombudsman.[72] In 2013, the number of cases referred to national or regional ombudsman or similar bodies was as high as 662.[73]

Signs of institutional maturation can be seen from an institution's agenda, membership and documentation articulating its intentions. The agenda of the Network seminars not only focuses on sharing experiences, case handling, communication and Network visibility, but also on substantive matters, such as the code for good administration and the role of ombudsmen in the protection of human rights.[74] The Network opens its biannual seminars to new participants, including representatives from countries applying for membership in the EU, but arrangements have also been made for regional ombudsmen to meet and interact with the EO. Seen as a key step in building a clearer public identity for the Network, the member ombudsmen, during the Network's Sixth Seminar of National Ombudsmen of EU Member States and Candidate Countries, adopted a statement that informs citizens and other potential users of ombudsmen services of 'the benefits that they can expect to obtain when they turn to a member of the Network about a matter that falls within the scope of EU law'.[75]

The ever-stronger Network represents a 'verticalization' of relationships. This has also happened in other parts of the EU's accountability landscape. Increasingly, in light of the expanding mandate, the institutions and bodies making up the EU's accountability landscape interact on multiple governmental levels, including supranational, inter-governmental, regional, and national levels. An example is the development of the Public Service Principles that were published to guide the conduct of EU civil servants. Before their publication in 2012, these principles were discussed within the Network and, thus, take into account best practices from the Member States.[76] Bearing in mind the expansion of this verticalization

---

[71] European Ombudsman, Annual Report 1997.
[72] European Ombudsman, Annual Report 2005.
[73] European Ombudsman, Annual Report 2013.
[74] European Ombudsman, Annual Report 2006–2013.
[75] European Ombudsman, Annual Report 2007: 103.
[76] European Ombudsman, Annual Report 2012.

trend, it is even more pertinent today, given the large number of new Member States that have recently joined the EU.

Given the turbulence of scale in which the administration continues to evolve, these vertical relationships between institutions have become essential. The development of the Network fits this context. The Network can be seen as a manifestation of verticalization on the part of the EO. In its quest for more democracy and accountability, the EO seems to have carved out a role for itself as the coordinator of standardization processes concerning good administrative behaviour and fundamental rights promotion and observance in the EU.

Legitimacy – A Pillar of Administrative Justice

It is crucial to the accountability capacity of the EO that it garners legitimacy. The legitimacy of the ombudsman is best understood and conceptualized through the recognition that ombudsman institutions all over the world are a central part of achieving 'administrative justice'.[77] There are generally two ways for ombudsman institutions to prevent maladministration giving rise to injustice: fire-fighting and fire-watching, on the one hand, and fire-prevention, on the other hand.[78] The first orientation is a reactive one and represents the traditional functions of most 'classical' ombudsmen. A second orientation, in addition to the core, classical complaint handling function, is a fire-prevention role in which monitoring and sometimes advising on reforms and administrative improvement represents a move towards a system-fixing understanding of the role of the ombudsman.[79]

The EO plays both roles. It ensures that European administrative bodies and those who exercise administrative functions make fair and just decisions. The EO's role as a complaint handler continues to be its core function: it is the main mechanism for providing redress when things go wrong. In this fire-fighting role the EO acts as a provider of individual administrative justice, assuring both minimal legal standards (the rule of law) and going beyond them (good administration) in protecting citizens from abuses of power.

---

[77] C. Gill (2014) 'The evolving role of the Ombudsman: a conceptual and constitutional analysis of the "Scottish Solution" to administrative justice', *Public Law*: 662–81.

[78] A. Stuhmcke (2012) 'The evolution of the classical ombudsman: a view from the antipodes', *International Journal of Public Law and Policy* 2(1): 83–95.

[79] A. Stuhmcke (2012) 'The evolution of the classical ombudsman: a view from the antipodes', *International Journal of Public Law and Policy* 2(1): 83–95.

But, the EO also operates more and more as a system-fixer. Using the knowledge that the EO draws from handling complaints, it develops alternative initiatives to improve administration by EU institutions and bodies. With an expanding case load, and with an interest in reducing or even avoiding future complaints of a nature already addressed, such alternative initiatives have, over time, become larger in scope. In a sense, this is where the EO started fire-watching and fire-preventing in addition to fire-fighting.

- One EO initiative shares lessons learned from earlier cases, by publishing 'star cases' in the EO's Annual Reports. These 'star cases' highlight best practices that show 'how best to react to issues that the Ombudsman raises'.[80]
- Another EO initiative develops codes or principles, such as the Public Service Principles (2012) and the Code of Good Administrative Behaviour (2013).
- A third EO initiative pertains to the EO's pro-active advocacy for such published principles, as well as for matters, such as making the Charter of Fundamental Rights legally binding, in order to firm up the principles of good administration by establishing a 'right to good administration'.

The 20-year trend, which indicates that the EO uses its discretion to refer complaints back to EU bodies while concentrating on systemic work, may raise concerns about the way in which that trend might affect the core role of the ombudsman. One of the perils is that the ability of the EO to resolve disputes and safeguard administrative justice through redress of complaints is, potentially, compromised by the EO's shift of emphasis. A strong focus on quality improvement may mean that the EO will run the risk of failing to protect individual complainants and, thus, remove an important mechanism available for the provision of redress for individual citizens. The move towards fire-prevention or the system-fix approach bears the risk, according to Gill,[81] that the EO is 'no longer a "citizen's defender" oriented towards citizens and focused on settling their disputes', but comes too close to being part of the EU machinery.

---

80 European Ombudsman, Annual Report 2009.

81 C. Gill (2014) 'The evolving role of the Ombudsman: a conceptual and constitutional analysis of the "Scottish Solution" to administrative justice', *Public Law*: 662–81.

CONCLUSION

The turbulence in the evolving EU administration has arguably turned the EO into a resilient institution. In terms of achieving administrative accountability, the EO has increasingly developed standards for good practice with an emphasis on transparency and principles of good administrative behaviour, while also using its networks to further improve swift and accurate complaint handling. Its contribution to the overall accountability landscape lies in this observation. Indeed, as the expanding EU accountability landscape has evolved over the past years, so has the EO. The accountability landscape 'verticalized' significantly as the EO engaged in multilevel governance networks. The multilevel European Network of Ombudsmen has matured over the past two decades and the EO has tried to build institutional capacity to operate in that multilevel administrative order. Moreover, environmental turbulence has been an important driver for the growth of the EO's institutional development (see Figure 2.1). This turbulence is seen in both the way the system is set up (administrative order and accountability landscape) and the way it works (practices). The question, however, remains as to the extent to which the multilevel nature of the EU politico-administrative system is captured by the EO. Whereas the EU politico-administrative order is a multilevel system, the EO may capture maladministration and misconduct mostly by EU-level institutions. One key challenge for the EO is, arguably, that the EU politico-administrative order produces turbulence of scale that is difficult to manage either by regulators or by account holders.

With the strong encouragement of the EP, the EO develops its capacity to be both an effective fire-watcher and fire-preventer. It is true that the EO's recommendations are not legally binding and it is not a formal lawmaker. Still, the EO's soft power seems to have a broad reach and has already shown itself to be able to instigate governance and legal reform. With its evolving networks, both horizontal and vertical, it is expected that such soft power will expand faster and will have a greater impact on administration at the national level.

REFERENCES

Ansell, C., J. Trondal and M. Ogard (eds.) (2017) *Governance in Turbulent Times*. Oxford: Oxford University Press.

Bach, T. and E. Ruffing (2013) 'Networking for autonomy? National agencies in European networks', *Public Administration* 91(3): 712–26.

Bach, T., E. Ruffing and K. Yesilkagit (2014) 'The differential empowering effects

of Europeanization on the autonomy of national agencies', *Governance* 28(3): 285–304. DOI: 10.1111/gove.12087.
Barma, N.H., E. Huybens and L. Viñuela (eds.) (2014). *Institutions Taking Root: Building State Capacity in Challenging Contexts.* World Bank Publications.
Bauer, M.W. and J. Trondal (2015) 'The administrative system of the European Union', in M.W. Bauer and J. Trondal (eds.) *The Palgrave Handbook of the European Administrative System.* Houndmills: Palgrave Macmillan.
Benz, A. (2012) 'The European Union as a loosely coupled multi-level system', in H. Enderlein, S. Wälti and M. Zürn (eds.) *Handbook on Multi-level Governance.* Cheltenham: Edward Elgar Publishing.
Benz, A. (2015) 'European public administration as a multilevel system administration: a conceptual framework', in M.W. Bauer and J. Trondal (eds.) *The Palgrave Handbook on the European Administrative System.* Houndmills: Palgrave Macmillan.
Bovens, M. (2007) 'Analysing and assessing accountability: a conceptual framework', *European Law Journal* 13(4): 447–68.
Brunsson, N. (1989) *The Organization of Hypocrisy: Talk, Decisions and Actions in Organizations.* Chichester: Wiley.
Buess, M. (2015) 'European Union agencies and their management boards: an assessment of accountability and democratic legitimacy', *Journal of European Public Policy* 22(1): 94–111.
Busuioc, M. (2012) 'European agencies and their boards: promises and pitfalls of accountability beyond design', *Journal of European Public Policy* 19(5): 719–36.
Busuioc, M. and M. Groenleer (2012) 'Wielders of supranational power? The administrative behaviour of the heads of European Union agencies', in M. Busuioc, M. Groenleer and J. Trondal (eds.) *The Agency Phenomenon in the European Union.* Manchester: Manchester University Press: 128–51.
Cyert, R.M. and J.G. March (1963) *A Behavioral Theory of the Firm.* Englewood Cliffs, NJ: Prentice-Hall.
Danielsen, O.A. and K. Yesilkagit (2014) 'The effects of European regulatory networks on the bureaucratic autonomy of national regulatory authorities', *Public Organization Review* 14: 353–71.
Dehousse, R. (2008) 'Delegation of powers in the European Union: the need for a multi-principals model', *West European Politics* 31(4): 789–805.
Diamandouros, P.N. (2005) 'Reflections on the Future Role of the Ombudsman in a Changing Europe', in The European Ombudsman (ed.) *The European Ombudsman: Origins, Establishment, Evolution,* Luxembourg: OPOCE: 217–40.
Eberlein, B. and E. Grande (2005) 'Beyond delegation: transnational regulatory regimes and the EU Regulatory state', *Journal of European Public Policy* 12(1): 89–112.
Egeberg, M. (ed.) (2006) *Multilevel Union Administration.* Houndmills: Palgrave Macmillan.
Egeberg, M. (2012) 'How bureaucratic structure matters: an organizational perspective', in B.G. Peters and J. Pierre (eds.) *The Sage Handbook of Public Administration.* London: Sage.
Egeberg, M. and J. Trondal (2009) 'National agencies in the European administrative space: government driven, commission driven, or networked?', *Public Administration* 87(4): 779–90.
Egeberg, M. and J. Trondal (2011) 'EU-level agencies: new executive centre

formation or vehicles for national control?', *Journal of European Public Policy* 18(6): 868–87.
Egeberg, M. and J. Trondal (2016) 'Why strong coordination at one level of government is incompatible with strong coordination across levels (and how to live with it). The case of the European Union', *Public Administration* 94(3): 579–92.
European Ombudsman, Annual Reports. Available from www.ombudsman.europa.eu/en/activities/annualreports.faces, accessed 4 January 2017.
Fenna, A. (2012) 'Federalism and intergovernmental coordination', in B.G. Peters and J. Pierre (eds.) *The Sage Handbook of Public Administration*. London: Sage.
Gill, C. (2014) 'The evolving role of the Ombudsman: a conceptual and constitutional analysis of the "Scottish Solution" to administrative justice', *Public Law* 4: 662–81.
Groenleer, M., M. Kaeding and E. Versluis (2010) 'Regulatory governance through EU agencies? The role of the European Agencies for maritime and aviation safety in the implementation of European transport legislation', *Journal of European Public Policy* 17(8): 1212–30.
Gulbrandsen, C. (2011) 'The EU and the implementation of international law: the case of "sea-level bureaucrats"', *Journal of European Public Policy* 18(7): 1034–51.
Hofmann, H.C.H. and A.H. Turk (eds.) (2006) *EU Administrative Governance*. Cheltenham: Edward Elgar Publishing.
Hooghe, L. and G. Marks (2001) *Multi-level Governance and European Integration*. New York: Rowman & Littlefield Publishers.
Jacobsson, B., J. Pierre and G. Sundstrom (2015) *Governing the Embedded State*. Oxford: Oxford University Press.
Kelemen, R.D. (2002) 'The politics of "Eurocratic" structure and the new European agencies', *West European Politics* 25(4): 93–118.
Kelemen, R.D. and A.D. Tarrant (2011) 'The political foundations of the Eurocracy', *West European Politics* 34(5): 922–47.
Laegreid, P. and K. Verhoest (eds.) (2010) *Governance of Public Sector Organizations*. Houndmills: Palgrave Macmillan.
Laegreid, P., T. Randma-Liiv, L.H. Rykkja and K. Sarapuu (2014) 'Introduction: Emerging coordination practices in European public administration', in P. Laegreid, T. Randma-Liiv, L.H. Rykkja and K. Sarapuu (eds.) *Organizing for Coordination in the Public Sector*. Houndmills: Palgrave Macmillan.
Laffan, B. (2003) 'Auditing and accountability in the European Union', *Journal of European Public Policy* 10: 762–77.
Maggetti, M. (2014) 'The rewards of cooperation: the effects of membership in European regulatory networks', *European Journal of Political Research* 53(3): 480–99.
Maggetti, M. and F. Gilardi (2011) 'The policy-making structure of European regulatory networks and the domestic adoption of standards', *Journal of European Public Policy* 18(6): 830–47.
Magnette, P. (2003) 'Between parliamentary control and the rule of law: the political role of the Ombudsman in the European Union', *Journal of European Public Policy* 10(5): 677–94.
Marks, G. (1993) 'Structural policy and multilevel governance in the EC', in A.W. Cafruny and G.G. Rosenthal (eds.) *The State of the European Community*. Colorado: Lynne Rienner.
Martens, M. (2008) 'Administrative integration through the back door? The role

and influence of the European Commission in transgovernmental networks within the environmental policy field', *Journal of European Integration* 30(5): 635–51.

McMillan, J. (2013) 'Commonwealth oversight arrangements – successes and challenges', paper to the Australasian Study of Parliament Group Annual Conference 2013. Available from www.aspg.org.au/conferences/perth2013/Conference%20Paper%20-%20John%20McMillan.pdf, accessed 24 January 2017.

Metcalfe, L. (2000) 'Reforming the Commission: will organizational efficiency produce effective governance?', *Journal of Common Market Studies* 38(5): 817–41.

Olsen, J.P. (2013) 'The institutional basis of democratic accountability', *West European Politics* 36(3): 447–73.

Olsen, J.P. (2015) 'Democratic order, autonomy and accountability', *Governance* 28(4): 425–40.

Ostrom, E. (1990) *Governing the Commons: The Evolution of Institutions for Collective Action*. New York: Cambridge University Press.

Pierre, J. and B.G. Peters (2005) *Governing Complex Societies*. Basingstoke: Palgrave.

Rokkan, S. (1999) *State Formation, Nation-Building and Mass Politics in Europe*. Oxford: Oxford University Press.

Stie, A.E. (2013) *Democratic Decision-making in the EU*. London: Routledge.

Stuhmcke, A. (2012). The evolution of the classical ombudsman: a view from the antipodes. *International Journal of Public Law and Policy* 2(1): 83–95.

Suvarierol, S., M. Busuioc and M. Groenleer (2013) 'Working for Europe? Socialization in the European Commission and Agencies of the European Union', *Public Administration* 91(4): 908–27.

Thelen, K. (2003) 'How institutions evolve: insights from comparative historical analysis', in J. Mahoney and D. Rueschemeyer (eds.) *Comparative Historical Analysis in the Social Sciences*. Cambridge: Cambridge University Press.

Trondal, J. (2007) 'The public administration turn in integration research', *Journal of European Public Policy* 14: 960–72.

Trondal, J. and B.G. Peters (2013) 'The rise of European administrative space: lessons learned', *Journal of European Public Policy* 20(2): 295–307.

Versluis, E. and E. Tarr (2013) 'Improving compliance with European Union law via agencies: the case of the European Railway Agency', *Journal of Common Market Studies* 51(2): 316–33.

Vogiatzis, N. (2014) 'Communicating the European Ombudsman's Mandate: an overview of the annual reports', *Journal of Contemporary European Research* 10(1): 106–23.

Wallace, H. (1993) 'European governance in turbulent times', *Journal of Common Market Studies* 31(3): 293–303.

Welsh, M. (2014) 'Resilience and responsibility: governing uncertainty in a complex world', *The Geographical Journal* 180(1): 15–26.

Wettenhall, R. (2012) 'Integrity agencies: the significance of the Parliamentary relationship', *Policy Studies* 33(1): 65–78.

Wilkins, P. (2014) 'Watchdogs as satellites of Parliament', *Australian Journal of Public Administration*, 75(1): 18–27.

Wille, A. (2016) 'The accountability landscape: moving to an ever denser union', *International Review of Administrative Sciences* 82(4): 694–717.

Wockelberg, H. (2014) 'Political servants or independent experts? A comparative study of bureaucratic role perceptions and the implementation of EU law in Denmark and Sweden', *Journal of European Integration* 36(7): 731–47.
Yesilkagit, K. (2011) 'Institutional compliance, European networks of regulation and the bureaucratic autonomy of national regulatory authorities', *Journal of European Public Policy* 18(7): 962–79.

3. 'Monitoring the law and independent from politics?' The relationship between the European Ombudsman and the European Parliament

Christine Neuhold

I INTRODUCTION: THE ROLE OF THE EUROPEAN OMBUDSMAN AND THE DEMOCRATIC DEFICIT

As is well known the European Union (EU) has been diagnosed as suffering from a malaise: the much proclaimed and debated democratic deficit. These 'democratic deficit allegations' as Zweifel calls this phenomenon, can, according to some, be traced back to discussions of the European Parliament's (EP's) draft treaty for a European union in the early 1980s and debates leading up to the 1986 Single European Act.[1] Others posit that the term has its origins in the ratification process surrounding the Maastricht Treaty.[2] But whatever the roots of this democratic deficit are, most scholars posit that it indeed exists.

In order to adhere to certain democratic norms, a representative system needs to govern in a way that citizens can see to be both 'of' and 'for' the people. On the one hand this implies that representatives must be chosen in such a way that citizens can see that their views and interests are in fact treated equally. On the other hand representatives must also take citizens' interests into account equally when making policy.[3]

While crucial decisions are taken at the European level, the processes of

[1] Thomas Zweifel, 'Who is Without Sin Cast the First Stone: The EU's Democratic Deficit in Comparison' *Journal of European Public Policy* (2002) No. 5, Vol. 9, 812–40.

[2] Richard Bellamy and Sandra Kröger, 'Representation Deficits and Surpluses in EU Policy-making' *Journal of European Integration* (2013) No. 5, Vol. 35, 477–97.

[3] Richard Bellamy and Sandra Kröger, 'Representation Deficits' (2013).

electing members of the European Parliament (MEPs) are, however, not seen as contests about the 'content or direction of EU policy'. The EU thus falls short on premises that are 'shared by a broad range of democratic theorists'.[4] Moreover it has been argued that the basic foundations of European democracy are lacking as the EU consists of peoples rather that one set of people. Europe is thus consisting of *demoi*, rather than a *demos*; but, as Weiler posits, without a *demos*, there can in fact be no democracy.[5]

This opens the question of how these 'citizens' can actually impact on decision-making in the EU and ties in with what Schmidt (2006) has coined as government 'with' the people.[6] Here one comes to a somewhat sobering conclusion.[7] On the one hand the fact that the EU is open to a plethora of different actors can be seen to allow for a rather high degree of participation. On the other hand, the very same system is also seen to be prone to the phenomenon of fragmentation.[8]

It has to be stressed, however, that this enhancement of 'procedural legitimacy',[9] where legitimacy may be strengthened as long as certain procedures – such as transparency, balance of interests, proportionality, legal certainty and consultation of stakeholders – are adhered to within the EU, ties in rather neatly with the creation of the European Ombudsman (EO) in 1995.

This body, as Magnette argues, illustrates a trend in the EU, which consists in subjecting the EU's institutions to a standard set of rules and procedures. It can be seen as a 'hybrid organ', formally a parliamentary

---

[4] Andreas Follesdal and Simon Hix, 'Why there is a Democratic Deficit in the EU: A Response to Majone and Moravcsik' *Journal of Common Market Studies* (2006) No. 2, Vol. 44, 533–62.

[5] Joseph Weiler 'Does Europe Need a Constitution? Reflections on Demos, Telos, and the German Maastricht Decision' *European Law Journal* (1995) No. 1, Vol. 3, 219–58.

[6] Vivien Schmidt quoted in: P. Kostatinova, 'Improving the Transparency and Accountability of EU Institutions: The Impact of the Office of the European Ombudsman' *Journal of Common Market Studies* (2015) No. 1, DOI:10111/jcms.12245, 1–17.

[7] Beate Kohler-Koch, 'The Organization of Interests and Democracy in the European Union' in B. Kohler-Koch and B. Rittberger (eds.), *Debating the Democratic Legitimacy of the European Union* (Lanham, MD: Rowman & Littlefield 2007) 255–71.

[8] Christopher Lord and Johannes Pollak, 'The EU's Many Representative Modes: Colliding? Cohering?' *Journal of European Public Policy* (2010) No. 1, Vol. 17, 117–36.

[9] C. Lord and P. Magnette, 'E Pluribus Unum? Creative Disagreement about Legitimacy in the EU' *Journal of Common Market Studies* (2004) No. 1, Vol. 4, 183–202.

body set up to control the institutions and bodies of the EU. On the other hand its role also comes close to that of a court as it is addressed by individuals putting forward complaints and it applies 'general principles' to these cases.[10] The Treaty on the Functioning of the European Union (TFEU) stipulates that the EO is to receive complaints from any citizen of the EU, or any natural or legal person residing or having its registered office in an EU Member State. Ombudsmen have, globally speaking, been associated with democratization.[11] As opposed to courts, in order to be able to address the EO one is thus not obliged to have formal standing, and there is no need to be affected by the case, i.e. one does not need to suffer any damages. If one goes to court however, one has to demonstrate standing and prove that the institution concerned has acted illegally.[12]

The hybrid nature of the EO[13] is reflected by the fact that he is appointed by the EP and there are close relations between the Ombudsman and the EP's Committee on Petitions. On the other hand the EO has to investigate 'complaints about maladministration' in the institutions, bodies, offices and agencies of the EU including the European legislature; the EP.[14]

This chapter addresses the question of how that possible tension plays out in the practical process by examining a series of cases brought forward to the EO and against the EP. The underlying question here is whether the EO acts as an 'independent' institution, as stipulated in the Treaty, vis-à-vis the EP and as such applies legal principles. In order to be able to grasp and operationalize this far-reaching concept of 'independence', we want to see whether there are any 'patterns' we can discern in this context: are there certain 'roles' that the EO adopts when deciding on cases against the EP? This conceptualization of roles is based on an examination of all decisions following an inquiry by the Ombudsman for cases against the EP for a ten year period.[15]

---

[10] P. Magnette, 'Between Parliamentary Control and the Rule of Law: The Political Role of the Ombudsman in the European Union' *Journal of European Public Policy* (2003) No. 5, Vol. 10, 677–94.

[11] Interview Director of EO, 20 May 2015 and Interview (former) Secretary General EO, 15 May 2015.

[12] Interview (former) Secretary General EO, 15 May 2015.

[13] The term Ombudsman comes from the Swedish language and is used in a gender neutral way (also in this chapter).

[14] Article 228 TFEU.

[15] Here one examined whether 'general principles' were applied to the cases under scrutiny and to what extent maladministration was found. Each case was summarized and categorized as regards to the issue at stake and how the EO decided in the specific case. This analysis is complemented by two interviews held

Against this background the approach and set-up of this chapter is as follows: First the relationship between the EP and the EO is sketched. After examining the scope of the activities of the EO, we probe into all decisions following an inquiry by the Ombudsman for cases against the EP. This concerns decisions that are closed for the period between 1 January 2005 and May 2015.[16] The chapter concludes with an attempt at conceptualizing the way the EO takes decisions according to certain 'roles' and links the latter to the more general debate on legitimizing the EU.

II THE LINK BETWEEN THE EP AND THE EO

As Magnette points out the idea of creating an Ombudsman at the European level goes back to the year of 1979, where it first came up in a resolution adopted by the EP.[17] But it was not until the intergovernmental negotiations leading up to the Maastricht Treaty that the office was actually created. It is noteworthy and also to some extent reflected in the way that the office is set up to this very day, that there were opposing positions when it came to the creation of the new office.

On the one side stood Member States such as Spain and Denmark that, based on their national traditions, pushed for the appointment of an Ombudsman in every EU Member State. These would be installed to ensure that individual rights are respected and would deal with complaints of citizens.[18] The proposals were somewhat differentiated; while Spain proposed a 'mediator' in each Member State, possibly together with an EO, to defend citizens' rights vis-à-vis the administrative authorities of *both* the Union and its Member States, Denmark proposed an Ombudsman with a mandate that was to be limited to the Community institutions.[19] The Spanish position was very much based on the experience that the introduction of an Ombudsman in their

with staff of the EO and interventions given at the European Ombudsman 20th Anniversary Colloquium (Brussels, 22 June 2015).

[16] This concerns decisions that are closed for this period. See www.ombudsman.europa.eu/ cases/decisions.faces, accessed 5 January 2017.

[17] Paul Magnette, 'Between Parliamentary Control and the Rule of Law (2003).

[18] Paul Magnette, 'Between Parliamentary Control and the Rule of Law' (2003).

[19] Ian Harden, 'External Scrutiny Institutions', in E. Jones, A. Menon and S. Weatherhill (eds.), *The Oxford Handbook of the European Union* (Oxford: Oxford University Press 2012) 380–91.

Member State was linked to general processes of democratization.[20] The eventual stipulations in the Treaty were based on the Danish proposal: an Ombudsman with a mandate limited to the EU institutions, with the Court of Justice falling outside the sphere of competence of the Ombudsman.

Moreover, one has to stress the fact that the EO is based on a Swedish concept[21] and the Austrian, Swedish and Finnish EU membership (and at the time even that of Norway) was lurking in the wings of the Treaty on European Union (TEU) negotiations so it comes as no surprise that such a 'Nordic' institution was to be established; to make the 'EU more recognizable to Nordic countries'. At the same time one wanted to counterbalance the economic dimension of the Maastricht Treaty by strengthening the link with the citizens.[22]

On the other side of the spectrum stood the other Member States and a majority of MEPs. The EP saw itself as *the* guardian of citizens' rights and the Ombudsman was seen as a possible form of competition. The Treaty of Maastricht reflects such tensions. On the one hand the role of the Ombudsman is clearly defined with no political competences. On the other hand, under the direct supervision of the EP, these competences could be extended.[23]

Accordingly, the relationship between the European Ombudsman and the EP is close and the EO is directly accountable to the European legislature. As a consequence, he is appointed by the EP. It is key to note that it is the EP alone that elects the EO, with no role for the Member States or the Commission or any other institution, for that matter. So far the EP has elected Ombudsmen that had a history of being national Ombudsmen and that were independent from the EU institutions and from their respective national governments. As such this can be seen as a 'success story'.[24] The close link between the EP and the EO is also reflected by the fact that the EO is based at the premises of the EP in Strasbourg and

---

[20] Interview Director of EO, 20 May 2015.

[21] Note that the office of an Ombudsman is a Swedish 'invention'. The King's Supreme Ombudsman was appointed in 1713. He had to ensure the observance of the law and that public officials carried out their tasks while the King was abroad. In 1809, the Swedish Parliament first elected an Ombudsman. Here, the main function was the supervision of the application of the laws by judges and other public officials (I. Harden 'External Scrutiny Institutions' (2012) 388).

[22] Interview Director of EO, 20 May 2015.

[23] Paul Magnette, 'Between Parliamentary Control and the Rule of Law' (2003) 680.

[24] Interview with (former) General Secretary of EO, 11 May 2015.

as such, for example, uses the Information and Technology Services of the EP. This form of cooperation is seen to work very well.[25]

The Treaty explicitly states that the Ombudsman shall be completely independent in the performance of his duties. In the performance of the latter he shall neither 'seek nor take instructions from any government, institution, body, office or entity'. Moreover, the Treaty states that the Ombudsman 'may not, during his term of office, engage in any other occupation, whether gainful or not'.[26]

The EO is appointed for the term of the European legislature and his term is renewable. He is moreover accountable to the EP insofar as at the request of Parliament, the Ombudsman may be removed by the Court of Justice if 'he no longer fulfils the conditions required for the performance of his duties or if he is guilty of serious misconduct' (Article 228 TFEU). In order to be accepted in the selection process via the EP, a candidate needs the support of at least 40 MEPs from at least two EU Member States. Those declared admissible will be asked (just like Commissioners 'to be') to present their priorities in a hearing in front of a specialized EP committee, in this case the EP Committee on Petitions. The EP elects the new Ombudsman by secret ballot and by majority of the votes cast.

In this context it is noteworthy that the fact that the EO can present a special report to the EP is seen 'of inestimable value' for the Ombudsman's work and these reports are seen as the Ombudsman's 'ultimate weapon'. Note that the mere existence of the power to make a special report to Parliament can already motivate an institution to adapt its behaviour. Especially when a draft recommendation is made, the fact that the next step could be a special report often helps the Ombudsman to 'persuade the institution or body concerned to alter its position'.[27] Special reports are therefore the exception rather than the rule. They are only drawn up in relation to 'important matters', on which Parliament could help persuade the institution or body concerned to change its position.[28]

It is important to note that the EO on the other hand will not investigate the *political* work of the EP and the concept of maladministration does not include the work of EP committees.[29] One has to stress that this is a 'bound-

---

[25] Interview with Director of EO, 20 May 2015.

[26] Article 228 TFEU.

[27] European Ombudsman, 'Speech by the European Ombudsman, Mr P. Nikiforos Diamandouros to the Committee on Petitions of the European Parliament' (Brussels, 13 September 2006).

[28] This is illustrated by the fact that over the period of 11 years, the EO has presented 13 special reports to the EP.

[29] For example, a complaint about the position taken by the EP in the context

ary' that the EO has set for himself and partly explained by the fact that 'from a Swedish perspective this was unthinkable'[30] to investigate political issues.

This is apparent from the first annual report of the first EO, which was approved by the EP:

> All complaints against decisions of a *political* rather than an administrative nature are regarded as *inadmissible*; for example, complaints against the political work of the EP's or its organs, such as decisions of the Committee on Petitions' (emphasis added).[31]

It is interesting to note that there are different views on this subject propagated by national ombudsmen. The former Danish Ombudsman, for example, stressed that an ombudsman shall not refrain from investigating cases just because they might (also) contain 'political substance'. It is seen as key, however, that in these cases the ombudsman shall confine the investigation to the legal elements of the case.[32]

Cooperation between the EO and the EP's Petitions Committee

As alluded to above, the EP's Petitions Committee saw itself as the 'guardian' of the rights of EU citizens, and as such the first EO Jacob Söderman was very concerned to manage any possible tensions; when first entering the Petitions Committee 'it was chilly in the room'.[33] There were two potential problems with that relationship:

- on the one hand the Petitions Committee *could* have seen the EO as its (potential) rival and limit the work of the EO by, for example, limiting its resources;
- on the other hand there was the inherent danger that the Petitions Committee would try to 'subordinate' the EO to its needs, i.e. that the EO would have to carry out dedicated work for the committee.[34]

---

of French nuclear tests in the Pacific (Complaint No. 281) was held inadmissible because it concerned a political decision, not a possible instance of maladministration (European Ombudsman, *Annual Report 1995* (Brussels 1996)).

[30] Oral intervention by first EO, at the European Ombudsman 20th Anniversary Colloquium (Brussels, 22 June 2015).

[31] European Ombudsman, *Annual Report 1995* (1996).

[32] Hans Gammeltoft-Hansen, The Ombudsman as a Marker of the Limits of Politics. Presentation given at a conference (Tallin: 7 March 2008).

[33] Oral intervention by first EO at the European Ombudsman 20th Anniversary Colloquium (Brussels, 22 June 2015).

[34] Interview with (former) General Secretary of EO (11 May 2015).

These problems have been, however, curbed and the relationship is described as being characterized by complementarity rather than by rivalry, with a clear division of competences between the two bodies. Petitions are seen as the 'bread and butter' of the Petitions Committee, with a clear division of competences between the two bodies.[35] The petitions that the Petitions Committee receives are very often about Member States' alleged failure to comply with EU law. These are matters where the EO cannot investigate. There is thus very little overlap in practice between the work of the EO and that of the Petitions Committee. The Petitions Committee's work overlaps much more with that of the Commission, in its role as Guardian of the Treaties, and that of national ombudsmen.

Note that the capacities of the EP's Petitions Committee are limited on issues of principle and it has to use one of its main tools, that of own-initiative reports, very sparingly. This is so as according to Rule 52 of the EP's Rules of Procedure the number of own-initiative reports are to be limited in number during the respective legislative period.[36]

The EP's Petitions Committee thus issues own-initiative reports following up an inquiry by the Ombudsman only in very selected cases (around one or two per year). One example is the own-initiative report which led to an EP resolution, concerning the Ombudsman's inquiry into complaint 2591/2010/GG against the European Commission in the case of Vienna Airport.[37] This inquiry follows complaints from 27 Austrian citizens' organizations concerning the absence of an environmental impact assessment (EIA) for several airport extensions. During his own investigation, the Ombudsman repeatedly pointed to problems with the EIA, which was eventually carried out retrospectively, including a potential conflict of interest involving the Austrian authorities.

Since the Commission failed to act on the Ombudsman's findings, he decided to submit a special report to the EP.[38] The EP stated in its resolution that efforts should be undertaken – also in the future – to carry out open and transparent mediation procedures ahead of projects with a potential

---

[35] Oral intervention by Chair of EP Petitions Committee at the European Ombudsman 20th Anniversary Colloquium (Brussels, 22 June 2015).

[36] During the first half of the legislative term each EP committee may simultaneously draft up to six own-initiative reports, and during the second half each committee can simultaneously draft up to three own-initiative reports.

[37] European Parliament, 'Resolution of 12 March 2013 on the Special Report of the European Ombudsman concerning his inquiry into complaint 2591/2010/GG against the European Commission' (Vienna Airport) (2012/2264(INI), (Brussels 2013).

[38] See www.ombudsman.europa.eu/en/press/release.faces/en/11567/html.bookmark, accessed 5 January 2017.

major impact on the local environment and human health. This is thus an example where the EP tried rather 'elegantly' to shift the focus of attention away from the specific instance of maladministration that had occurred 'towards systemic improvements for the future'.[39]

III THE SCOPE OF THE ACTIVITIES OF THE EO

As mentioned above, according to the TFEU, the EO's main function is to inquire into, and report on instances of, 'maladministration' arising from activities of the EU institutions and bodies.[40] Only the Court of Justice, acting in its judicial capacity, falls outside the Ombudsman's mandate. Inquiries may not only be opened in response to complaints from citizens or residents of the Union, but can also be based on the initiative of the EO himself. It has to be noted that neither the Treaty nor the Statute of the Ombudsman actually defines what is meant by the term of 'maladministration'. In the practical process, the EO has consistently adhered to the position that this concept includes – but is not limited to – unlawful behaviour.[41] The scope of cases that the EO can look into is, however, limited by three factors:

- First, given that the case is (or has been) the subject of legal proceedings, the EO cannot conduct inquiries.
- Second, the EO tries not to duplicate the work of institutions that have circumscribed and specialized mandates, such as the office to combat fraud: OLAF,[42] which has the clear mandate of fighting fraud within the EU.[43]
- The role of the EO is not, therefore, to investigate individual wrongdoing in the EU institutions, such as corruption, fraud or harassment. Rather, the EO can inquire into whether those who *do* have such responsibility (i.e. the institutions themselves and OLAF)

---

[39] Oral intervention by first EO, at the European Ombudsman 20th Anniversary Colloquium (Brussels, 22 June 2015).

[40] Article 228 TFEU.

[41] Ian Harden, 'Presentation given at 10th Anniversary Conference of the European Ombudsman' Vilnius, 14–15 April 2005; see www.lrski.lt/en/international-relations/26-international-relations/10th-anniversary-conference/presentations/44-presentation-by-prof-ian-harden-head-of-the-legal-department-the-european-ombudsman.html, accessed 5 January 2017.

[42] OLAF is an office set up to combat fraud and is the abbreviation from the French: Office Lutte Anti-Fraud.

[43] Ian Harden, 'Presentation given at 10th Anniversary Conference of the European Ombudsman' (2005).

> have carried out their 'functions properly and whether the relevant administrative systems are fit for purpose'.[44]

The EU institutions can be induced, but not forced to modify their activities as a response to investigations into specific cases, where the EO issues critical remarks or as response to recommendations issued by the EO. It has to be noted that the EO receives a very large number of complaints each year[45] and so first has to see whether these are actually admissible. Once a case is seen as admissible there are several possible outcomes: either the EO could propose a friendly solution with the institution against which a complaint is filed, or the EO could find that no maladministration has in fact occurred or that no further inquiries are justified. Note that one will not find the term 'friendly solution' in the Statute of the EO, nor in the Treaties. This concept was very much shaped by the first EO.

The Statute laid down by Parliament mentions that the EO would be seeking a 'solution' if he makes a finding of 'maladministration', but there was no explicit provision for the EO to try to solve a problem without making a definite finding of maladministration. The rationale behind this is the somewhat 'hybrid' mode the EO operates under.[46]

Similarly, there is no express provision in the Treaty or the Statute of the EO if the EO wants to issue recommendations even if there is no maladministration. Hence the EO also came up with the option of 'further remarks'. The two modes are not exclusive and it is a matter of judgment, which is likely to be most useful in dealing with a specific case, or a specific point in the handling of a case. As the EO has no power to order an institution to put matters right and is not a prosecutor, he can only issue critical remarks. If it is not possible to persuade the institution to rectify the matter, the only solution envisaged by the Treaty and Statute is to report the issue to Parliament by way of a special report, as alluded to above. However, there is a limit to the number of such reports Parliament can deal with effectively. Furthermore, in some cases, the maladministration cannot be put right. To fill the gap the first EO 'borrowed' the concept of critical remarks from the practice of the Swedish and Finnish ombudsmen. These critical remarks were somewhat overused at the beginning, but now one resorts

---

[44] Ian Harden, 'Protecting the Whistleblowers – Asian and European Perspectives. The Role of the European Ombudsman as a Protector of the Public Interest', 13. International Anti-Corruption Conference, Athens, 31 October 2008; see www.asef.org/images/docs/1265-IanHarden.pdf, accessed 5 January 2017.

[45] 2,420 complaints were registered in 2013.

[46] Paul Magnette, 'Between Parliamentary Control and the Rule of Law' (2003).

much more to friendly solutions and draft recommendations in cases where the institution can and should rectify the matter. Before 2006 there was no follow-up on critical remarks, but this has since changed and the respective institution has six months to follow up the matter by indicating what action it has taken to avoid similar maladministration in the future. These cases are later followed up to ensure whether the respective institution has complied with the recommendations.[47] The follow-up measures taken as a response to critical remarks are published annually.

If we examine some of the recent data available, i.e. number of inquiries for 2013, we find that 350 inquiries were opened by the EO. If we then zoom in on how many inquiries concerned which EU institutions, we find that the Commission is clearly in the lead, with 225 (64.3 per cent of cases). EU agencies then follow suit with 84 cases (or 24 per cent). Comparatively speaking, only a fraction of cases were opened against the EP (15 cases or 4.3 per cent). The latter, i.e. the cases brought before the EO against the EP, are the focus of this chapter.

IV DECISIONS BY THE OMBUDSMAN FOLLOWING AN INQUIRY AGAINST THE EP

All decisions following an inquiry by the EO against the EP that were published on the EP website were examined for the period of 1 January 2005 until May 2015.[48] These decisions were classified according to the nature of the case and to what extent and on what grounds maladministration was found.

Note that the EO website does not contain all decisions on all cases, as it does not contain information on the so-called 'telephone' procedure. Here the (office of the) EO will phone the institution in question or contact that institution by email and the matter would be solved. These would be matters of minor administrative oversight that can be easily solved. These decisions are, however, still traceable by way of an internal database. Here there would be usually no issue of principle involved.[49]

These cases where the EO did conduct a formal inquiry were examined in order see to what extent the Ombudsman acted as an 'independent institution' and applied legal principles. In order to be able to capture the

---

47 Interview with (former) General Secretary of the EO, 11 May 2015.

48 See www.ombudsman.europa.eu/cases/decisions.faces, accessed 5 January 2017.

49 Interview with (former) General Secretary of EO, 11 May 2015.

Table 3.1 Decisions of EO following an inquiry against the EP 2010–2015[1]

Maladministration and critical remark	No maladministration/EP has settled the case
36[2]	76[3]

Notes:
1 Only cases were examined where a case was opened against the EP as the sole institution. Cases where the complainant withdrew were not considered.
2 In two cases no critical remark was issued.
3 In 12 cases the EO issued further remark(s).

concept of independence, we wanted to see whether there are any patterns we can discern according to which the EO decides in cases against the EP. The results are shown in Table 3.1.

When examining the cases against the EP and the respective EO decisions, we find that in a majority of cases no maladministration was found or the EP has settled the case. In around a third of the cases under scrutiny, the EO did, however, find certain instances of maladministration and in a large majority of these cases resorted to the tool of issuing critical remarks. In a majority of the cases these critical remarks are issued in cases concerning alleged violations of EP staff regulations and issues relating to transparency, i.e. requests for information and access to documents of the EP.

An example of alleged violations of staff regulations would be the complaint of a (former) official of the EP.[50] He was seconded to another Community institution. In this context problems with his promotion and the award of merit points arose.[51] The Ombudsman then closed his inquiry into this complaint with the critical remark, which falls into the realm of 'good administrative practice'.

Accordingly, an Appointing Authority should conduct procedures leading to the award of merit points in line with the applicable rules. This includes carrying out a 'proper comparative assessment' of the merits of its staff members. In the case under scrutiny the EP failed to conduct such an assessment. This is thus seen to constitute a case of maladministration. In the future the position of the EO could give guidance to comparative cases of secondment to EU institutions.

---

50 Case: 344/2007/(WP)BEH.

51 According to Article 37 of the Staff Regulations of officials of the European Communities an official on secondment 'shall continue to enjoy all his rights under the conditions contained in Articles 38 and 39 . . . as an official of his parent institution'.

When examining the cases relating to alleged unfair and irregular decisions relating to recruitment procedures of officials to the EP, it is noteworthy that in general the Ombudsman considers that selection boards are to have a certain margin of discretion when taking decisions in recruitment procedures.[52]

What is seen as problematic, however, and where the EO has issued several critical remarks, is the provision of information to applicants by the EP on why, for example, certain decisions were taken. An example of this would be the case of an individual who applied for an open competition organized by the EP in the field of general security.[53] In this context the complainant was informed by the President of the Selection Board that he could not be admitted to the competition because he did not enclose enough supporting documents as regards his professional experience. After his inquiry into the case, the EO sustained the allegation that contradictory information was supplied to the complainant and as such made a critical remark. Accordingly, the EP failed to indicate clearly to the complainant the grounds for the decision not to admit him to the competition. This is seen as an instance of maladministration and note that this did not go unnoticed by the EP's administration. Accordingly, the EP acknowledged and apologized for its error. This case also sheds light on the extent to which the EO can assume the role of an 'arbitrator' between an individual and the EU institutions, in this case the EP.

If one then zooms in on the issues that actually gave rise to complaints to the EO against the EP, most cases relate to alleged unfair treatment in competition and selection procedures organized by the EP (see Table 3.2). Although some of these cases, as alluded to above, give rise to critical remarks, one can also very much see the 'conciliatory' role that the EO plays. Moreover, in several cases patterns of best practices for future selection procedures are established. An example would be where an individual participated in a recruitment procedure for administrators organized by Parliament, but was informed that he was excluded from participation due to lack of professional experience.[54] Although the EO did not find maladministration related to the content of the case as such, a solution was found insofar as the EP decided to clarify certain issues relating to future recruitments procedures.[55]

In this context one also has to stress the fact that a large number of cases

---

52 Case: 2222/2004/TN.

53 Case: 755/2004/OV.

54 Case: 2222/2004/TN.

55 This pertains to the issue of how parental leave is taken into account when calculating qualifying periods for professional experience.

Table 3.2 Overview of matters giving rise to complaints to the EO against the EP: alleged violations of staff regulations and alleged unfair treatment in selection procedures

Alleged unfair treatment in competition and selection procedures organized by EP	Alleged violations of staff regulations[1]	Alleged violations of staff regulations: Financial issues[2]
28	24	23

Notes:
1 A majority of these cases (around 20) cover issues such as issues of promotions within the EP on the basis of annual staff assessments, which can result in the award of a certain number of merit points. One exceptional cost of alleged harassment of an EP staff member also falls into this category.
2 This category covers issues such as award of allowances and reimbursement of pension costs.

that concern the alleged violation of staff rules concern the allocation of merit points related to the promotion of staff working within the EP. These complaints relating to such evaluation procedures have repeatedly given rise to findings of maladministration. Interestingly, the Ombudsman was requested in a particular case that he should consider submitting a special report to the EP.[56] The EO did not, however, decide to do so although the complaint – pertaining to the lack of impartiality – does raise an issue, which is seen to possibly affect officials and other agents working for Parliament. Interestingly, the case under scrutiny was seen as 'not important enough to merit Parliament's attention in its role as a political body designed to represent EU citizens'. In the future this issue could, however, as a matter of principle give rise to a special report. The EO closed the case by way of issuing a critical remark, which again falls into the sphere of 'good administration'. Accordingly, situations should be avoided 'where the impression is given that a person or authority called upon to decide on a matter might be perceived as being partial'. However, this risk is seen clearly to exist when the individual or authority 'dealing with a complaint against a decision was closely involved in the adoption of that very same decision'.

A substantial number of cases that also relate to (alleged) violations of staff regulations are issues with financial implications and relate to the questions such as the award of allowances and reimbursement of pension costs.

---

56 See Case: 3289/2008/BEH for more references on related cases.

Table 3.3 Overview of matters giving rise to complaints to the EO against the EP: general 'institutional matters'

Alleged problems when dealing with requests for information and access to documents[1]	Alleged unfair treatment in award of tenders or grants by the EP	Alleged issues with other institutional matters (such as access to the EP)[2]
16	11	10

Notes:
1 Issues with the EP website also fall into this category.
2 Within this category fall issues such as the question of access to the EP as an institution or the issue of access of visitor groups or treatment of individuals by EP security services.

Some cases also relate to tendering procedures conducted by the EP.[57] A somewhat exemplary case in this context is the case of an individual who formed part of a consortium that had submitted a bid in response to a call for tenders organized by the EP in 2004.[58] This case is interesting as it sheds light on the use of further remarks as setting 'best practices' for future procedures. While on the basis of the Ombudsman's inquiries into this complaint, there appears to have been no maladministration by Parliament, the further remark goes into the direction of declaring any conflict of interests. The EP is thus called upon to contemplate adopting measures that could prevent such problems as were prevalent in this case arising in future cases. All persons who deal with tenders should thus not only declare any potential conflict of interest but also provide information on any previous dealings with, or activities involving, tenderers, which might be relevant to the outcome of the tender.

A substantial number of cases relate, moreover, to the way that the EP deals with requests for information and access to documents (see Table 3.3). A notable case in this context,[59] which sheds light on the hybrid nature of the EO alluded to above, is a case where the EP refused to grant the complainant,[60] public access to documents relating to the negotiations leading up to the finalization of the Anti-Counterfeiting Trade Agreement (ACTA). While the EO applied 'general principles' to this case and came

[57] Case: 3732/2004/GG.

[58] Call for tenders PE-INTERP/2004-01 – Study concerning the constraints arising from remote interpreting.

[59] Case: 2393/2011/RA.

[60] This is an association of 28 digital civil rights associations from 18 European countries known as European Digital Rights (EDRi).

to the conclusion that there had been no maladministration by the EP, he issued further remarks to enhance the role of the EP as *the* European legislature representing EU citizens. Accordingly, the Parliament, as a 'political body' is called upon to intervene with the other EU institutions (in this case Commission and the Council) in order to ensure that, in future, the 'very nature of Parliament, which is to openly deliberate on issues' that could have an impact on citizens such as ACTA, is not undermined.

A related case that sheds more light on the role of the EO as a 'transparency watchdog' ensuring the right of citizens or citizens' organizations to access to information is again related to ACTA.[61] This time, the complainant made a request for public access to the minutes of meetings of *coordinators* of several EP committees relating to the ACTA negotiations. The EP flagged up the fact that in general no separate minutes of the meetings of committee coordinators exist, and that these minutes are included in the minutes of the committee meetings themselves. The complainant then turned to the EO with the complaint that the EP fails to include the minutes of committee coordinators in its register of documents. Based on this claim, the Ombudsman made a recommendation to the EP that, when such minutes are drawn up, Parliament should include them in its public register of documents. The European legislature then agreed that, in the quest for promotion of greater transparency, recommendations or decisions adopted by the coordinators would, after their endorsement by the respective EP committee, be included in the committee minutes, which are accessible in the public register as of July 2014 onwards. The EO then came to the conclusion that the Parliament has thus taken appropriate measures to implement his draft recommendation.

On the other hand, some cases relating to transparency transgress (even) more into the political sphere. A case in point is the EP's refusal to give public access to details of MEPs' allowances. This dates back to the year of 2005, where the EP refused to give insight into MEPs' allowances,[62] allegedly due to reasons of data protection. The Ombudsman consulted the European Data Protection Supervisor, who advocated that the public has a right to be informed about the behaviour of MEPs. The Ombudsman then called on the EP to disclose the requested information, in the light of the public's legal right of access to documents. The EP maintained its refusal again with the argument of data protection. It announced,

---

61 Case: 262/2012/OV.

62 In this case a journalist wanted to have insight into the allowances paid to five Maltese MEPs. The journalist argued that taxpayers have a right to know how MEPs spend public money.

however, that it would publish general information on MEPs' allowances on its website and alluded to the possibility of re-assessing the situation in 2009.[63] The complainant was not satisfied with the EP's reaction and did not withdraw his complaint. The Ombudsman issued a critical remark but had and has no legal recourse to annul the decision itself.[64] By way of media coverage, however, this case came into the public domain and gave rise to a more general debate on MEPs' allowances.

In a somewhat related case, the EP refused to give access to the names of MEPs participating in the EP's supplementary pension scheme. The Ombudsman made a preliminary finding of maladministration and proposed a friendly solution, which the EP rejected. One has to note, however, that the Parliament as a whole voted down a concrete proposal from its Budgetary Control Committee to publish the list of names. The Ombudsman thus decided to close the case as the EP's action has made the issue one of 'political responsibility'. The underlying reasoning was that in this case the European legislature is accountable to the European electorate and not to the Ombudsman.[65]

Both cases are examples of cases which arguably contained political substance but where the Ombudsman confined his investigation to the legal elements of the case. He did so by way of investigating whether maladministration had occurred and/or actions taken by the EP violated the principle of transparency.

A recent decision (from 2015) reflects the extent to which the Ombudsman takes the side of citizens as a 'mediator' in what the EO described as a contemporary 'David and Goliath' type struggle between an individual employee and the powerful bureaucracy of a European institution, in this case the EP. The case concerned the EP's decision to disregard the derogation from the mobility it had granted to one of its officials on account of her daughter's severe and irreversible disability. After the inquiry into the issue the Ombudsman came to the conclusion that the EP could 'not lawfully revoke its derogation'. She made a proposal to the European legislature in this regard, which the EP however rejected. The Ombudsman thus made a draft recommendation, requesting the EP to allow the complainant the continuing benefit of the derogation for as long as her daughter's situation required the mother's presence, even if this meant indefinitely. The EP, while refusing to acknowledge that its

---

63 This was to be done in 2009.

64 The full decision is available at www.ombudsman.europa.eu/recommen/en/053643.htm, accessed 5 January 2017.

65 The full decision is available at www.ombudsman.europa.eu/decision/en/060655.htm, accessed 5 January 2017.

position was not warranted, accepted the Ombudsman's recommendation and the case was closed.[66]

Categorization of the 'Roles' the EO Adopts vis-à-vis the EP

At the outset of this chapter, the question was raised whether the EO acts as an independent institution vis-à-vis the EP. In order to be able to capture this very far-reaching concept of independence, it was decided to try to conceptualize this by way of roles that the Ombudsman adopts when deciding on cases against the EP.

After having examined decisions against the EP over a ten-year period, the EO can thus be seen to adopt four main 'roles' vis-à-vis the EP:

- assuming the role of '*arbitrator*' or '*mediator*' between complainants and the EP, leading in a majority of the cases to a settlement of the case;
- setting '*best practices*' when it comes to 'good administration' within the EP and thus giving guidance beyond the specific issue or case at stake;
- acting as a '*transparency watchdog*' by ensuring that certain documents – for example in the ACTA case – come into the public domain. This is crucial not only for the EU institutions in general but also for the EP in particular as the EU legislature is to deliberate openly on issues concerning EU citizens;
- (leading to) the '*politicization of issues*', for example in the Vienna Airport case, where the EP's Petitions Committee not only issued an own-initiative report but this also led to an EP resolution. This in turn can enhance media coverage on specific topics and, as such, issues get into the public domain, giving rise to public debate.

These roles have to be put into the more general context of the way the EO pursues his work, i.e. beyond the specific context of cases against the EP as an institution. To just give one example: transparency of the way that decisions are taken and access to key documents is crucial in a Union where some procedures are increasingly 'informalized'.[67] One case in point is the Ordinary Legislative Procedure (OLP), where decisions are, to an increasing extent, taken in first reading behind closed doors in

---

[66] Case: 118/2013/AN.

[67] Thomas Christiansen and Christine Neuhold. 'Informal Politics in the EU' *Journal of Common Market Studies* (2013) Vol. 51, No. 6, 1196–206.

so-called trilogues or the 'fast-track' procedure, bringing together selected key players from the EP, the Council and the European Commission.[68] In this context it is important to note that the EO just very recently opened a case in its role of 'transparency watchdog' on the disclosure of documents relating to trilogues.[69]

This in turn could not only shed light on issues at stake, in the specific cases under scrutiny, but could in general lead to more transparency and accountability of decisions that are taken via the 'fast-track' and lead to more political and (possibly) more public debate on the way decisions are taken in the EU. The incumbent EO brought it to the point by saying that:

> I am, in this context, very mindful of the specific role that I have been elected . . . to, within its mandate, support our emerging European citizenship. Transparency, democratic accountability and public trust are central to that citizenship.[70]

This case on increasing transparency of trilogues in turn is an example of a strategy that the incumbent EO increasingly pursues, which is that of own-initiative inquiries. According to the Treaty the EO is 'invited to conduct inquiries on his own initiative into the activities of the Union institutions, bodies, offices or agencies'.[71] By increasingly adopting this strategy, this enables the EO to address key questions and as such he can be a spokesperson for both non-governmental organizations (NGOs) and a 'vessel' for citizens' interests. Two examples of this strategy are the own-initiative inquiry into the implementation by FRONTEX[72] of its fundamental rights obligations[73] or the inquiry into how the European Citizens' Initiative (ECI) is working. According to the ECI a group of one million EU citizens can call on the European Commission to propose new EU legislation. In January 2014, the EO invited organizers (ECIs) to see how well the ECI is working and, as such, contributed to the public debate on this topic.

---

68 Christine Reh, 'Is Informal Politics Undemocratic? Trilogues, Early Agreements and the Selection Model of Representation' *Journal of European Public Policy* (2013) Vol. 21, No. 6, 822–41.

69 Case: OI/8/2015/FOR. The case was opened on 26 May 2015.

70 Emily O'Reilly, 'Trilogues and Transparent Law-making', Speech given at 'International Right to Know Day 2015' (Brussels, 28 September 2015).

71 Article 228 TFEU.

72 European Agency for the Management of Operational Cooperation at the External Borders of the Member States of the European Union (Frontex).

73 OI/5/2012/BEH-MHZ.

V CONCLUDING REMARKS

In a quest to counterbalance the economic dimension of the Maastricht Treaty and to make the EU more 'recognizable' to its new 'Nordic' Member States, an EO was established. Just like in many EU Member States, the Ombudsman has no power to make legally binding decisions but is a 'moral authority'.[74]

The EO is appointed by the EP and by the EP only, without any role for any other EU institutions or the EU Member States for that matter. He can also be removed by the Court of Justice at a request of the EP, *inter alia* if he is guilty of serious misconduct. Accordingly, there is a close relationship with the EP but at the same time the mandate of the EO covers the Community institutions including the EP. Note, however, that the political work of the EP, including the work of its committees, does not fall within the sphere of the EO and that this 'division' was already established in the first year that the EO took up his work. The EO does, however, probe into questions of maladministration within the EP and examines issues such as the refusal of access to documents or decisions taken within open competitions and selection procedures for the EP.

If one examines the decisions of the EO in cases against the EP over a time-span of ten years, we find that in a majority of the cases no maladministration was found to have occurred or that the EP settled the case. The EO thus successfully plays the role of 'arbitrator' or 'mediator' between the complainant(s) and the EP. In the cases where the EO found maladministration to have occurred and issued critical remarks these concerned for the most part (alleged) violations of EP staff regulations and issues relating to transparency. The critical remarks for the most part relate to principles of good administration that are to set best practices within the EP and provide guidance beyond the specific case at stake.

In other selected cases where maladministration was found, for example when the EP refused to give access to the names of MEPs participating in the EP's supplementary pension scheme, these were matters of political salience and at the end fell under the political responsibility of the European legislature. Although this on the one hand reflects the limits of the work of Ombudsmen in general and the EO is only one case in point here, it also sheds light on the potential 'spin-off' of the inquiries conducted by the EO. On the one hand debates about certain issues, such the allowances of MEPs, shift into the public domain, *inter alia* by way of ensuing media coverage. On the other hand it can lead to more

---

[74] Ian Harden, 'External Scrutiny Institutions' (2012) 383.

political debate both within the EP's committees and plenary and also lead to concrete action points such as publishing general information on MEPs' allowances. Moreover, it also reflects the fact that even when the EO has to investigate into cases that might contain political substance or might have political implications, he confines his investigation to the legal elements of the case.

Initial reservations of the EP's Petitions Committee about the creation of an EO can be seen to have been unfounded and the relationship seems to be characterized more by complementarity rather than by rivalry. Both institutions have successfully joined forces in selected cases in the past, for example in the case of the construction of Vienna Airport. Here an EO inquiry led not only to an own-initiative report by the Petitions Committee, but also to a resolution by the EP. By way of 'bundling' forces and legal tools, the public's attention and public debate on certain issues can be channelled and heightened.

One can thus observe that the EO is not only an 'independent' institution, acting according to legal principles but one can discern certain patterns according to which decisions are taken. After having examined decisions against the EP over a ten-year period, the EO can be thus seen to adopt four main 'roles' vis-à-vis the EP, reaching from the role of 'arbitrator' to that of a 'transparency watchdog'.

These roles are very much linked to a more general process of attempting to legitimize the EU by way of what has been coined as government 'with' the people or 'procedural legitimacy'. Moreover, one has to stress the fact that the EO, by way of own-initiative inquiries, seeks to strengthen the link with NGOs and citizens and at the same time conducts inquiries into issues of great political salience such as the respect of fundamental rights.

In sum, we thus find that the EO is not only an independent institution but one that can be more generally associated with attempts of 'legitimizing' the EU.

4. Public awareness of EU rights and the functions of the European Ombudsman: some unpleasant findings

George Tridimas and Takis Tridimas

INTRODUCTION

The present chapter focuses on the level of awareness of citizens of European Union (EU) of the role of the European Ombudsman (EO).[1] Section 1 offers a short description of the responsibilities of the EO to pursue accountability at the supranational authorities of the EU. Recognizing that the EO can only succeed if citizens are informed about their EU rights and know who to turn to in support of those rights, Section 2 uses the findings of a relatively recent (2011) special Eurobarometer survey to assemble such information. It finds that the replies regarding knowledge of citizen rights and their advocate vary considerably from Member State to Member State. Section 3 argues that the cross-country variation in survey replies can be attributed to a host of economic and political factors that vary across the Member States; these include income, intra-EU trade, length of EU membership, tradition of democratic government, domestic governance arrangements relating to voice and accountability, government effectiveness, the rule of law, and control of corruption. Section 4 reports the empirical results from estimating the effect of said explanatory variables on the pattern of national replies to the survey. Section 5 concludes.

[1] The term 'ombudsman' is always used without a sense of gender and without recognizing the gender of the current occupant of the position.

1 THE ACCOUNTABILITY ROLE OF THE EO

Delegation of decision-making in the EU is an inherently complicated process. For a growing range of issues of public interest, the governments of the sovereign Member States, acting as the agents of their respective national citizens, assign decision-making competencies to supranational organs, particularly to the EU Commission, which plays the role of a supranational administrative and executive body. Popular folklore, as well as formal research, has identified major political accountability deficits at the EU level, where accountability is defined as a relationship between an actor and a forum in which the actor has an obligation to explain and justify its conduct, the forum is entitled to ask questions and pass judgment, and the actor may be rewarded or sanctioned (Bovens 2007 and 2010).

As the EU's supranational authorities are not subject to the same scrutiny by the European Parliament (EP) as national authorities of Member States are by their national parliaments, accountability at the EU level has been complemented by additional forms of governance.[2] The EO is one of the most prominent institutions for accountability purposes (the others being the Court of Justice of the European Union (ECJ) and the European Court of Auditors (ECA)). The EO's function is to examine and report on complaints, submitted by EU citizens and legal persons residing in the Union of maladministration by the EU institutions.

The Maastricht Treaty, in 1992, established the Office of the EO to monitor the supranational bodies, which was conceived as a step towards reducing the accountability deficit. The idea of a supranational ombudsman originated in the 1970s, but as Member States could direct complaints about political matters to the EP's existing Committee of Petition (the CoP), neither the EP nor the Commission was receptive thereto (Song and Della Sala 2008). Sometime later, Denmark and Spain took the lead in lobbying for an Office of the EO, but for different reasons (ibid.). The Danish motivation was to control the EU institutions and keep the integration process in check. The Spanish motivation, on the other hand, due to Spain's observation that most of the Community policies affecting the public were actually implemented by the Member States, was to develop and protect the principle of European citizenship that granted rights and protections to individuals, therefore strengthening the legitimacy of the EU. 'The principle of good

---

[2] For a recent detailed discussion of this and related points, see amongst others Lord and Pollak (2010).

administration, then, could appeal to those who wanted to enhance the basis of European citizenship as well as those who simply wanted to keep a tighter rein on EU institutions and their officials' (ibid., p. 487). Both those favouring further integration and those who were against it saw the usefulness of setting up the new body. For integrationists, the establishment of the EO strengthened the legitimacy of the EU, while Eurosceptics saw the EO as a restriction on the powers of the EU's centralizing organs.

The right to good administration is enshrined in Article 41 of the Charter of Fundamental Rights of the European Union (the 'Charter'). It confirms a person's right to impartial, fair and timely handling of his affairs by the EU bodies; his right to be heard; to have access to his file; to receive damages for EU institution wrongdoings; and to use his preferred language in addressing or being addressed by the EU institutions. It further confirms the administration's obligation to justify its decisions. The EO takes the position that failure to apply the Charter is 'maladministration'. Maladministration takes place 'when a public body fails to act in accordance with a rule or a principle which is binding upon it. [It] includes unlawful activity and errors of legal reasoning and interpretation, failure to respect a legal rule or principles of good administration or fundamental rights' (Peters 2005, p. 702). It encompasses all kinds of poor or improper administrative behaviour, from late payment for EU projects to the unjustified refusal to release a document or information. The EO's mandate covers maladministration by EU institutions, but excludes maladministration by the national authorities of the Member States; the latter is taken up by national ombudsmen. The EO's investigations of maladministration relate to the acts of the EU's executive agents and exclude political, legislative or judicial acts. Mirroring the relationship that developed between the ECJ and national courts (Tridimas and Tridimas 2004, and the literature cited therein), the EO has fostered the establishment of networks of national ombudsmen by referring complainants whose cases cannot be pursued by the EO because they relate to national authorities, to the national ombudsmen.

Most complaints examined by the EO are directed against the Commission, whose decisions often have a direct impact on citizens. The most frequent complaints relate to late payment, contract disputes, arbitrary discrimination, and access to documents. The role of the EO is to *scrutinise the limits* of Commission discretion (Peters 2005, p.720). The EO's pursuit of EU administration accountability promotes transparency, as manifested by the EO consistently demanding public access to documents, and forces the authorities to explain their decisions. Through this process, citizens become better informed about their rights and duties, which not only enhances the rule of law, but also increases their ability to participate in the political process.

2 CITIZEN INFORMATION ABOUT EU RIGHTS AND THE EO

It follows from the brief discussion above, that, in order for the EO to help EU administration to be transparent, effective and citizen friendly, it is crucial that citizens be well informed about their EU rights and know to whom they can turn to support those rights. A special 2011 Eurobarometer survey,[3] commissioned by the EP (the 'Survey') sheds some light on these and related questions. A sample of 26,836 European citizens from all 27 (at the time) Member States were interviewed, face-to-face. Table 4.1 assembles a summary of the main findings by Member State. Question A asked whether citizens are informed about the Charter. Questions B1–B3 inquired how satisfied citizens are with the effectiveness, service mindedness and transparency of EU administration, respectively. Questions C and D related directly to the functions of the EO, notably its responsibility to ensure that EU citizens know about their rights and information about the responsibilities of the EO. Finally, Questions E1–E4 examined the importance citizens attach to the right to: free movement, good administration, submit complaints to the EO, and petition the EP. The numerical entries in Table 4.1 show the percentage of respondents from each Member State that agreed fully with the question asked.

The replies show notable differences from Member State to Member State, regarding the respondents' level and depth of knowledge about EU citizen rights and their advocate, but all-in-all they reflect poor levels of knowledge.

- Less than one in six respondents (14 per cent) replied that they felt fully informed about the Charter; on the contrary, almost three quarters of them (72 per cent) were not totally informed – not shown in Table 4.1. Luxembourg records the highest familiarity with rights (25 per cent) and Latvia the lowest (6 per cent).
- A bare majority of the respondents (52 per cent) reported that the most important function of the EO was to ensure that EU citizens know their rights and how to use them, while slightly less than half

[3] The full survey can be downloaded from www.ombudsman.europa.eu/en/press/statistics/eb751_eb_factsheet.faces, accessed 2 March 2015.

Table 4.1 *Survey responses to EU citizen rights and the functions of the EO*

Country	A	B_1	B_2	B_3	C	D	E_1	E_2	E_3	E_4
Belgium	12	13	11	8	53	59	52	49	35	30
Bulgaria	9	15	16	15	52	34	55	36	35	6
Czech Republic	22	18	17	16	46	39	34	33	40	16
Denmark	13	7	7	3	69	32	63	33	39	8
Germany	15	7	6	5	60	48	70	30	31	24
Estonia	13	14	14	12	49	44	68	12	25	15
Greece	11	19	18	15	50	54	33	47	46	36
Spain	10	8	10	8	47	58	31	41	35	19
France	8	6	6	6	66	55	47	33	28	24
Ireland	15	9	8	8	43	45	42	35	33	18
Italy	21	13	11	14	47	59	28	44	35	19
Cyprus	12	13	12	11	66	74	55	47	42	53
Latvia	6	9	11	8	61	30	64	22	21	10
Lithuania	8	15	18	16	49	43	64	18	16	12
Luxembourg	25	10	11	9	52	64	57	30	28	19
Hungary	10	18	18	15	54	39	52	21	39	13
Malta	12	26	20	19	49	62	33	37	41	28
Netherlands	14	15	8	10	50	54	58	52	28	14
Austria	18	11	11	10	57	52	58	42	40	24
Poland	11	14	11	10	49	42	54	15	32	18
Portugal	11	7	7	7	43	39	33	29	34	18
Romania	8	22	22	21	38	44	50	30	28	25
Slovenia	18	11	12	11	56	54	60	29	44	14
Slovakia	19	26	26	24	58	21	65	20	37	16
Finland	10	14	15	17	56	39	74	35	43	43
Sweden	19	6	8	5	69	49	73	38	30	11
United Kingdom	13	4	5	4	46	42	39	24	26	19
EU27	14	10	10	9	52	49	48	33	32	32

Notes:

A Percentage of respondents who are 'totally' informed about the Charter.

B_1 Percentage of respondents who are very satisfied with the Effectiveness of the EU administration.

B_2 Percentage of respondents who are very satisfied with the Service Mindedness of the EU administration.

B_3 Percentage of respondents who are very satisfied with the Transparency of the EU administration.

C Percentage of respondents who agree that the most important responsibility of the EO is to ensure that EU citizens know about their rights and how to make use of them.

D Percentage of respondents who are 'totally' interested in being informed about the responsibilities of the EO.

E_1 Percentage of respondents who consider the right to move and reside freely in the EU as the most important right.

E_2 Percentage of respondents who consider the right to good administration by EU institutions as the most important right.

E_3 Percentage of respondents who consider the right to submit complaints to the EO as the most important right.

E_4 Percentage of respondents who consider the right to petition the EP as the most important right.

(49 per cent) reported that they were interested in being informed about the responsibilities of the EO.

- The survey indicates that the four most important citizen rights are: (1) the right to move and reside freely in the EU; (2) the right to good administration by EU institutions; (3) the right to submit complaints to the EO; and (4) the right to petition the EP.[4]
- The survey also recorded low levels of satisfaction with the effectiveness, service-mindedness, and transparency of the EU administration. The EU averages of the former two stand at 10 per cent and of the latter at 9 per cent. No country recorded more than one-quarter of its citizens as totally satisfied with service-mindedness.
- Again, there are considerable cross-border variations in the responses. For example, the UK, French, Portuguese, and Swedish respondents are considerably less satisfied with these three aspects of the EU administration than the Slovak, Romanian, Czech, and Greek respondents. Similarly, 74 per cent of the Cypriot respondents are interested in being informed about the responsibilities of the EO, as opposed to only 21 per cent of the Slovaks. Further, for 74 per cent of the Finnish and 70 per cent of the German, but only for 31 per cent of the Spanish respondents, the right to move and reside freely in the EU is the most important right. The right to submit complaints to the EO features highest in the Greek responses at 46 per cent and lowest in Lithuania at 16 per cent.

3 EXPLAINING SURVEY RESPONSES TO EU RIGHTS AND THE EO

A question that has yet to be considered in EO scholarship is 'What factors may account for such cross-border differences in the survey responses?' Given the economic and political dimensions of the EU, we expect that a host of economic, political and governance variables are pivotal in explaining the observed pattern of cross-border variation in each of the nine replies. The empirical validity of our theoretical hypotheses (explained in more detail below) is put to the test, using regression analysis; the results are reported in Section 4.

In the context of economic variables, we expect that the per capita

[4] The list also included the right to vote in European elections if someone moves to another Member State, the right to have access to documents of the EU institutions, and the right to propose legislation through a citizens' initiative.

income of a Member State and the size of its intra-EU trade, either together or separately, will prove to be important determinants of the national responses. The level of per capita income captures the size of economic activity and, arguably, its complexity; it is a standard explanatory variable. For example, the higher the level of per capita income, the better informed citizens are about their rights and the mechanisms to enforce them. In addition, the higher the level and sophistication of the economy, the more likely it is that disputes will arise in connection with exchanges, rights, and obligations of private and state actors, generating more frequent referrals to formal channels of adjudication, like the EO. We denote per capita income by Y, which is measured by per capita gross domestic product (GDP) in Purchasing Power Standards (PPS) for 2010, the year preceding the survey.

Inclusion of the size of intra-EU trade is motivated by research findings regarding the dynamics of legal and economic integration in Europe, which identifies a strong positive relationship between intra-EU economic activity and legal integration, where the latter is measured by the number of references for preliminary rulings to the ECJ by national courts. In pioneering work, Stone Sweet and Sandholtz (1997) and Stone Sweet and Brunell (1998) argued that economic integration led to legal integration, in the sense that an increasing volume of transnational transactions in the EU generated a supranational system of dispute resolution in which the ECJ is the court of last resort. The main instrument of this legal order is the reference for preliminary ruling submitted by national courts to the ECJ, whereby national courts request the ECJ to rule on the applicability and interpretation of EU law. Using time-series and cross-sectional data, Stone Sweet and Brunell estimated regression models where the level of nominal intra-EU trade was the key variable to explain the number of references for preliminary rulings made by the national courts to the ECJ. Employing a richer data set and more careful specification of variables to measure the relative size of intra-EU trade and references for preliminary rulings per capita for each country, Pitarakis and Tridimas (2003) carried out Granger causality tests,[5] which showed that causality ran the opposite way, from references for preliminary rulings to intra-EU trade. Analytically, establishing EU law, removing barriers to trade, and forming a single market increased trade among the EU Member States.

[5] Simply put, Granger temporal causality means that if the past history of variable X explains the present values of another variable Y, then X Granger – causes Y. It bears noting that temporary causality may be unidirectional, bi-directional or may not exist at all.

Carrubba and Murrah (2005) and Hornuf and Voigt (2015) present further refinements by including additional economic variables and political explanatory variables, as well as performing additional statistical tests to explain why some Member States have drawn upon the procedure more often than others. From the perspective of the present inquiry, it is, therefore, expected that the more a Member State trades with other Member States, the more it is affected by EU legislation and administration, which, in turn, leads its citizens to be more familiar with EU matters, more affected by EU administration, and more likely to lodge complaints about such matters. Thus, we use intra-EU trade (denoted as ITEU) as an explanatory variable and measure it as the sum of a Member State imports from and exports within the EU as a percentage of such Member State's 2010 per capita GDP.

To account for the possibility that the respondents' replies reflect, more generally, positive or sceptical views about the EU, rather than direct answers to the survey questions, we also use, as a conditioning variable, the percentage of respondents from each Member State that tend to trust the EU (denoted by TRUST), a figure regularly published by the Eurobarometer survey. We use the figures published in the Eurobarometer 75 of Spring 2011.[6]

It is further presumed that citizen knowledge and familiarity with EU principles and practices grow with the length of a particular Member State's membership. Thus, we expect that citizens of countries that have been Members of the Union for a long time will display more knowledge about their rights and the EO's functions. To capture this effect, we include, as an additional independent variable, the number of years (NY) of EU membership of each Member State through 2011, with 59 being the highest for the six founding Members (starting from the foundation of the predecessors to the current Union in 1952) and with two being the lowest (for Bulgaria and Romania).

Further, acknowledging that the different political histories of the Member States have shaped attitudes towards EU membership, we add a dummy variable to capture the length of each Member State's Democratic Tradition (denoted by DT). DT takes the value of 2 for those Member States that have been uninterrupted democracies (i.e., all Western democracies from the Cold War period and beyond); the value of 1 for Greece, Spain, and Portugal, each of which shook off military dictatorships and democratized in the mid-70s; and 0 for post-communist Member States.

---

[6] Available at http://ec.europa.eu/public_opinion/archives/eb_arch_en.htm, accessed 2 March 2015.

In addition to the above variables, we hypothesize that the experience that citizens accumulate from domestic governance arrangements also affects their attitudes and expectations towards international governance and, consequently, their responses to EO-related questions. 'Domestic governance' refers to the institutional arrangements of a Member State intended to serve the interests of its citizens. According to the World Bank:

> This includes the process by which governments are selected, monitored and replaced; the capacity of the government to effectively formulate and implement sound policies; and the respect of citizens and the state for the institutions that govern economic and social interactions among them.[7]

The World Bank publishes a range of such political governance indicators, but for the purpose of our inquiry, we focus on the possible effects of: Voice and Accountability, Government Effectiveness, Rule of Law, and Control of Corruption. The definitions are as follows.

- Voice and Accountability (VA) reflects perceptions of the extent to which a country's citizens are able to participate in selecting their government, as well as freedom of expression, freedom of association, and a free media.
- Government Effectiveness (GE) reflects perceptions of the quality of public services; the quality of the civil service and the degree of its independence from political pressures; the quality of policy formulation and implementation; and the credibility of the government's commitment to such policies.
- Rule of Law (RL) reflects perceptions of the extent to which agents have confidence in and abide by the rules of society, in particular the quality of contract enforcement, property rights, the police and the courts, as well as the likelihood of crime and violence.
- Control of Corruption (CofC) reflects perceptions of the extent to which public power is exercised for private gain, including both petty and grand forms of corruption, as well as 'capture' of the state by elites and private interests.

Figures for these governance indicators range from approximately -2.5 (weak) to 2.5 (strong) governance performance. However, it is not clear that experience with domestic good governance (high values of the above indicators) is, a priori, associated with positive attitudes towards the EU

---

[7] Source: http://info.worldbank.org/governance/wgi/index.aspx#home, accessed 2 March 2015.

(e.g., high percentages of satisfaction with the EU administration, interest in the function of the EO, or support for a particular EU right). For example, respondents from a country characterized by high domestic government efficiency may find the EU institutions fall below their national standard and report low levels of satisfaction therewith (and vice versa for respondents from a country with low national government efficiency). Alternatively, respondents may extend their national experience to the EU, reporting high satisfaction with it.

Given the wide range of questions covered by the Survey, we do not presume that each of the independent variables mentioned above affects all nine dependent variables. Rather, we expect that different explanatory variables will account for the cross-border variation in each reply. To give a simple example, there is no reason to believe that the same factors determine how informed respondents are about EU rights, how satisfied they are with the transparency of the EU administration, or what is the most important responsibility of the EO. Only the two economic variables, Y and ITEU are used as independent variables in all regressions, as suggested by the dynamics of legal and economic integration, as well as the TRUST variable. Be that as it may, our empirical inquiry is severely handicapped by the small size of our sample, that is, we only have 27 observations, which is another reason why, in each estimated specification, we use only a subset of the governance regressors.

4 RESULTS

The results from our Ordinary Least Squares estimation are shown in Tables 4.2 to 4.4.

(a) Information about EU Rights

The estimates reported in Column 1 of Table 4.2 show that the higher the Member State's per capita income and the larger its percentage of intra-EU trade, the higher the percentage of respondents who are informed about the EU fundamental rights, just as our priors suggested. However, somewhat paradoxically, the lower the percentage of people who trust the EU, the higher the percentage of those who are informed about EU rights. Two possible explanations may account for this finding. First, the less the respondents trust the EU, the greater the need to know more about EU rights. Alternatively, what the statistical findings might be picking up is a kind of reverse causality; because the respondent citizens know their EU rights, they trust the EU less (the Eurosceptic argument). In view of the

Table 4.2 Determinants of percentage of respondents

	Who are informed about EU Rights		Who are satisfied with EU administration					
			Effectiveness		Service		Transparency	
Explanatory variables	(1)	(1A)	(2)	(2A)	(3)	(3A)	(4)	(4A)
Y	0.1193** 3.90	0.0697** 3.89	0.0019 0.56		0.0241 0.85		0.0347 1.20	
ITEU	0.0864* 2.38	0.0662* 2.17	0.0953* 2.34	0.1064** 3.49	0.0640# 1.73	0.550* 2.16	0.0231 0.71	
TRUST	−0.2179* −2.01	−0.0959 −1.00	0.0319 0.26		0.1016 1.02		0.1755# 1.87	0.2295** 2.92
NY	−0.1185# −1.94		−0.1862* −2.72	−0.1785** −3.45	−0.1587** −2.81	−0.0987** −2.68	−0.1279* −2.47	−0.0872# −1.96
DT	1.7076 0.95		5.1358** 2.55	5.5207** 3.10	2.7112 1.46		2.7050# 1.75	2.3691# 1.76
GE					−6.0703** −2.89	−3.0788* −2.34		

CofC							−5.6789** −4.06	−4.688** −3.80
RL	−3.9982# −1.78		−8.5605** −3.39	−8.2490** −4.13				
Constant	12.5877* 2.52	7.3564# 1.60	12.3261** 2.20	14.1441** 5.53	9.3742* 2.07	15.3293** 6.70	3.6291 0.84	4.2579 1.00
SSR R–SQ $F(n_1,n_2)$ Prob>F	254.911 0.5728 4.47(6,20) 0.0050	319.787 0.4640 6.64 (3,23) 0.0022	320.862 0.6358 5.82(6,20) 0.0012	328.507 0.6271 9.25(4,22) 0.0002	245.4447 0.6695 6.75(6,20) 0.0005	318.386 0.5713 10.22(3,23) 0.0002	234.881 0.6836 7.20(6,20) 0.0003	261.644 0.6475 10.10(4,22) 0.0001

Notes:
Second row figures denote t – statistics.
** significant at 1%.
* significant at 5%.
\# significant at 10%.

facts that the Charter is a recent development in comparison to the foundation of the EU (including its predecessor communities) and the Charter only became legally binding with the entry into force of the Lisbon Treaty in 2009, while the EU and its predecessors have been part of Europe's institutional landscape since 1957, we find the former as a more plausible explanation than the latter.

The length of a Member State's EU membership exerts a similar negative effect (albeit statistically significant only at or above the 10 per cent level) – that is, the longer a country has been a Member of the EU, the lower the percentage of respondents who are informed about EU fundamental rights. The latter may be indicative of a kind of 'inertia', where the longer a country has been in the EU, the more its nationals have been exposed to the effects of EU rule-making and, hence, the less urgent it is for them to know about EU rights. A similar negative effect is detected for the rule of law (again at or above the 10 per cent level) – that is, the higher a country scores in domestic application of the rule of law, the less its respondents are informed about EU rights. Insofar as this finding can be inverted (i.e., the lower a country scores in domestic application of the rule of law, the more its nationals are informed about the rule of law), it points to the operation of a substitution effect, where citizens consider that if the rule of law is not respected in their country, they seek to obtain information about another layer of rights. Finally, the democratic tradition of a country has no statistically significant effect on the percentage of those who are informed about EU fundamental rights. Given the small size of our sample, Column (1A) of Table 4.2 presents the results from using per capita income, intra-EU trade, and trust only as explanatory variables (i.e., those whose estimates were statistically significant at or above the 5 per cent level). With that information in mind, it turns out that only per capita income and intra-EU are statistically significant and have the expected positive sign.

(b) Attitudes towards the EU Administration

The results from testing attitudes towards the EU administration are shown in Table 4.2, Columns (2)–(4); as before, Columns labelled with an 'A' show the estimates after dropping the statistically insignificant explanatory variables. Columns (2) and (2A) reveal that the percentage of those satisfied with the effectiveness of the EU administration is positively related to income and democratic tradition, but depends negatively on length of membership and the rule of law. That is, as was the case with the percentage of those informed about EU rights, the longer a country has been an EU member and the greater it scores on the rule of law, the

Table 4.3 Determinants of percentage of respondents

	Who say the EO's most important responsibility is to ensure that citizens know about their rights		Who say they are totally interested in being informed about the responsibilities of the EO	
Explanatory variables	(1)	(1A)	(2)	(2A)
Y	0.0148 0.27		0.1523# 1.84	0.1091 1.57
ITEU	−0.0223 −0.34		−0.0114 −0.12	
TRUST	0.0367 0.21		−0.0076 −0.03	
DT	−1.2608 −0.44		10.2445* 2.328	8.3968** 2.61
VA	−34.0650* −2.11	−34.3961** −2.87		
GE	24.1643** 3.42	23.5559** 3.90		
CofC			−9.7110* −2.43	−8.3346* −2.31
Constant	63.0651** 5.13	64.6338** 8.79	32.4868** 2.65	34.8489** 6.98
SSR R–SQ $F(n_1,n_2)$ Prob>F	887.903 0.4781 3.05(6,20) 0.0275	898.682 0.4718 10.72(3.23) 0.0005	1922.682 0.4651 2.90(6,20) 0.0336	2044.083 0.4314 5.82(3,23) 0.0041

Notes:
Second row figures denote t – statistics.
** significant at 1%.
* significant at 5%.
# significant at 10%.

less satisfaction it reports with EU effectiveness. We may, then, infer that when the rule of law is weakly respected domestically, citizens view the EU administration as presenting a better alternative.

Regarding the determinants of satisfaction with EU service (Columns (3) and (3A)) we observe that it increases with intra-EU trade, a result that accords with prior intuition, but it decreases with the length of EU membership and the effectiveness of domestic government. None of the other explanatory variables has any significant effect.

Turning to the determinants of the percentage of respondents who are satisfied with EU transparency, the estimates of Columns (4) and (4A) indicate that the greater the trust in the EU and the stronger the democratic tradition, the greater the satisfaction. On the other hand, once again, the longer the length of EU membership, and the greater the score of domestic Control of Corruption, the lower the percentage of those satisfied.

(c) Attitudes towards the EO

Table 4.3 focuses on the factors that shape the views of the respondents towards the EO.[8] The lower the Voice and Accountability score and the higher the Government Effectiveness score, the higher the percentage of respondents who agree that the EO's most important responsibility is to ensure that citizens know about their rights (see Columns (1) and (1A)). The former implies that citizens appeal to the EO as a substitute for low domestic Voice and Accountability. The latter implies that experience of high domestic Government Effectiveness leads citizens to also demand strong transnational governance, in the form of the EO ascertaining their rights.

With respect to interest in the responsibilities of the EO, the findings reported in Columns (2) and (2A) indicate that such interest is higher the longer the Member State has had a democratic tradition but lower when its Control of Corruption is high. Thus, a long democratic experience fosters demand for information regarding accountability, while poor domestic governance (Control of Corruption is low), fosters a need to compensate by turning to the EU. On the other hand, neither the two economic variables (per capita income and intra-EU trade) nor trust in the EU affect the views of the respondents about the EO.

(d) Determinants of EU rights

Table 4.4 presents the determinants of EU rights. The importance of the right to move freely in the EU varies positively with TRUST in the EU and Government Effectiveness, it is negatively related to the length of the Member State's Democratic Tradition, but is not affected by either per

---

[8] Since the office of the EO was established in 1995 a country's length of EU membership is excluded from the set of explanatory variables.

Table 4.4 Determinants of percentage of respondents who say the most important European citizens' rights is the right to:

	Move and reside freely in the EU		Good administration by EU institutions		Submit complaints to the European Ombudsman		Petition the European Parliament	
Explanatory variables	(1)	(1A)	(2)	(2A)	(3)	(3A)	(4)	(4A)
Y	0.0512 0.59		0.0021 0.04		0.0115 0.18		0.0302 0.39	
ITEU	−0.0664 −0.65		0.0296 0.42		0.0581 0.73		−0.0370 −0.41	
TRUST	0.5647* 2.09	0.5047* 2.23	−0.1050 −0.54		−0.1104 −0.51		0.1333 0.55	
NY					−0.1946# −1.72	−0.1653# −1.81		
DT	−14.1499** −2.48	−9.1768** −2.80	11.6777** 3.74	12.2072** 5.89	5.7692 1.56	3.7697# 1.83	7.1917# 1.83	8.1069** 2.95
VA	−31.0059 −1.25				−5.4414 −0.04		−52.7532* −2.37	−51.2279** −2.92
GE	34.2158** 3.15	20.5201** 4.22	7.8049 1.13				19.6816* 2.03	19.0918* 2.22
RL			−19.0086** −2.79	−11.8377** −3.53				

Table 4.4 (continued)

	Move and reside freely in the EU		Good administration by EU institutions		Submit complaints to the European Ombudsman		Petition the European Parliament	
Explanatory variables	(1)	(1A)	(2)	(2A)	(3)	(3A)	(4)	(4A)
Constant	10.2816 0.77	14.7757 1.21	34.8924** 3.60	32.1021** 10.76	38.7529** 2.75	33.2325** 15.11	41.6962* 2.47	46.8399** 4.31
SSR	2102.594	2363.877	1061.480	1163.159	1155.453	1191.057	1679.58	1729.02
R–SQ	0.5783	0.5259	0.6332	0.5981	0.1646	0.1389	0.4178	0.4037
F (n_1,n_2)	4.57(6,20)	8.5(4,22)	5.75(6,20)	17.86(2,24)	0.66(6,20)	1.94(2,24)	2.39 (6,20)	5.19(3,23)
Prob >F	0.0045	0.0006	0.0013	0.0000	0.6846	0.1662	0.066	0.0069

Notes:
Second row figures denote t – statistics.
** significant at 1%.
* significant at 5%.
# significant at 10%.

capita income or intra-EU trade (see Columns (1) and (1A)). Intuitively, TRUST in the EU and the experience of a non-democratic regime both translate into valuing the right to free movement. Further, the more effective the government of a Member State, the more its citizens value free movement. The reason may be that good domestic governance protects individual liberties, including the freedom to move. The estimated parameters of Columns (2) and (2A) show that respondents from Member States with a strong Democratic Tradition and low observance of the Rule of Law support the right to good administration by the EU, but neither the two economic variables nor TRUST in the EU affect views towards that right. Thus, in an echo of the earlier findings on interest in the responsibilities of the EO (Table 4.3, Column (2)), a long Democratic Tradition encourages demand for good EU administration, while poor application of the Rule of Law is counterbalanced by turning to the EU. The importance of the right to submit complaints to the EO varies with the length of the Member State's Democratic Tradition but is inversely related to the length of that Member State's EU membership, although both results are statistically significant only at or above the 10 per cent level (see Column (3A)). Finally, the importance of the right to petition the EP depends positively on Democratic Tradition and Government Effectiveness, but negatively on Voice and Accountability. Analytically, a long Democratic Tradition and good quality of domestic policy institutions lead citizens to demand greater participation with the EU policy-making organs. On the other hand, when citizens enjoy high levels of participation in domestic politics, demand for participation at the EU level subsides.

5 CONCLUSIONS

The purpose of this chapter has been to explain the diverse pattern of national responses to the Survey questions relating to information about EU citizen rights, the responsibilities of the EO, and the importance of different EU citizen rights. We summarize our empirical findings by discussing how the proposed economic and political explanatory variables affect the responses. The pattern of empirical estimates allows the following inferences:

- As the level of per capita income rises, so does information about citizen rights.
- An increase in intra-EU trade leads to more information about EU rights and higher satisfaction with EU Administration effectiveness and service.

- The more citizens trust the EU, the less they are informed about rights; the more they are satisfied with EU transparency, the greater importance they place on the right to free movement, but the lower importance they place on the right to submit complaints to the EO.
- The longer a country has been a Member of the EU, the lower the percentage of those informed about EU rights, and in what is probably an indictment for the EU, the lower the percentages of those who are satisfied with the performance of the EU administration on service, effectiveness and transparency. Seen from a different perspective, the latter implies that the longer a country has been a Member State, the more flawed its citizens find EU administration.
- Longer experience of democratic governance is associated with higher satisfaction with the effectiveness and transparency of the EU administration and the importance of the rights to good administration, and to petition the EP. On the other hand, it is also associated with lower interest in information about the responsibilities of the EO, and renders less important the rights to free movement and to submit complaints to the EO.
- The effects of domestic governance variables are varied and diverse. The higher a country's score on Voice and Accountability, the lower the importance its citizens place on the EO ensuring that they know of their EU rights and their right to petition the EP. Citizens from Member States with greater effectiveness of their national governments give higher importance to the responsibility of the EO to ensure that citizens know their EU rights and to the rights to free movement and to petition the EP, but they are less satisfied with the effectiveness of the EU administration. The more the Rule of Law is respected, the fewer citizens are informed about EU rights, the less they are satisfied with the effectiveness of the EU administration, and the lower they prioritize the right to good administration by the EU. Finally, citizens of Member States that successfully control corruption are less satisfied with the transparency of EU administration and less interested in obtaining information regarding the responsibilities of the EO.

It is perhaps comforting to find that some standard theoretical predictions are consistent with the data (e.g., the effect of per capita income and intra-EU trade). It is also worth noting that citizens turn to the EU, including the EO, only when they consider domestic governance defective. But, we also note the negative effect of the length of EU membership on the percentage of those informed about EU rights, and those who are satisfied with the performance of the EU administration. Given that this inquiry is the first of its kind, we consider our results to be preliminary and tentative, and call for a closer examination. We are also well aware of the acute problem of our small sample size. Use of more rigorous examination with a larger and richer set of replies is of paramount importance. Be that as it may, we hope that our results can serve to open an informed debate.

REFERENCES

Bovens, M. (2007) 'New forms of accountability and EU-governance', *Comparative European Politics* 5, 104–20.

Bovens, M. (2010) 'Two concepts of accountability: accountability as a virtue and as a mechanism', *West European Politics* 33, 946–67.

Carrubba, C., and L. Murrah (2005) 'Legal integration and the use of the preliminary ruling process in the European Union', *International Organization* 59, 399–418.

Hornuf, L., and S. Voigt (2015) 'Analyzing preliminary references as the powerbase of the European Court of Justice', *European Journal of Law and Economics*, 37, 287–311.

Lord, C., and J. Pollak (2010) 'Representation and accountability: communicating tubes?', *West European Politics* 33, 968–88.

Peters, A. (2005) 'The European Ombudsman and the European Constitution', *Common Market Law Review* 42, 697–743.

Pitarakis, J.-Y., and G. Tridimas (2003) 'Joint dynamics of legal and economic integration in the European Union', *European Journal of Law and Economics* 16, 357–68.

Song, W., and V. Della Sala (2008) 'Eurosceptics and Europhiles in accord: the creation of the European Ombudsman as an institutional Isomorphism', *Policy & Politics* 36, 481–95.

Stone Sweet, A., and T.L. Brunell (1998) 'Constructing a supranational constitution: dispute resolution and governance in the European Community', *American Political Science Review* 92, 63–81.

Stone Sweet, A., and W. Sandholtz (1997) 'European Integration and Supranational Governance', *Journal of European Public Policy* 4, 297–317.

Tridimas, G., and T. Tridimas (2004) 'National courts and the European Court of Justice: a public choice analysis of the preliminary reference procedure', *International Review of Law and Economics* 24, 125–45.

5. Advancing transparency in the European Union: the role of the European Ombudsman

Dacian C. Dragos and Bogdana Neamtu

INTRODUCTION

The principle of free access to administrative documents has become extremely widespread in Europe and throughout the world[1] being regarded as a precondition and standard practice for well-functioning democracies. The European Union (EU), one of the most fascinating constitutional projects in the world today, also faces challenges regarding the relationship between public authority and the citizen but in a way that is quite different from what we are used to in the context of the national states.[2] Despite the fact that it is quite hard to draw direct comparisons with national approaches in the realm of free access to documents, the fact that the EU is perceived as rather opaque may be a reason for concern. After the release of the 2014 European Commission's report on public access to institutional documents in the summer of 2015, several critical voices argued that despite the somewhat positive outlook cast by the figures in the report, the EU is less transparent than many of its Member States, at least with respect to access to legislative documents.[3] There are at least two main reasons for concern from the perspective of transparency. First,

[1] Right2Info, 'Access to Information Laws: Overview and Statutory Goals' (20 January 2012), www.right2info.org/access-to-information-laws, accessed 19 November 2015.

[2] Sophie van Bijsterveld, 'Transparency in the European Union: A Crucial Link in Shaping the New Social Contract between the Citizen and the EU', Transparency in Europe II, proceedings of conference hosted by the Netherlands during its Chairmanship of the EU Council (25 and 26 November 2004), www.ip-rs.si/fileadmin/user_upload/Pdf/clanki/Agenda__Bijsterveld-Paper.pdf, accessed 19 November 2015.

[3] Transparency International, 'EU Institutions are less Transparent than Many Member States' (EurActiv.com, 02 September 2015), www.euractiv.com/sections/

there is a general lack of access to information about EU decision-making and limited interest on the behalf of the EU institutions with regard to proactive disclosure of such documents, including documents outlining the negotiating positions of the three EU institutions or 'four column documents' when they meet behind closed doors during 'trilogues'.[4] Second, the institutions must do more to ensure that already published documents can actually be found. In the EU integrity study published in 2014, 78 per cent of the requested documents were already in the public domain but the applicants simply could not find them.[5]

An important lesson from comparative law relates to the existence of bodies entrusted with guaranteeing compliance with the right of access.[6] The European Ombudsman (hereafter EO), in a rather similar fashion to the national ombudsmen, represents a combination of an independently functioning mechanism of public scrutiny as well as a low-threshold mechanism to deal with the complaints of individual citizens.[7] It is perhaps worth noting the fact that the EO has helped to give direction to standard setting with regard to access to information.[8] Also, recent developments in the EU have pointed toward the interesting and innovative role assumed by the EO in ensuring the transparency of the decision-making process of the EU. Emily O'Reilly, the current EO, has adopted a strategy of launching a suite of systemic investigations at her own initiative. It is a departure from previous Ombudsmen, who used own-initiative investigations more sparingly.[9] Using this strategy, she looked into transparency in the EU-US trade deal, the Transatlantic Trade and Investment Partnership (TTIP), Commission expert advisory groups, revolving doors between the public and private sector, and the European Citizens' Initiative.[10]

This chapter endeavours to investigate the role of the EO in the realm of

trade-society/eu-institutions-are-less-transparent-many-member-states-317240, accessed 19 November 2015.

[4] Ibid.

[5] Ibid.

[6] Henri Labayle, 'Openness, Transparency and Access to Documents and Information in the European Union' (2013), www.europarl.europa.eu/RegData/etudes/note/join/2013/493035/IPOL-LIBE_NT%282013%29493035_EN.pdf, accessed 19 November 2015, p. 31.

[7] Van Bijsterveld (note 2) p. 4.

[8] Ibid. p. 5.

[9] James Crisp, 'Secretive "Trialogue" Talks to Agree EU Law Face Investigation' (EurActiv.com 21 April 2015), www.euractiv.com/sections/eu-priorities-2020/secretive-trialogue-talks-agree-eu-law-face-investigation-313936, accessed 19 November 2015.

[10] Ibid.

free access to documents and information, with a focus on describing and analysing the underlying norms and principles which form the ombudsprudence in this field. The main research question we try to answer is whether the institution is indeed involved in creating norms of good administration in individual decisions and if yes, to be able to make an inventory of these norms. The empirical research was inspired by a similar research conducted by De Leeuw in 2009 in the field of public tenders.[11] However, as opposed to the cited research, the authors of this chapter do not assume a normative position with regard to the role the EO should play.

Part I of the chapter represents a brief theoretical analysis of the role and function of the EO with an emphasis on the normative standards used for review and the involvement of the institution in the production and codification of these standards. Part II, dedicated to empirical research, comprises a description of the methodology, of the role of the EO vis-à-vis free access to documents and two mini-studies connected to the main research objective.

PART I: THE ROLE OF OMBUDSMAN INSTITUTIONS IN ADVANCING GOOD ADMINISTRATION

1 National Ombudsmen as Creators of Norms of Good Administration

The figure of the ombudsman has become familiar in many democratic systems over the last half-century,[12] with new offices being created even after 2000[13] (Luxembourg in 2004 and Bulgaria in 2005), and there is no shortage of historical overviews of the emergence of ombudsman

---

[11] Magdalena E. de Leeuw, 'An Empirical Study into the Norms of Good Administration as Operated by the European Ombudsman in the Field of Tenders' (EUI Working Papers, 2009), http://cadmus.eui.eu/bitstream/handle/1814/11234/EUI_RSCAS_2009_20.pdf?sequence=3, accessed 19 November 2015, pp. 1–75.

[12] Herwig C.H. Hofmann, Gerard C. Rowe, and Alexander H. Türk, *Administrative Law and Policy of the European Union* (Oxford University Press 2011) p. 780.

[13] Nikiforos Diamandouros, 'The Ombudsman Institution and the Quality of Democracy' (Occasional paper based on the lecture with the same title offered at the University of Siena, Italy on 17 October 2006), www.circap.org/uploads/1/8/1/6/18163511/diamanduros.pdf, accessed 19 November 2015, p. 2.

institutions in Europe[14] and elsewhere. This section offers first a brief discussion regarding the types of ombudsman institutions that currently exist in Europe, based on the observation that they have been created for different purposes and hence have been assigned different tasks and powers.[15] In other words, the flexibility of the institution which makes it readily adaptable to different constitutional, cultural, legal and political environments implies diversity.[16] The main goal is to highlight whether a specific type of ombudsman is more likely to foster the role of this institution as creator of norms of good administration.

While prior to the Second World War the ombudsman institution has been limited to a handful of countries, being mostly a Nordic experiment,[17] from the 1960s onwards two main developments occurred: first, the proliferation of ombudsman institutions at various levels (a trend often described as 'ombudsmania')[18] and then their diversification.[19] In addition to governmental ombudsmen with general jurisdiction over administrative conduct,[20] other types of ombudsman institutions have been created: single purpose ombudsmen (health service ombudsman), human rights ombudsmen, private ombudsmen, etc.[21]

Another general trend observable in the last decades regards not only the increase in the number and types of ombudsman institutions but also significant changes in the functions originally associated with the concept.[22] A first shift regards the transition from disciplining errant public servants and maintaining a good standard within the public service to the provision of remedies in individual cases.[23] Additional functions of the institution in various national settings include: identification of systemic

---

14 Magdalena E. de Leeuw, 'The European Ombudsman's Role as a Developer of Norms of Good Administration' (2011) 17/2 *EPL* p. 349.

15 Ibid.

16 Diamandouros (note 13) p. 2.

17 Milan Remac, 'Standards of Ombudsman Assessment: A New Normative Concept?' (2013) 9/3 *Utrecht Law Review* p. 62.

18 Ana Maria Moure Pino, 'The European Ombudsman in the Framework of the European Union' (2011) 38/3 *Revista Chilena de Derecho* p. 426.

19 Milan Remac, *Coordinating Ombudsmen and the Judiciary* (Intersentia 2014) pp. 3–4.

20 Roy Gregory and Philip Giddings, 'The Ombudsman Institution: Growth and Development', in Roy Gregory and Philip Giddings (eds.), *Righting Wrongs: The Ombudsmen in Six Continents* (IOS Press 2000) pp. 6–7.

21 Mary A. Marshall and Linda C. Reif, 'The Ombudsman: Maladministration and Alternative Dispute Resolution' (1995) XXXIV/1 *Alberta Law Review* pp. 215–39.

22 Gregory and Giddings (note 20) p. 11.

23 Ibid. p. 12.

faults in the functioning of public administration and the provision of recommendations of a general nature regarding good administrative practices; promotion of 'open government', in that ombudsmen are authorized to deal with complaints about the way in which public bodies have handled requests under the code of practice or relevant legislation operative in their country; auditing telephone intercept records; protection of whistle-blowers; employing mediation and conciliation with the purpose of finding an outcome satisfactory to the complainant and the agency concerned, as quickly as possible and with a minimum of formality ('quick fix'); and an educational role, especially in countries from Eastern Europe and Latin America.[24]

Remac offers an extensive inventory of the literature and argues that various authors identify various models and stages in the development of the ombudsman institution.[25] Based on his analysis, we included in our work the following authors and possible models: (1) Gregory distinguishes two main ombudsman models: a 'classical ombudsman of mature liberal democracies' and an 'ombudsman connected with regime transformations in new or emerging democracies';[26] (2) Reif also distinguishes two models of ombudsmen but she talks about a 'classical ombudsman', i.e. an ombudsman that complies with the definition of an ombudsman as proposed by the International Bar Association in 1978 and a 'hybrid ombudsman' that is vested with some additional authority;[27] (3) Kucsko-Stadlmayer distinguishes three types of ombudsmen in connection with their powers: the basic or classical model, the rule of law model, and the human rights model.[28]

Heede offers a somewhat different categorization and argues that there are mainly two dimensions based on which a distinction should be operated among various national ombudsman institutions (especially in terms of the functions performed).[29] The main difference between the models is the primary function of an ombudsman: redress or control. A redress

---

[24] Ibid. pp. 12–18.

[25] Remac (note 17) pp. 63–4.

[26] Roy Gregory, 'The Parliamentary Ombudsman in the United Kingdom', in Joachim Jens Hesse and Theo A.J. Toonen (eds.), *The European Yearbook of Comparative Government and Public Administration*, Volume III. (Nomos Verlagsgesellschaft 1997).

[27] Linda C. Reif, *The Ombudsman, Good Governance, and the International Human Rights System*. (Martinus Nijhoff Publishers 2004).

[28] Gabriela Kucsko-Stadlmayer, *European Ombudsman-Institutions: A Comparative Legal Analysis Regarding the Multifaceted Realisation of an Idea* (Springer 2008).

[29] Cited in De Leeuw (note 14) pp. 349–50.

ombudsman seeks to remedy an individual grievance by negotiating and mediating between parties while a control ombudsman acts for the benefit of all citizens and is involved in rule development.[30] Next, the models are distinguished on the basis of the ombudsman's position in relation to other mechanisms of control and redress (overlapping or non-overlapping mandates).[31]

These categorizations do not always include the legislative standard of the ombudsmen's control. In order to assess the role of various national ombudsmen as creators of norms of good administration, it is important to identify their legislative standard of control and, in close connection, their assessment criteria. Remac distinguishes four types of legislative standards of control, associated with four generations of ombudsman institutions (these generations are defined from a historical, evolutionary perspective): legality (first generation – oldest ombudsmen institutions in Europe, Sweden and Finland); general normative concept such as good administration or good government (second generation – Danish Ombudsman, Dutch National Ombudsman); human rights (third generation – Eastern Europe, after the fall of the communist regimes); and fighting against corruption (fourth generation – African countries).[32] Very often these legislative standards of control are combined in practice.[33]

The standard of assessment used by the ombudsman institutions is different from the legislative standard of control but should be understood in close connection with the latter. Remac argues that a very general distinction should be operated between legal rules as assessment standards and 'something else'.[34] Based on this distinction, his classification of assessment standards includes legal norms, other norms (good or proper administration), and human rights. Human rights, despite being a separate category, operate in a similar way to the legal rules, mainly because human rights are stated in laws. In systems where the ombudsmen use good administration as the main standard of assessment, they are also providing content for what good administration means.[35] Thus, they may produce checklists of good administrative practice, publish codes of good administrative behaviour and take initiatives to tackle systemic maladministration.[36] The sets of norms they produce are inherently open-ended and

30 De Leeuw (note 14) p. 350.
31 Ibid.
32 Remac (note 17) pp. 63–7.
33 Ibid. p. 66.
34 Ibid. pp. 67–9.
35 Diamandouros (note 13) pp. 9–10.
36 Ibid. p. 10.

subject to continuous updating, due to specific circumstances that may change and develop rapidly.[37] When providing this content, depending on their philosophy regarding the mission and role of the institution, they can regard the law as an obligatory condition of good administration (placing in this case a high emphasis on legality) or they can have a more flexible approach, meaning that they regard the law as an existing standard to be complemented by other normative standards or they do not consider the law relevant at all, mainly because the complaints they receive are not covered by the law.[38]

Only the ombudsmen whose main legislative standard of control is good administration can be included in the category of developers of norms. The other ombudsmen will be limited to applying the existing legal provisions to the cases they are dealing with. However, even in the case of the former, a significant difference can occur, based on the degree of discretion and the ombudsmen's attitudes regarding the interaction between the law and the standards they develop.

2 The EO as Creator of Good Administration Norms

The main question this section tries to answer is how the EO fits into the previously analysed categories and whether it can be regarded as a creator of norms of good administration.

The main roles that the EO institution is entrusted with are to be found in the political debates predating the creation of this function. Thus, the ombudsman institution created by the Maastricht Treaty, owes its inspiration to a combination of Spanish enthusiasm for European citizenship and Danish concern for administrative efficiency and fairness.[39] Thus, from a political perspective, the main role of the institution is to help bridge the gap between citizens and the Union's institutions[40] by establishing a relationship of confidence between the institutions and the citizen, based on transparency in the Community's administration.[41] The enhancement of the relationship between the European administration and the citizen has continued ever since the creation of the institution to remain an important

---

[37] Ibid. pp. 9–12.

[38] Remac (note 17) p. 76.

[39] Roy Gregory, 'The European Union Ombudsman', in Roy Gregory and Philip Giddings (eds.), R*ighting Wrongs. The Ombudsmen in Six Continents* (IOS Press 2000) pp. 155–74.

[40] Aklexandros Tsadiras, 'Maladministration and Life beyond Legality: The European Ombudsman's Paradigm' [2015] 11 *International Review of Law* p. 2.

[41] Gregory (note 39) pp. 156–7.

mission of the EO.[42] From a legal perspective, the EO's main function is to strengthen the protection of citizens' rights and interests in the Union territory vis-à-vis the Community institutions through the creation of a non-litigious mechanism for delivery of administrative justice.[43] This mechanism was envisioned as an alternative to the litigation before the courts and it had to be cheap, flexible and accessible.[44]

The EO is said to have been modelled according to the Danish Ombudsman plan, one of the most widely copied ombudsman models.[45] The EO is described as the only example of a fully-fledged, classical ombudsman at the international level.[46] Remac argues that the Danish Ombudsman pertains to the second generation Ombudsmen, namely those having as a legislative standard of control a general normative concept, less stringent than the legal norms.[47] This is not to say that legality is excluded as a standard of review from the Danish Ombudsman's activity – the largest category of complaints regards the merits of administrative decisions, which are, furthermore, assessed through a legality review.[48]

The EO is tasked to investigate instances of maladministration in the activities of institutions, bodies, offices and agencies of the EU, with the exception of the Court of Justice of the European Union (CJEU) acting in its judicial role. Besides dealing with individual complaints about maladministration, the EO can also conduct own-initiative inquiries into more structural problems of maladministration.[49] In the case of the EO, the standard of review is not defined per se as good administration but rather as its opposite, maladministration. Diamandouros defines the scope of the EO's activity by comparing it to the one of the courts and argues that 'while for the courts the major realm of activity and concern is to ensure adherence to legality on the part of state and the citizens, for the ombudsman the equivalent realm is the promotion of good administration and the avoidance of maladministration'.[50]

The concept of maladministration is a rather ambiguous one as it has no official definition in European law. In the 1995 Annual Report,[51] the

---

42 Moure Pino (note 18) p. 246.
43 Tsadiras (note 40) p. 2.
44 De Leeuw (note 14) p. 351.
45 Ibid. p. 352.
46 Moure Pino (note 18) p. 433.
47 Remac (note 17) p. 65.
48 De Leeuw (note 14) p. 352.
49 Ibid.
50 Diamandouros (note 13) p. 10.
51 European Ombudsman, *Annual Report 1995* (22 April 1996), www.ombudsman.europa.eu/activities/annualreports.faces, accessed 19 November 2015, pp. 8–9.

EO put together an indicative list of elements constituting maladministration: administrative irregularities and omissions, abuse of power, negligence, unlawful procedures, unfairness, malfunction or incompetence, discrimination, avoidable delay, and lack or refusal of information. In 1997, the European Parliament requested a clearer definition. In response, the EO declared in his 1997 Annual Report that 'maladministration occurs when a public body fails to act in accordance with a rule or principle which is binding upon it'.[52] He also stated that 'when the Ombudsman investigates whether a Community institution or body has acted in accordance with the rules and principles which are binding upon it, his first and most essential task must be to establish whether it has acted lawfully'.[53]

Maladministration should be understood as a double-layered notion: the first layer, which forms the basis of the concept, concerns legality and comprises the legally binding provisions of the primary and secondary EU law, as well as the case law of the Union courts. The second layer, more flexible and under continuous development, pertains to propriety and consists of rules and principles that the EO considers to regulate the EU's administrative attitude.[54] In a similar vein, Mendes argues that good administration, the opposite of maladministration, is also composed of three interconnected layers.[55] With regard to the first two layers, she distinguishes between procedural guarantees that are meant to protect the substantive rights of the people dealing with EU bodies (Article 41 of the Charter of Fundamental Rights, which elevates good administration to the status of a fundamental right) and legal rules that structure the exercise of the administrative function by reference to the public interest. With regard to good administration, the terminology is quite confusing, because, based on the context, one needs to distinguish among good administration as a fundamental right, principle or standard.[56]

The European Code of Good Administrative Behaviour proposed by the EO in 1999 to the European institutions and then approved through

---

[52] European Ombudsman, *Annual Report 1997* (20 April 1998), www.ombudsman.europa.eu/activities/annualreports.faces, accessed 19 November 2015, pp. 22–4.

[53] Ibid.

[54] Tsadiras (note 40) p. 6.

[55] Joana Mendes, 'Good Administration in EU Law and the European Code of Good Administrative Behavior' (EUI Working Papers, September 2009), http://cadmus.eui.eu/bitstream/handle/1814/12101/LAW_2009_09.pdf?sequence=3&isAllowed=y, accessed 19 November 2015, pp. 4–5.

[56] Ibid. p. 3.

a resolution by the European Parliament on 6 September 2001, represents the main tool detailing the rules and principles against which the EO could assess cases of maladministration. In addition, the Code was intended to serve two other main purposes: to provide a guide for the staff of Community institutions and bodies regarding their relationship with the public and to inform the citizens about their rights and the standards of administration they may expect.[57] In the literature there are two conflicting views with regard to whether or not the role of the Code was simply to explain in more detail what the Charter's right to good administration enshrined in Article 41 should signify in practice.[58] A better understanding of this issue can be depicted from the analysis of the main principles/rules and their nature included in the Code.

The different opinions about what good administration means are reflected in the way in which various scholars categorize the rules and principles included in the Code, which lacks a formal structure and has an eclectic character. Table 5.1 portrays two main approaches to the categorization of the principles and rules included in the Code. The first is in line with a normative approach which considers the EO as the developer of own standards of review; the second draws more on the distinction between legality and 'something else'.

Despite the different jargon and philosophies behind the categorization of the principles and rules from the Code, most authors admit that the Code takes account of the principles of European administrative law contained in the case law of the Court of Justice and also draws inspiration from national laws; in addition it includes rules and principles which are not enshrined in the law.[59] While some of the principles from the Code are clearly derived and/or overlap with Community law, others have an extra-legal character, especially those referring to 'care and consideration in how citizens are treated' and 'the good functioning of the administrative service'.[60] Remac states that the Code of the EO may be perceived as having a more pronounced legalistic character (compared to the other codes/lists of good administration standards) as it was adopted through

---

57 Ibid. p. 1.

58 While Moure Pino (note 18) p. 440 argues that this was the sole goal of the Code, Mendes (note 55) p. 6 claims that the distinctive feature of good administration lies in the combination and partial overlap between legality and aspects of good administration that stand beyond legality and this is why the Code should not be regarded as explicating the right to good administration as envisaged in Article 41 of the Charter.

59 De Leeuw (note 14) p. 354; Mendes (note 55) p. 12.

60 De Leeuw (note 14) p. 355.

Table 5.1 Categorization of norms and principles comprised in the Code

	1st approach	2nd approach
Main categories	Traditional and new human rights ● Principles of non-discrimination and equality; ● Right to be heard; ● Privacy and data protection; and ● Requests for access to documents.	General principles of European administrative law ● Legality; ● Non-discrimination; ● Proportionality; ● Absence of abuse of power; ● Respect for legitimate expectations; and ● Transparency.
	Substantive principles ● Absence of abuse of powers; ● Proportionality; ● Objectivity; and ● Legitimate expectations.	Procedural and substantive rights and duties which result from express rules of Community law ● Data protection, the right to complain to the EO (fundamental rights enshrined in the Charter). ● Right to have his or her affairs handled impartially, the right to be heard and to make statements, fairly and within a reasonable time, the duty to state reasons, language rights (Article 41 of the Charter).
	Formal principles ● Principles of impartiality and independence; and ● Duty to state reasons.	Rules of administrative practice in line with the idea of providing a good service to the public ● Duty to advise the public in the handling of the case, to act courteously, to transfer a file to the competent services, rules on how to handle request for information and on keeping records.

Table 5.1 (continued)

	1st approach	2nd approach
	Principles of good administration that aim at behaving with care and consideration in contacts with the public or duties relating to the good functioning of the administrative service a) *Courtesy and fairness* b) *Active and adequate provision of information* • Advising the public on how a matter which comes within his remit is to be pursued and how to proceed in dealing with the matter; • Replying letters in the language of the citizen; • Acknowledgment of receipt and indication of competent official; and • Indication of possibilities of appeal. c) *Adequate organization of the administration* • Transferring letters/complaints to the competent service; and • Keeping of adequate records. d) *Timeliness of decisions*	

Source: Compiled by the authors based on Magdalena E. de Leeuw, 'The European Ombudsman's Role as a Developer of Norms of Good Administration' (2011) 17/2 EPL, pp. 354–5 and Joana Mendes, 'Good Administration in EU Law and the European Code of Good Administrative Behavior' (EUI Working Papers, September 2009), http://cadmus.eui.eu/bitstream/handle/1814/12101/LAW_2009_09.pdf?sequence=3&isAllowed=y, accessed 19 November 2015, pp. 6–7.

resolution by the European Parliament (though the resolution does not make it legally binding).[61]

One question arising from the literature is whether the standards used by the EO are completely independent from the law or, despite being something 'extra', they cannot be dissociated from the law. So far, two main divergent opinions have been identified. A first group of authors claims that the standards invoked by the EO should be completely separated from the law,[62] having a strong ethical dimension which should be assessed in the context of each case. The possible combinations that exist between good administration and the law are summarized in the matrix in Table 5.2. A second group of authors argues that while the EO can bring something extra in addition to the law, it is impossible to have an action/decision which is unlawful but otherwise labelled as good administration.[63] This view is also in accordance with the view of the EO institution, which puts legality at the core of good administration. The current EO, Emily O'Reilly, clearly argues that good administration cannot exist outside of legality: 'An Ombudsman should never ask a public institution to act contrary to the law; but an Ombudsman will expect an institution to do whatever is possible within the law in order to achieve outcomes which are fair and reasonable in all of the circumstances.'[64] A similar view is also expressed by the former EO Diamandouros, who claims that 'the rule of law requires public administration to act lawfully: thus, it cannot be good administration to violate the law. However the converse is not necessarily true. In other words, the fact that a public authority has acted lawfully does not preclude the possibility that it might have failed to comply with the principles of good administration.'[65]

---

[61] Remac (note 17) p. 77.

[62] Philip M. Langbroek and Peter Rijpkema, 'Demands of Proper Administrative Conduct: A Research Project into the Ombudsprudence of the Dutch National Ombudsman' (2006) 2/2 *Utrecht Law Review* pp. 81–98; Magdalena E. de Leeuw, 'An Empirical Study into the Norms of Good Administration as Operated by the European Ombudsman in the Field of Tenders (EUI Working Papers 2009), http://cadmus.eui.eu/bitstream/handle/1814/11234/EUI_RSCAS_2009_20.pdf?sequence=3, accessed 19 November 2015, pp. 1–75; De Leeuw (note 14); Milan Remac and Philip M. Langbroek, 'Ombudsman's Assessment of Public Administration Conduct: Between Legal and Good Administration Norms' (2011/2012) IV/2 *The NISPAcee Journal of Public Administration and Policy* pp. 87–115.

[63] Mendes (note 55).

[64] European Ombudsman, *Good Administration in Practice: The European Ombudsman's Decisions in 2013* (2014), www.theioi.org/downloads/9d5gm/EU_OM_Good%20administration%20in%20practice_Oct%202014_EN.pdf, accessed 19 November 2015, p. 2.

[65] Diamandouros (note 13) p. 11.

Table 5.2 Interaction between law and good administration

Administration	Good	Not good
Lawful	Lawful and good	Lawful and not good
Unlawful	Unlawful and good	Unlawful and not good

Source: Leah Grolman, 'Life beyond Legality: Lessons from the EU and UK for an Australian Charter or Principles of Good Administration' (1 June 2014), http://papers.ssrn.com/sol3/papers.cfm?abstract_id=2568293, accessed 12 December 2015, p. 19.

It is clear that the EO's standards for assessment include both legal rules and other normative standards pertaining to the umbrella concept of good administration. It is, however, less clear if the EO can be described as mostly conducting a review based on other normative standards than the legal rules. Various scholars argue that whether the EO employs a rather legalistic approach depends on the specific thematic field in which the complaint is made. Thus, empirical research in the field of public tenders showed that complainants in this area are legal persons and therefore are rather interested in obtaining a purely legalistic approach.[66] In other areas, such as transparency in EU recruitment competitions and individual's rights in the centralized infraction process of Article 258 of the Treaty on the Functioning of the European Union (TFEU), the EO has had a rather different role than in public tenders, by expanding the realm of proper administrative conduct beyond the narrow confines of legality.[67] It is also suggested in the literature that the EO's own understanding of the role played by the institution will determine how legalistic the review is. Thus, the first EO, Söderman, based on his experience as the national Ombudsman of Finland, has adopted a narrow and legalistic approach, seeing the EO institution as a surrogate court (at least in his first years as EO).[68] The next incumbent, Diamandouros, argued that public bodies should not just act lawfully but they should also be service-minded and ensure that members of the public are properly treated and enjoy their rights fully.[69] Diamandouros is also famous for his widely quoted expression 'there is life beyond legality'.[70] The current EO, Emily O'Reilly,

[66] De Leeuw (note 14) p. 359.
[67] Tsadiras (note 40) p. 6.
[68] Damian Chalmers, Christos Hadjiemmanuil, Giorgio Monti and Adam Tomkins, *European Union Law: Text and Materials* (Cambridge University Press 2008) p. 344.
[69] Diamandouros (note 13) p. 12.
[70] Ibid.

similar to her predecessor Diamandouros, argues that the main role of the institution is to make sure that all EU citizens and businesses will be treated fairly, reasonably and sensitively by the EU administration and that their encounters with EU administration are marked by civility and courtesy.[71]

PART II: EMPIRICAL RESEARCH INTO THE ROLE OF THE OMBUDSMAN AS CREATOR OF NORMS OF GOOD ADMINISTRATION IN THE AREA OF ACCESS TO PUBLIC DOCUMENTS AND INFORMATION

This section is the most extensive one, as it contains the outcome of several mini-research projects conducted over the last several years in the areas of transparency, free access to documents and information, and the role of the EO in promoting transparency and good administration. This section includes a brief description of the methodology, a general analysis on the ombudsprudence of the EO in the area of free access to documents and a more applied research on whether or not the EO acts as a creator of norms of good administration when handling complaints in the area of free access to documents.

1 Methodology

The research objective of this empirical study is twofold: (1) to analyse the role of the EO in the area of guaranteeing free access to documents and information; and (2) to identify whether the EO can be described as a creator of norms of good administration and to identify if there is room for more in this respect.

The research method used is content analysis of the individual decisions of the EO from 2010–2014 which pertain to the area of free access to public documents. The total number of decisions reviewed is just over 500, accessed directly from the website of the institution. The empirical research comprised several stages. During the first stage of the research, each of the 500 decisions was briefly summarized and categorized based on the main provisions included in Regulation No. 1049/2001 (beneficiaries, access to documents versus access to information, exceptions, etc.). The aim of the first stage was to produce a descriptive report regarding

[71] European Ombudsman (note 64) p. 2.

main problems pertaining to access to documents at EU level but most importantly to highlight the role of the EO in this area and to point out if major developments occurred due to his/her intervention (presented in Part II, section 3). During the second stage of the research, the decisions were revisited and re-examined from the perspective of the norms employed by the EO in each case. An Excel file was created containing the following aspects: type of maladministration alleged; the assessment of the EO (whether or not maladministration was found; whether a specific principle of good administration was invoked; whether only legal norms were invoked; how the case was settled). The aim was to determine if the EO in the individual decisions clearly spells out the principle of good administration involved and offers indications about how it should have been applied by the institutions concerned in that specific case. Based on this, an analysis of the role of the EO as creator of norms of good administration was made (presented in Part II, section 4).

2 EO and Free Access to Documents

Governments worldwide are faced with increasing demands for opening up and making their decision-making processes more transparent and accessible to their citizens. The EU is also subject to this demand, especially due to the fact that law and policy processes seem to be cumbersome and are perceived to take an inordinate amount of time.[72] The right of access to documents is one important aspect/dimension of transparency.[73]

In the EU, the journey toward more transparency and openness has involved the transition from access to documents seen as a challenge to be surmounted by Community institutions to access as a right of the individual.[74]

The link between transparency of the EU decision-making process and public access to documents was first recognized in 1992 in Declaration No. 17 annexed to the Maastricht Treaty. According to the Declaration, transparency of the decision-making process strengthens the democratic

---

[72] Sophie van Bijsterveld, 'Transparency in the European Union: A Crucial Link in Shaping the New Social Contract between the Citizen and the EU' (Transparency in Europe II, proceedings of conference hosted by the Netherlands during its Chairmanship of the EU Council, 25 and 26 November 2004), www.ip-rs.si/fileadmin/user_upload/Pdf/clanki/Agenda__Bijsterveld-Paper.pdf, accessed 19 November 2015, p. 2.

[73] European Ombudsman (note 64) p. 6.

[74] Labayle (note 6) p. 5.

nature of the institutions and the public's confidence in the administration.[75] Two Commission communications on transparency and access to documents were then published, followed by a 'Code of Conduct' adopting the principle of public access to Council and Commission documents.[76] In 1997, the Treaty of Amsterdam enshrined these principles into primary law,[77] consecrating public access to documents as an EU citizens' right (Article 255 TEC).[78] Regulation (EC) No. 1049/2001 regarding public access to European Parliament, Council and Commission documents was adopted in order to give content to this right. The effect was immediate. The Regulation, which became applicable on 3 December 2001, has led to a steep and sustained increase in requests for access to documents – at least in the first years after its adoption, the Commission estimates that the number of access requests increased by around 50 per cent every year. Since on average two-thirds of requests were granted, it can be argued that the Regulation had opened to the public a considerable amount of previously unpublished documentation.[79] Before the adoption of this Regulation, only a few years before, the Union institutions had operated on the basis that confidentiality was the rule and that giving access to information and documents was a discretionary exception to that rule.[80]

The Lisbon Treaty has brought important changes with regard to the right of access to documents in the EU. First of all, the Charter of Fundamental Rights makes this access a fundamental right. Article 42 under the heading 'Right of access to documents', states that 'any citizen of the Union, and any natural or legal person residing or having its registered office in a Member State, has a right of access to documents of the institutions, bodies, offices and agencies of the Union, whatever their medium'. This provision expands the realm of entities which should

[75] Milena Mihaylova, 'Implementation of the Concept of Transparency by EU Institutions: Access to Documents' (2013), http://campus.hec.fr/global-transparency/wp-content/uploads/2013/10/Mihaylova-Implementation-of-the-concept-of-transparency-by-EU-institutions.pdf, accessed 19 November 2015, p. 2.

[76] Labayle (note 6) p. 7.

[77] Ibid.

[78] Mihaylova (note 75) p. 2.

[79] European Commission, 'Public Access to Documents Held by Institutions of the European Community, A Review (Green Paper 2007), http://eur-lex.europa.eu/legal-content/EN/TXT/PDF/?uri=CELEX:52007DC0185&from=EN, accessed 19 November 2015, p. 2.

[80] João Sant'Anna, 'The European Ombudsman as the Guardian of Transparency' (Presentation for the conference Europe 2020 – the Civic Visions, Sofia, 29–30 January 2010), http://old.europe.bg/en/htmls/page.php?category=397&id526997, accessed 19 November 2015.

provide free access to documents beyond the three main institutions of the Community. This provision is also reinforced by the TFEU. The TFEU itself has also changed the legal environment of the right of access. Article 15(3) states in more precise terms than Article 255 TEC the ways of exercising the right of access to documents on a compulsory basis.[81]

In light of the Lisbon Treaty, Regulation (EC) No. 1049/2001 needs to be revised. In addition, the revised Regulation should include the experience achieved so far in its application, initiatives that the European institutions themselves have adopted in recent years to favour transparency and access to documents, and also the case law doctrine of the CJEU in this area.[82] Though various initiatives have existed over the last years, a revised version of it is still to be achieved in the future.

Protection of the citizens' right to access the documents and information held by the Community institutions is one of the areas in which the activity of the EO is highly significant. As observed by De Leeuw, the types of complaints that are commonly dealt with by the office of the EO are of a different nature than those made to the national ombudsmen, mainly because there is less direct contact between the Community administration and the citizens of the Member States.[83] There is, however, one area in which the activity of the EO is rather similar with that of the national ombudsmen (in terms of volume), namely transparency and access to public documents. According to the 2014 annual report, for several years now, 20 per cent to 30 per cent of the complaints that the EO's office investigates have concerned transparency. The most common transparency issues raised are the institutions' refusal to grant access to documents and/or information.[84] Year after year, the main issues included in complaints are: excessive delay in dealing with applications; the narrow interpretation of the exceptions to access; and breach of the requirement that each institution should have a public register of documents to facilitate the exercise of the right of access.[85]

It is important to note that from the perspective of the concept of good administration, access to documents and information can be categorized

---

[81] Labayle (note 6) p. 11.

[82] Síndic de Greuges de Catalunya, 'The Right of Access to Public Information' (Monographic Report, March 2012), www.sindic.cat/site/unitFiles/3151/Report%20access%20to%20public%20information.pdf, accessed 19 November 2015, p. 7.

[83] De Leeuw (note 11) p. 15.

[84] European Ombudsman, *Annual Report 2014* (26 May 2015), www.ombudsman.europa.eu/activities/annualreports.faces, accessed 19 November 2015, p. 7.

[85] Sant'Anna (note 80).

from several different perspectives. Thus, it can be considered a procedural right if it refers to access to file, enshrined in Article 41(2) first indent, or to the right of access to documents under Article 15(3) TFEU. Or, it can be considered a non-legal rule if the information requested is not covered by Regulation No. 1049/2001 or by the rules applicable to access to the files, but its availability is regarded to favour good administration (as reflected in Article 22 of the Code).[86]

3 *Ombudsprudence* on Specific Issues of Access to Information

3.1 The freedom of information request

3.1.1 Clarity and precision Article 6 of Regulation No. 1049/2001 states that applications for access to a document shall be made in any written form, including electronic form, in one of the languages of the EU and in a *sufficiently precise manner* to enable the institution to identify the document. The applicant is not obliged to state reasons for the application. The obligation to ask for clarifications is also a right of the petitioner, and the institution shall assist the applicant in providing the clarification, for example, by providing information on the use of the public registers of documents. Informal ways of communication are also envisaged, when the application relates to a very long document or to a very large number of documents, the ultimate scope being the identification of a fair solution.

The institutions have discretion as to how to interpret the concept 'sufficiently precise manner' used by Regulation No. 1049/2001. Here we can see how the EO may play a role in fostering a certain interpretation of the concept that is in line with the good administration principle. Thus, in some cases, the EO praised the Commission for attempting to informally find out more about the scope of the request, to identify the information sought after by the applicant. In other cases, the Commission was criticized for interpreting the requests too narrowly, which was favoured by the lack of any explanatory inquiries addressed to the applicants.

For instance, in a case where the complainant requested the European Agency for Reconstruction (EAR) documents relating to certain tenders, the absence of a reply was followed by a confirmatory application which EAR also failed to deal with. The intervention of the EO by the way of an inquiry[87] led to a reply from EAR that sought to obtain more detailed information so as to identify the documents to which the complainant

---

[86] Mendes (note 55) p. 6.
[87] Case: 671/2007/PB.

wanted public access. The fact that the identification of the documents was apparently not possible in the case appeared to suggest that the record-keeping at the EAR was unprofessional, and not that the details provided by the complainant were insufficiently clear.

As to the way in which applications are formulated, the EO has found that sometimes requests were too vague or open-ended, but this did not excuse the Commission from seeking further clarifications. For instance, when a company requested access, under Regulation No. 1049/2001, to 'all data, documents, emails, correspondence, reports, meeting minutes, internal memos, and any other material related to our company, our contract and our relations with the awarding authority', the EO agreed with the Commission that the scope of the request was unclear and open-ended. Further on, the reference to 'all the contacts that the Commission had with . . .. in relation to our company' is unclear as it covers access to information, and not simply access to documents, while a reference to 'copies of all the correspondence sent and received by the Commission in relation to the case' was sufficiently precise to allow the Commission to process it effectively. In procedural terms the EO was referred to prematurely, as no confirmatory request was yet addressed; however, this fact did not impede the EO to stress the importance of the good administration principles when dealing with requests that are not clearly formulated, leading to an obligation to assist the applicant and to answer those parts of the application that are clear and precise.[88]

3.1.2 Vexatious or repetitive requests The right of citizens to receive a reply to their inquiries submitted to institutions, and the duty of the latter to provide a reply are, however, not absolute. A reason often used for turning down requests for public information is that the application is unreasonable and vexatious, or simply repetitive. This is recognized also by the EO, based on the provisions of the Code of Good Administrative Behaviour, which in Article 14(3) states that in cases where correspondence from citizens is abusive because of its excessive number or of its repetitive or pointless character, no reply needs to be sent. However, the EO considers that this exception to the general principle that institutions have to reply to citizens' correspondence must be applied strictly. The citizens concerned have to be explicitly informed of the institution's decision to discontinue correspondence with them and of the reasons for that decision.

In cases where the institutions invoked this ground for refusal, the EO

---

[88] Case: 465/2010/FOR.

stated that the decision that correspondence sent by a citizen is improper, for example, because it is repetitive, abusive and/or pointless, must be based on an individual and substantive assessment of a citizen's correspondence.[89] In all cases, the EO performed a careful review and found that, for instance, 18 emails which were not even all distinct in substance cannot be considered vexatious, repetitive or pointless requests.[90] The number of applications is not per se an indication that the applicant is sending vexatious requests. Apart from that, the obligation to inform the applicants that the reason for refusal or discontinuance of correspondence is their repetitive or pointless requests still stands.

In another case, when asked to provide detailed information relating to the work of the Common Sickness Insurance Scheme or, alternatively, documents from which the applicant himself could extract that information, the Commission provided some documents but considered that it was not obliged to meet his request in full because it was excessive. The EO came to the conclusion that the Commission had not adequately justified its refusal to grant access to the information or the documents concerned and this also led to a wider inquiry into the handling of the case.[91] In the recommendations, the EO referred to 'an appropriate level of service-mindedness, diligence and objectivity', the lack of which amounts to maladministration. Consequently, the Commission was encouraged to adopt guidelines in order to deal with complex requests of information that are not obviously abusive. The refusal to grant access should be based on an objective *approximate estimation* of the time or resources that the services would otherwise have to invest to meet the information request.

The disproportionate administrative burden placed on the institution was also a reason for rejecting access to documents, and the institution invoked the principle of proportionality. The EO noted that the principle of proportionality on its own does not constitute a separate justification for a refusal to provide access to the requested reports, so the institution should have carried out a concrete, individual examination of the request. The case law of the CJEU cited by the institution (that involved access to documents that amount to 47,000 pages)[92] needs to be interpreted in a different manner – as allowing the institution to skip the assessment of every piece of document for a categorization of the documents. The institution cannot rely on the principle of proportionality per se instead of carrying

---

[89] Case: OI/7/2011/EIS.

[90] Case: 1825/2009/IP.

[91] Case: 56/2007/PB.

[92] T-2/03 – *Verein für Konsumenteninformation v Commission* ECLI:EU:T:2005:125.

out an assessment of the request at hand to see if it is proportional or not. The institution on the other hand invoked the volume of work required as a justification, in itself, for not agreeing to the request for access. The EO reaffirmed that refusal to grant access must be based exclusively on the exceptions to the 2001 Regulation.[93]

3.1.3 Applications erroneously addressed to a non-competent public authority There are three main possible solutions for the frequent situations when the petitioner addresses the request for public information to an institution that does not possess that information: (1) the application is set aside as wrongly addressed; (2) the petitioner is informed about the competent institution, but a new application is necessary to that competent institution; (3) the petitioner is informed about the competent institution *and* the application is transferred to that institution.

Regulation No. 1049/2001 does not have rules for transferring incorrectly addressed requests. On the other hand, in environmental matters, the Aarhus Convention requires that institutions that are not competent to solve the request must promptly inform the requester and either transfer the request to the appropriate agency or inform the requester which authority may have the requested information.[94]

However, such an obligation seems to have been extended by the EO as a matter of good governance through the Code of Good Administrative Behaviour (Article 23). Thus, the EO found that failure of the Commission to forward to its Secretariat-General the complainant's request for access is also an instance of maladministration.[95] In another section of the decision, the EO conceded that at the very least the complainant should have been informed of where to submit his request, as a matter of *courtesy*, a principle enshrined in Article 12(2) of the Code of Good Administrative Behaviour.

In the same context the EO dealt with situations where due to erroneous information on the website of the institution, the applicant asked for a decision with a wrong identification number, and the institution used this argument in order to disregard his application altogether.[96] In other cases, the EO found that a simple suggestion to the complainant that he approach a different institution would have been more citizen-friendly.[97]

---

93 Case: 2493/2008/(BB)(TS)FOR.
94 Aarhus Convention, Article 4 para. 5.
95 Case: 2493/2008/(BB)(TS)FOR.
96 Case: 2101/2009/BEH.
97 Case: 2632/2009/(SIT)(PF)JF.

3.2 Response

As a general trait of the cases investigated by the EO relating to freedom of information issues, in most cases the intervention of the Ombudsman triggers the answer of the institution or a friendly resolution of the conflict through explanations. The over-arching principle here is courtesy, enshrined in Article 12 of the Code of Good Administrative Behaviour.

In cases where the communication with the complainant is carried out in an improper manner (for instance a reply such as 'see you in court' triggered by the continuous request of the complainant to be given a formal answer[98]), the EO has stressed the importance not only of the resolution of the dispute on merits, but also of the way in which the relation with the applicants is carried out. The staff of the institutions should be courteous and thus build up and maintain trust between citizens and European public administration, and that the institutions should make efforts in taking the necessary measures in order to sensitize their staff to the above needs.

Courtesy must be observed even in cases when the information is not held by the institution, but it can be retrieved from other sources known to the institution. For instance, rather than simply stating that the information sought is not published on its website, it would be appropriate for the institution to refer the person in question to the notice of competition that contains such information.[99]

All refusals, total or partial, must be accompanied by a clear reasoning as to the *grounds* of refusal. The EO has contributed to the understanding of this notion by stating that the requirement that the reasons for non-disclosure must be *concrete and specific* does not imply that the institution must merely make a clear statement to the effect that it carried out a concrete and specific examination.[100] Rather, it must be concrete and specific to the *applicability of the exceptions* to the *actual documents* in question. In absence of such information, the applicant cannot assess the validity of the refusal and decide accordingly as to the review mechanisms available. Not to mention that the review process will also be lengthier due to the need to ask for explanations from the institution.

3.3 The relation between *documents* and *information*

In comparative literature, there is a distinction between 'public information' and 'public document'. It is evident that the widest scope of a

---

98 Case: 884/2010/VIK.

99 Case: 2470/2009/(TS)TN.

100 Case: 943/2007/PB.

Freedom of Information Act from the applicant's point of view is assured by granting access to 'public information', not to 'public documents', because in this way the public authority is required to provide the public information even when it is enclosed in a document not entirely open to the public, or, more importantly, search for information not enclosed in a single document or make a new document for the purpose of the request. However, many jurisdictions restrict the access to only information structured in an existing document, with no possibility to ask for the compilation of a new document for the purpose of the request.[101]

Regulation No. 1049/2001 provides for access to 'documents of the institutions'. 'Document' means any content whatever its medium (written on paper or stored in electronic form or as a sound, visual or audio-visual recording) concerning a matter relating to the policies, activities and decisions falling within the institution's sphere of responsibility. The Court of First Instance and the CJEU (T-14/98 *Hautala/Council*[102]) established the principle of access to the elements of information contained in the documents which are not covered by an exception to the right of access.

However, the Regulation does not require European institutions to create new documents to respond to an application. Consequently, when the information requested is not enclosed in one or more existing documents, involves research in different sources, drafting new documents and/or collation of data, the application clearly goes beyond the scope of the Regulation.

Nevertheless, the request may be handled as a request for information in line with the administrative rules of the institution concerned. The Parliament, the Council and the Commission have adopted codes of good administrative conduct comprising rules relating to the handling of requests for information. In practice, however, it is not always easy to distinguish a request for information from an application for access to documents (particularly in the case of databases).[103]

---

101 See for comparative view Patrick Birkinshaw, *Freedom of Information. The Law, the Practice and the Ideal* (Fourth Edition, Cambridge University Press 2010), Chapter 12, and Open Society Justice Initiative, 'Transparency and Silence: A Survey of Access to Information Laws and Practices in Fourteen Countries' (2006), www.opensocietyfoundations.org/publications/transparency-and-silence-survey-access-information-laws-and-practices-14-countries, accessed 6 January 2017.

102 Reports of Cases 1999 II-02489.

103 Report from the Commission on the application in 2011 of Regulation (EC) No. 1049/2001 of the European Parliament and of the Council regarding public access to European Parliament, Council and Commission documents. COM (2012) 429 final, 2 August 2012.

In the course of 2008, the EO conducted a survey on the public's right of access to information in databases held by public bodies.[104] The survey was carried out within the framework of the European Network of Ombudsmen. The specific background to the survey was a complaint submitted by a Danish-German journalist in 2005, which concerned a request for access to national reports on EU farming aid. The reports submitted to the Commission by the national administrations were transmitted electronically to a database, and their content was instantly 'absorbed' by that database. The question, therefore, arose as to whether the request concerned access to documents or access to information. The key legislation on openness in the EU administration only gives a right of access to documents, which means that it does not give citizens a general legal right of access to information held by the EU administration. The case made one thing abundantly clear: if the content of electronic databases falls outside the scope of the EU's most important legislation concerning openness in the EU administration, the very purpose of that legislation probably cannot be fulfilled. As a result of the inquiry of the EO, a practice has evolved according to which the result of a normal search in the database is considered a document in the sense of Regulation No. 1049/2001. However, the Commission was not willing to modify the existing search parameters of the database in order to be able to retrieve the information requested.

In other cases, the EO reiterated that any 'meaningful' set of 'content' recoverable from a database constitutes an individual 'document'.[105]

In the context of the same discussion of *document vs. information*, the EO took the view that an annex to a document to which access is requested is not a separate document, but forms an integral part of the document to which it is attached, so the assessment as to whether or not it may be disclosed should thus be made at the same time as the one concerning the main document.[106] The EO also made it clear that institutions cannot decide that a certain part of an existing document constitutes a 'sub-document' or another document simply because it contains a different kind, or type, of information. Furthermore, references to attachments should be treated as forming part of the document concerned, and should, therefore, not be excluded from an institution's analysis when dealing with a request for access to the document.[107]

---

[104] See www.ombudsman.europa.eu/en/resources/otherdocument.faces/en/4160/html.bookmark, accessed 6 January 2017.

[105] Case: 2493/2008/(BB)(TS)FOR.

[106] Case: 1111/2012/AN.

[107] Case: 1633/2008/DK.

Internal documents, emails or other correspondence drafted in preparation of an official letter may also represent public documents.[108] This is in line with Holkeri's view that access to information pertaining to issues of general importance is a prerequisite for the social debate that precedes or explains decision-making. Thus, the principle should be that all the preparatory documents relating to the decision-making come into the public domain, at the very latest when the decision has been made. Within these preparatory documents, of great importance are the studies, statistics and other research related to a project of general interest.[109]

3.4 Excepted information

3.4.1 Scope of the exceptions An important aspect of all freedom of information applications is the restrictions or exceptions from the access to information or documents, namely instances where the information is shielded from the public based on over-arching interests. The exceptions listed in Regulation No. 1049/2001 are of strict interpretation, no other exceptions may be invoked in order to deny access. This has been made clear by the EO in its decisions. Thus, the danger arising from 'allowing misleading and unreliable data to circulate' (it regarded serious adverse reactions contained in the EudraVigilance database) was considered by the EO to be exceeding the exceptions listed in the Regulation and consequently not a valid ground for refusal. Also, in the same case, the argument of administrative burden was also considered invalid.[110]

Good practices have been identified by the EO in dealing with such requests. Thus, in order for an institution to be able to determine if exclusion grounds apply, it must first identify all documents pertaining to the request. This is a prerequisite for assessing whether or not an exclusion ground is present. Then, the relationship between personal data/public information has to be treated with care. Individual access to information containing personal data should be granted under Article 13 of Regulation No. 45/2001. However, Regulation No. 1049/2001 aims to ensure the widest public access possible to the documents held by the EU institutions. Consequently, when an applicant submits a request for access, under Regulation No. 1049/2001, to a document which was previously disclosed to the same applicant pursuant to Article 13 of Regulation No. 45/2001,

---

[108] Case: 122/2014/PMC.

[109] Katjo Holkeri, 'Public Scrutiny and Access to Information in Finland' in OECD, *Public Sector Transparency and Accountability – Making It Happen*, 2002, pp. 151–63.

[110] Case: 2493/2008/(BB)(TS)FOR.

the institution must still carry out an individual and concrete examination of that document under Regulation No. 1049/2001. Nevertheless, if the request for access under Article 13 of Regulation No. 45/2001 led to the disclosure of the entire document to which access is subsequently requested under Regulation No. 1049/2001, the institution could consider explaining that there is no real use in carrying out the examination.

3.4.2 Non-existence of the document – the Glomar doctrine Relating to some exempted information, a public authority may refuse to confirm or deny the existence or non-existence of requested information whenever the very fact of their existence or non-existence is itself classified or can jeopardize the secrecy of the information requested. It is the Glomar doctrine[111] or the 'glomarization' of the response under the Freedom of Information Act.[112]

The 'Glomar' response is not an exclusively American freedom of information application feature; it is also permitted by Regulation No. 1049/2001 on access to documents in the EU, which in Article 9 (4) provides that 'an institution which decides to refuse access to a sensitive document shall give the reasons for its decision in a manner which does not harm the interests protected in Article 4'. Implicitly, this provision allows the institution refusing access to sensitive documents to respond in such a manner that would neither deny nor confirm the existence of the document sought after, or even to state that such document does not exist in order to protect certain interests.

---

[111] *Glomar Explorer*, a large salvage ship built by the CIA for its covert 'Project Jennifer' – an attempted salvaging of a sunken Soviet nuclear submarine – was about to be the subject of an article in the *Los Angeles Times*; aware of its imminent publication, CIA sought to stop it, but journalist Harriet Ann Phillippi requested that pursuant to the Freedom of Information Act the CIA provide disclosure of both the Glomar project and its attempts to censor the story. CIA chose to 'neither confirm nor deny' both the project's existence and its attempts to keep the story unpublished. Applicant's case was rejected (Case: *Phillippi v CIA* 1976), though when the Ford administration was replaced by the Carter administration in 1976, the government position on the particular case was softened and both of Phillippi's claims were confirmed. See Clyde W. Burleson, *The Jennifer Project* (College Station: Texas A&M University Press 1997). The 'Glomar response' precedent still stood, and has since had bearing in Freedom of Information Act cases such as in the *American Civil Liberties Union v Department of Defense* 2005, wherein a Federal Judge rejected the Department of Defense and CIA's use of the Glomar response in refusing to release documents and photos depicting abuse at Abu Ghraib prison in Baghdad.

[112] FOIA Update, Vol. VII, No. 1, Page 3 (1986). 'OIP Guidance: Privacy "Glomarization"'. United States Department of Justice.

The CJEU has held that 'it is clear from the wording of Article 4(1)(a) of Regulation No. 1049/2001 that, as regards the exceptions to the right of access provided for by that provision, refusal of access by the institution is mandatory where disclosure of a document to the public would undermine the interests which that provision protects, without the need, in such a case and in contrast to the provisions, in particular, of Article 4(2), to balance the requirements connected to the protection of those interests against those which stem from other interests'.[113]

Consequently, in matters like these, the investigation of the EO is restricted to finding out whether the exception applies, and cannot go further and look into whether a public interest test was performed. For that reason, the EO has reaffirmed the fact that there is a presumption of legality as regards an institution's statement that a document does not exist.[114]

In another case,[115] the EO considered the response of an institution as to the impossibility to identify the document as being plausible, and that an on-site visit to search for the document would have been unreasonable and it would have to be performed only in exceptional circumstances (without giving any indication as to what such circumstances might be). The fact that the applicant did not challenge the non-existence of the document also helped to bring the case to an end.

3.4.3 Partial disclosure The simple existence of some exempted information in a document should not impede the applicant to access the other information from the document, information that does not fall under exceptions listed in the Regulation. Thus, the provisions of Article 4 section 6 of Regulation No. 1049/2001 – 'if only parts of the requested document are covered by any of the exceptions, the remaining parts of the document shall be released' – have been issued in order to put an end (at least theoretically) to the practice of refusing to partially release documents which contain secret information only to a limited extent, a practice sanctioned by the Court of First Instance in several cases.

The EO strengthened this approach by requiring institutions to assess whether they could grant the complainant partial access to internal documents pursuant to Article 4(6) of Regulation No. 1049/2001 and failure to do so amounts to maladministration.[116]

---

[113] Case: C-266/05 P *Sison v Council* [2007] ECR I-1233, para. 46; see also Case: T-264/04 *WWF v Council* [2007] ECR II-911, para. 44.

[114] Case: 1392/2012/DK.

[115] Case: 671/2007/PB.

[116] Case: 1861/2009/(JF)AN.

3.4.4 International relations Another important matter considered to be worth protecting under the freedom of information regime is the international relations of the state or, in other words, foreign policy of the state. Article 4 of Regulation No. 1049/2001 only mentions international relations, without further details. Under this section can also be included Article 5 of the same Regulation, aimed at resolving conflictual situations according to which a Member State receiving a request for a document in its possession, originating from a European institution, has to determine if it is clear that the document shall or shall not be disclosed; if in its determination the Member State is facing difficulties, it has two options: (1) to consult with the institution concerned in order to take a decision that does not jeopardize the attainment of the objectives of the Regulation; or (2) to refer the request to the institution for decision. The case law of the CJEU dealt with documents relating to Council decisions concerning the fight against terrorism.[117]

International agreements still pending the process of ratification might be refused from disclosure by the parties, either on this ground alone or on the ground that one of the parties has not given its consent. Thus, a non-governmental organization which monitors the activities of the international financial institutions in Central and Eastern Europe, required the assistance of the EO in accessing the Framework Agreement signed by the European Investment Bank and the Republic of Tajikistan in 2009.[118] The refusal was first grounded on Article 33 of the Bank's Public Disclosure Policy – as a third-party document and that the Tajikistan authorities did not give their consent for disclosure. Upon complaint, the European Investment Bank Complaints Office acknowledged that the rejection of the complainant's application had not been correctly grounded as regards the classification of the Agreement as a third-party document, but it cannot still be disclosed as it was still undergoing the process of ratification by the competent authorities of Tajikistan. The matter was resolved after the signing of the agreement by its public release.

The powers of the EO were put to test in 2008, in a case where public access to any Council documents relating to discussions which took place between EU and United States' (US) representatives on 3 May 2006 in Brussels on the subject of 'rendition' and 'extraordinary rendition' was requested[119] The refusal to disclose the documents (classified as 'RESTREINT EU') was based on the exceptions set out in the Regulation

---

[117] See also C2005/171/26 in Joined Cases T-110/03, T-150/03 and T-405/03 *Jose Maria Sison v Council of the European Union*, Official Journal C 171, 09/07/2005 P. 0015 – 0015.

[118] Case: 2145/2009/RT.

[119] Case: 944/2008/OV.

under Article 4(1)(a), third indent, (protection of the public interest as regards international relations), and Article 4(3) (protection of the institution's decision-making process). The Council stated that the document in question 'contains the report of the EU–US meeting held in the framework of the transatlantic dialogue, during which sensitive issues in the field of the fight against terrorism were discussed. It reports in detail on the positions taken by both sides. It contains an analysis and comments on this area of cooperation and an assessment on how the issues have so far been addressed by the two parties. Given the sensitive content of the document, the Council considers that its disclosure would be detrimental to the good functioning of the relations between the EU and the US, and this stance was confirmed by the EO upon inspection of the documents at issue.

A similar request regarded a document held by the Council of the EU – a note on the alleged use of European Countries by the US Central Intelligence Agency for the transportation and illegal detention of prisoners. Public access was refused in its entirety pursuant to Article 4(1)(a), third indent (protection of the public interest with regard to international relations) of Regulation No. 1049/2001, on the basis that disclosure would undermine the efforts that have been made to protect the relations between the EU and the Russian Federation, disclosure would put assessments concerning the visa issue, which were not shared with the Russian delegation, in the public domain, and that disclosure would weaken the EU's negotiating position.

The EO took into account the fact that, according to the case law of the EU courts, the interests protected by Article 4(1)(a) of Regulation No. 1049/2001 are of a particularly sensitive nature, which entails institutions enjoying a wide discretion in determining whether disclosure could undermine the public interest, not without checking whether the refusal came after an inspection of the document and upon a proper assessment of its sensitivity in terms of public interest.[120]

A third important case involved full access to documents concerning the negotiation of a new Anti-Counterfeiting Trade Agreement (ACTA). The documents to which the complainant requested full access contained only procedural aspects, not substantial information that the complainant sought after, so upon a phone conversation facilitated by the EO, the matter was resolved. However, the EO took the opportunity to state that the Council was entitled to apply the exception foreseen in Article 4(1)(a) in order to refuse access to the documents concerned.[121]

---

[120] Case: 1051/2010/BEH.

[121] Case: 90/2009/(JD)OV.

3.4.5 Third-party consent Article 3 of Regulation No. 1049/2001 provides that 'third party' shall mean any natural or legal person, or any entity outside the institution concerned, including the Member States, other Community or non-Community institutions and bodies and third countries. The procedure for disclosing third-party originated documents that are being held by the EU institutions or bodies involves consultation of the third party with a view to assessing whether an exception is applicable, unless it is clear that the document shall or shall not be disclosed. Following such a consultation, a Member State may request the institution not to disclose a document originating from that Member State without its prior agreement.[122] However, the institution remains solely responsible for granting or refusing access.

The EO has dealt with requests for access to information refused on the ground that the state where the documents originated has not given its consent for disclosure. However, in this regard the case law of the CJEU on this matter is relevant in order to see how much room for manoeuvre the EO enjoys. Thus, the Commission relied on the ruling of the Court of First Instance in Case T-168/02[123] to refuse access to the documents originating from Spain. In that case, the Court of First Instance had stated that a request made by a Member State under Article 4(5) of Regulation No. 1049/2001 constitutes an instruction to the institution not to disclose the document in question. However, the EO in its recommendation noted that the CJEU had, in Case C-64/05 P[124] http://www.ombudsman.europa.eu/en/cases/decision.faces/en/5517/html.bookmark – _ftn10 overruled, in part, the Court of First Instance's ruling in Case T-168/02. The CJEU held that a Member State's prerogative, under Article 4(5) of Regulation No. 1049/2001, to request that a document not be disclosed, is delimited by the substantive exceptions set out in Articles 4(1) to (3) of Regulation No. 1049/2001. The Member State is merely given, in this respect, a power to take part in the Community decision as regards access. Understood in this way, the '*prior agreement*' of the Member State referred to in Article 4(5) of Regulation No. 1049/2001 is not a discretionary right of veto as regards access, but rather a form of assent, by which the Member State confirms that none of the exceptions apply. The EO noted that the Member State's intervention does not affect the Community nature of the decision as regards access.[125] In other words, the refusal to disclose

---

[122] Article 4, section 4 of Regulation No. 1049/2001.

[123] Case: T-168/02 *IFAW Internationaler Tierschutz-Fonds gGmbH v Commission* [2004] ECR II-4135.

[124] Case: C-64/05 P *Sweden v Commission and others* [2007] ECR I-11389.

[125] Case: 355/2007/(TN)FOR.

the documents cannot be based solely on the Member State's opposition to disclosure. The institutions need to carry out an assessment of the document to see whether it would undermine the interests protected by the exceptions from Regulation No. 1049/2001. Such was the case with protection of court proceedings and legal advice in case of infringement procedures.[126]

In a different case, the complainant contested the European Commission's decision not to disclose documents relating to a proposed investment project for the construction of a new nuclear power plant in Bulgaria.[127] The Commission's refusal was based on the fact that neither the Bulgarian authorities nor the investor company had consented to the documents' disclosure. In the Commission's view, Article 44 of the Treaty establishing the European Atomic Energy Community (the 'Euratom Treaty') meant that access to documents concerning an investment project has to be denied as long as both the investor and the Member State concerned have not given their explicit consent to disclosure. The EO carried out a detailed analysis of the relationship between the Euratom Treaty and the general access to documents regime established by Article 15 TFEU and Regulation No. 1049/2001. He made the preliminary finding that the Commission's position was not convincing. He invited the institution to reassess its interpretation of Article 44 of the Euratom Treaty and to consider adopting a more proactive approach to disclosing the documents referred to in Articles 43 and 44 of the Euratom Treaty. This was a case that went bad in the end from the EO's point of view – upon refusal of the Commission to change the interpretation; the EO expressed his disappointment at the fact that the Commission had failed to engage with his arguments, the case being finalized with critical remarks.

Summarizing the good administration practices recommended by the EO in cases relating to third-party consent we identify the following traits: if a third party needs to be consulted there needs to be a proper deadline established for its response; if the third party does not respond within the set deadline, the institution should proceed to an examination of the documents without any need to carry out new consultations; third-party reservations cannot represent by themselves a ground for refusal regarding disclosure; and the third-party's request to find out the identity of the applicant has no bearing and it should not delay the response of the third party.

---

126 Case: 2073/2010/AN.
127 Case: 2335/2008/(VIK)CK.

3.4.6 Protection of personal information and privacy Article 4 of Regulation No. 1049/2001 provides that 'the institutions shall refuse access to a document where disclosure would undermine the protection of . . . privacy and the integrity of the individual, in particular in accordance with Community legislation regarding the protection of personal data'. The complementary legislation to which this text makes reference is Regulation No. 45/2001 of the European Parliament and of the Council of 18 December 2000 on the protection of individuals with regard to the processing of personal data by the Community institutions and bodies and on the free movement of such data. A balancing test is required every time such issues appear (Article 8(b) of Regulation No. 45/2001), to see whether the public interest in disclosure overrides the protection of personal data.[128]

In some instances, the disclosure of information might involve no invasion of privacy because, fundamentally, the information is of such a nature that no expectation of privacy exists. For example, public officials generally have no expectation of privacy regarding their names, titles, grades, salaries (the amount that corresponds to a specific position), or regarding the parts of their successful employment applications that show their qualifications for their positions.

The request for information about absences of Members of the European Parliament (MEPs) due to medical grounds and for statistics from the European Parliament concerning medical certificates submitted by MEPs are considered to be falling under the concepts of 'processing of personal data' in a manner which infringes the rules set out in Regulation No. 45/2001. A key question was also whether individual MEPs can be identified from the statistics, and the EO agreed with the Parliament that specific circumstances might still enable the identification of individual MEPs even if only aggregated statistical data were disclosed.[129]

The relationship between personal data/public information needs special attention in this context. The EO is of the opinion that privileged individual access to information containing personal data should be granted under Article 13 of Regulation No. 45/2001; on the other hand, Regulation No. 1049/2001 has as its scope giving the widest access possible to the documents held by the EU institutions. A request for access under Regulation No. 1049/2001 regarded a document previously disclosed to the same applicant under Regulation No. 45/2001. The EO stated that there is a need for an individual and concrete examination under Regulation

---

[128] Case: 2510/2011/CK.

[129] Case: 2682/2008/(MAD)(TN)ELB.

No. 1049/2001 to see whether the document may be released. However, if based on Regulation No. 45/2001 the institution has disclosed the entire document to which access is subsequently requested under Regulation No. 1049/2001, the institution could 'consider explaining that there is no "*effet utile*" in carrying out the examination mentioned above'.[130]

Regarding the numerous requests to disclose the names of Selection Board members,[131] the EO has recommended agencies to reconsider their position regarding disclosure of the names of Selection Board members so that such information would be provided to all candidates and not only to those who explicitly request it.[132] Also, as a proactive approach, he advised the Commission to systematically inform interest representatives, in advance of meetings with Commission staff members, that the Commission intends to release the names of interest representatives, if so requested in the context of applications for access to documents under Regulation No. 1049/2001.[133]

3.4.7 Decision-making This exception, present in the majority of jurisdictions,[134] can be divided into three distinct components: (1) advice given to deciding entities or officials; (2) deliberations of public authorities; and (3) internal rules and regulations of public authorities regarding their personnel and functioning.

At the EU level, Article 4 section 3 of Regulation No. 1049/2001 provides:

> access to a document drawn up by an institution for internal use or received by an institution, which relates to a matter where the decision has not been taken by the institution, shall be refused if disclosure of the document would seriously undermine the institution's decision-making process, unless there is an overriding public interest in disclosure. Access to a document containing opinions for internal use as part of deliberations and preliminary consultations within the institution concerned shall be refused even after the decision has been taken if disclosure of the document would seriously undermine the institution's decision-making process, unless there is an overriding public interest in disclosure.

---

[130] Case: 1108/2012/RT.

[131] The Good Practice Guidelines are available at www.ombudsman.europa.eu/cases/correspondence.faces/en/54521/html.bookmark, accessed 6 January 2017.

[132] Report on visits to Agencies, www.ombudsman.europa.eu/en/activities/visitreport.faces/en/59248/html.bookmark#_ftnref1, accessed 6 January 2017.

[133] Case: 277/2012/RA.

[134] See for a comparative view, Birkinshaw (note 101), Chapter 12; Open Society Justice Initiative (note 101); Herke Kranenborg and Wim Voermans, *Access to Information in the European Union: A Comparative Analysis of EC and Member States Legislation* (Europa Law Publishing 2005).

The EO has been dealing with cases where institutions refused access to the documents on the ground that they formed part of an internal communication which took place in preparation of one of the Commissioners' reply to a parliamentary question and that the exchange of correspondence between institutions was 'internal'.[135] The final position of the Commission was that a final text representing the position taken by an institution, as a result of internal deliberations and consultations, necessarily differs from its first draft, and disclosing the different versions of the evolving draft of this text to the public would reveal the substance of the internal discussions thereon. Such a disclosure would make officials involved in the decision-making process reluctant to express their honest views on the issue, undermining the effectiveness of the deliberations. On top of that, the Commission maintained that the complainant had provided no arguments for the existence of an 'overriding public interest in disclosure'.[136] The EO agreed with the institution that the exception has been correctly applied and consequently has facilitated the communication between the Commission and the applicant in view of better explanation of this position. In other cases, the applicant has agreed to a future disclosure of the document, after it becomes final.[137]

On the other hand, the EO has not accepted the Commission's refusal to grant access to the evaluation sheet containing the Selection Board's final assessment of the complainant's written test. In this case, the European Personnel Selection Office (EPSO), following the EO's own-initiative inquiry on the issue of transparency in EU recruitment,[138] agreed that selection boards should use a model evaluation sheet for written tests and that candidates who failed the written tests or who were not invited to an interview could obtain such evaluation sheets upon request. Although even the EPSO has not followed this commitment fully,[139] the EO concluded that it is not clear why such practice is not embraced by the Commission in its own procedures of selection and this is an instance of maladministration.[140] In a similar way, a request that EPSO release the number of candidates invited to the oral test does not

[135] Case: 172/2010/ANA.
[136] Case: 172/2010/ANA.
[137] Case: 297/2010/GG.
[138] Decision of the European Ombudsman closing his own-initiative inquiry OI/5/2005/PB.
[139] Case: 18/2010/IP.
[140] Case: 62/2010/RT.

undermine the competition in question.[141] Furthermore, denial of access to the (anonymized) reports of the individual experts who evaluated a proposal on the basis that it would prevent experts giving their full and frank opinion in the decision-making process is not sufficiently justified and amounts to maladministration.[142]

In all these circumstances, the EO stressed the need to better justify the decisions of non-disclosure in terms of their coverage by the existent exceptions from Regulation No. 1049/2011. Thus, Articles 4(1) to 4(3) of Regulation No. 1049/2001 do not contain any exception which would justify a refusal to grant access based only on the argument that the institution holding the document considers that the document is not 'relevant' for the public. Requiring members of the public to demonstrate that the documents were 'relevant' for that individual in order to obtain access amounts to maladministration.[143] Similarly, internal audit reports are not covered by the exception and the EO has convinced an agency to make a change in its policy regarding access to such documents.[144]

Summarizing the EO's findings in most of these cases, it may be noted that EU bodies have offered insufficient reasoning for refusal when the latter was grounded on protection of decision-making process, and that often access was granted after the EO's intervention. The main recommendation of the EO regards proactive disssemination of such documents where there is interest for them.

3.4.8 Commercial interest EU institutions may refuse access to a document where disclosure would undermine the protection of commercial interests of a natural or legal person, including intellectual property (Article 4 of Regulation No. 1049/2001). For instance, if documents to which access was requested went to the heart of a company's importing business, since they indicated the market shares, commercial strategy and the sales policy of the undertakings in question are covered by the exception;[145] precise information relating to the cost structure of an undertaking constitutes business secrets, the disclosure of which to third parties is likely to undermine that undertaking's commercial interests.[146] However,

---

141 Case: 2470/2009/(TS)TN.

142 Case: 2781/2008/(TS)FOR.

143 Case: 2493/2008/(BB)(TS)FOR.

144 Case: 2914/2009/DK.

145 Joined Cases T-355/04 and T-446/04 Co-*Frutta Soc. coop. v Commission* [2010] ECR II-00001, para. 128.

146 Case: T-380/04 *Terezakis v Commission* [2008] ECR II-11 (summary publication), para. 95.

the exception tends to be excessively applied, prompting the Court of First Instance (now the General Court) to state in the same judgment,[147] that if all information relating to a company and its business relations were regarded as being covered by the protection given to commercial interests in accordance with Article 4(2), first indent, of Regulation No. 1049/2001, effect would not be given to the general principle of giving the public the widest possible access to documents held by the institutions.

In short, the EO has found that such requests for information pose the following problems: not all information about a company is commercially sensitive, so a test should be performed every time to see whether the exception applies. In many cases the EO found insufficient reasoning of refusal. Also, the opposition of the economic operator regarding disclosure is not binding on the EU's institutions (which can 'overrule' a third-party's objection).

In one case that reached the EO office, the Commission refused to grant access to three letters which Porsche AG had sent to former Vice-President Verheugen, written when the Commission consulted key stakeholders concerning the review of the Community Strategy to reduce carbon dioxide emissions from passenger cars. It was therefore likely that the three letters contained information on Porsche AG's business relations. However, the EO's inspection of the documents established that these letters and/or their annexes, did not relate exclusively to the protected commercial interests described above.[148] Third-party objections are not mandatory for the Commission, which retains the discretion as to carry out its own assessment.

Moreover, the EO remarked that even if all the information was the kind that falls within the definition of commercial interests in a broad sense (market share; commercial strategy; industrial, financial, banking or commercial data, including information relating to the company's business relations or contracts; its methods of assessing costs; and company know-how), a test should be performed to see whether the disclosure would undermine the commercial interest of the company. The justification of the Commission for its refusal, which made reference only to Porsche AG's 'specific position on the automobile market', without any other reference to the individual facts of the case, is not acceptable as a reasoning for non-disclosure, consequently the opposition of Porsche AG to the disclosure is not binding on the Commission.

In another case, the European Medicines Agency (EMA) decided

---

147 See Case: T-380/04, *Terezakis v Commission*, para. 93 [2008] ECR-II-11.
148 Case: 676/2008/RT.

to refuse access, invoking Article 3(2)(a) of its own rules of access to documents, which refers to the protection of 'commercial interests of a natural or legal person, including intellectual property'.[149] The applicants sustained that it was unlikely that clinical study reports would contain anything that could undermine the protection of a natural or legal person's commercial interests, and that anyway, commercial interests of the drug industry should not override the welfare of patients. The EO agreed with EMA that neither legislation nor the case law of the CJEU provides for a clear definition of 'commercial interests'; however, the interpretation of the concept given by EMA, which rested on the *potential for benefit, disproportionate prejudice and serious* harm, seems to be too wide to be in line with the more narrow approach of the CJEU in the few cases it has dealt with. In the end, EMA accepted the interpretation of the EO and released the documents; moreover, it committed to future practices along the suggested line of interpretation.[150]

3.4.9 Ongoing proceedings and investigations This exception is based on the presumption that withholding the information would prejudice the criminal proceedings or the effectiveness of tests and audits conducted by a public entity and keeping secrecy over this type of information would serve the public interest better than disclosure. The exemption applies only when information is obtained from confidential sources, so that the public should be encouraged to participate with information in public proceedings and investigations without the fear of being exposed. When the exemption is not absolute, it has to involve consultation of the person interested before deciding for disclosure. Sometimes, though, the exemption is absolute, meaning that it permits an agency to respond to a request under a Freedom of Information Act as if the records in fact did not exist.

From a practical standpoint, this exemption relates to, for example, *preliminary investigations in criminal cases*. On the other hand, some aspects in connection with preliminary investigations in criminal cases are not subject to secrecy – the decision to open legal proceedings, not to launch a preliminary investigation or to discontinue a preliminary investigation should not be subject to secrecy. In most cases, final judgments upon a case do not include any confidential elements, but this rule also has exceptions, when, for instance, the judgment includes information of a sensitive personal nature as in the case of sex crimes.

---

149 Case: 2560/2007/BEH.

150 Not all the other cases were dealt with accordingly, though – see Case: 1701/2011/(BEH)ANA.

Following this pattern, European institutions are allowed to refuse access to a document where disclosure would undermine the protection of court proceedings and legal advice, and the purpose of inspections, investigations and audits, unless there is an overriding public interest in disclosure (Article 4 of Regulation No. 1049/2001).

From the practice of the EU, several conclusions may be drawn. First, the concept of 'ongoing investigation' is still unclear and needs further guidance on how it should be interpreted.[151] The case law of the CJEU has dealt with cases such as T-409/05 *A.S.TER v Commission* and T-290/05 *Friedrich Weber v Commission*, but there is still no clear definition of the concept.

Another question is whether the burden of proof of the possibility to prejudice an investigation should be on the applicant or on the institution? The EO made it clear that the institution is the one that has to come up with arguments why such disclosure would jeopardize the procedure, and the exception does not apply automatically.[152]

The EO has also stressed the fact that the risk of a protected interest being undermined must be reasonably foreseeable and not purely hypothetical, and that for each individual document institutions need to prove that disclosure would undermine the investigation.[153] The EO merely made a correct application of the case law of the CJEU on this matter. Thus, the Court of First Instance[154] was the first one to state in *Franchet and Byk v Commission* that 'the third indent of Article 4(2) of Regulation No 1049/2001 must be interpreted in such a way that this provision, the aim of which is to protect "the purpose of inspections, investigations and audits", applies only if disclosure of the documents in question may endanger the completion of inspections, investigations or audits'.

A general recommendation of the EO regarded the need for various agencies to clarify their rules on public access in the case of ongoing complaints in their rules of procedure[155]

When the judicial proceedings are over, the documents that served in the procedure may be released. In its recent judgment *My Travel*,[156]

---

[151] Case: 452/2010/BEH.

[152] Case: 3699/2006/ELB.

[153] Case: 3699/2006/ELB.

[154] Joined Cases: T-391/03 and T-70/04 *Franchet and Byk v Commission* [2006] ECR II-2023.

[155] Case: 755/2014/BEH.

[156] Case: C-506/08 P *Sweden v MyTravel and Commission*, judgment of 21 July 2011, Reports of Cases 2011 I-06237, para. 76; Appeal Case before the Court of Justice C-506/08 P.

the CJEU held in respect of the second subparagraph of Article 4(3) of Regulation No. 1049/2001 that once the decision is adopted, the requirements for protecting the decision-making process are less acute. The EO enforced this interpretation when an initial refusal of the Commission to release documents based on the exception regarding ongoing judicial procedures was continued and even after the proceedings were over.[157] The Commission's statement that disclosure might jeopardize investigations into 'ongoing and future infringements of similar characteristics' was considered to be generic: it could be used to oppose non-disclosure of any document, in any administrative (or other) procedure, since *in abstracto* it is always possible that an institution uses the same strategy, arguments or methods in more than one case, or that it changes them radically, thereby departing from previous practice.

3.4.10 The overriding public interest Article 4(2) and Article 4(3) of Regulation No. 1049/2001 provide that an institution must not release a document to the public if one of the interests set out in those provisions applies, unless there is an *overriding public interest* in disclosure. This raises the question of burden of proof – namely who has the obligation to invoke the public interest? The institution *ex officio* or the applicant?

A debate has arisen in connection with the conflicting scope of the inner provisions of Regulation No. 1049/2001. In an independent study focused on the implementation of the Regulation,[158] the most serious problem was considered the manner in which each institution applies the Article on exceptions (Article 4) to the citizen's access to documents. Specifically, in many occasions Article 4 is not being applied in connection with Article 2, which enshrines the *right* to access information, meaning that in many cases Article 4 is treated as a *rule* rather than as an *exception* to the rule. The institutions use Article 4 as a protecting tool against disclosure, almost never applying the 'public interest test' in determining whether 'there is an overriding public interest in disclosure'. Article 4 of Regulation No. 1049/2001 does not even specify what a public interest test is or how such a test should be applied or performed, therefore a part of the problem is the lack of procedures or standards in place to assist those working in the institutions to perform public interest tests, resulting in personal interpretations and inconsistency in performance across different

---

[157] Case: 1861/2009/(JF)AN.

[158] Jason Ferguson, Improving Citizens' Access to Documents: ECAS Recommendations to the European Commission and Other Institutions (Brussels: ECAS 2003).

institutions. The conclusion of the study was that the Commission should propose to revise Article 4 and allow for guidelines to be developed by each institution, including specific procedures or a concrete framework that those applying public interest tests can perform such tests accurately and consistently.

The Commission is of the opinion that in order for an overriding public interest to apply, there must be a public interest which outweighs the interest protected by the exception to the right to public access, and that the complainant needs to put forward any arguments that would show the existence of a public interest. The EO on the other hand, noted that an institution to which a request is made pursuant to Regulation No. 1049/2001 is required to apply the Regulation in full.[159] This involves carrying out a full analysis to determine whether an overriding public interest in disclosure exists. The EO underlines that, in this respect, it is certainly correct for the institution to which a request for public access is made to examine arguments put forward by an applicant in relation to overriding public interests. However, the EO notes that the institution concerned should also, *ex officio*, carry out its own examination as regards whether there is an overriding public interest in disclosure. The EO considers that, in relation to its future practice, the Commission should clearly indicate that it has also, *ex officio*, considered whether there may be an overriding public interest in disclosure.[160] However, in other cases, the Commission seems to rely again on the arguments put forward by the complainant.[161] In other cases, the Commission has not even assessed the arguments put forward by the complainant. In the latter case, it was about the interest of the population of the Vera conurbation to know why, despite the Court's judgment declaring that Spain had failed to fulfil its obligations, the latter had still not executed that judgment and the population still continued to suffer the consequences of that failure.[162]

Summarizing the good practices promoted by the EO on how to deal with the public interest test, the institution has made it rather clear that institutions must carry out a full analysis to determine whether an overriding public interest in disclosure exists. It is certainly correct that the institution to which a request for public access is made to examine arguments put forward by an applicant in relation to overriding public interests, but the institution concerned should also, *ex officio,* carry out its

---

159 Case: 1039/2008/FOR.
160 Case: 1039/2008/FOR.
161 Case: 172/2010/ANA.
162 Case: 2073/2010/AN.

own examination as regards whether there is an overriding public interest in disclosure. In that regard, the EO welcomes any internal guidelines or rules that the institutions may decide to update in order to ensure that its services are aware of the obligation to carry out the said examination.

4 Deadlines for Answering the Requests

The deadlines in freedom of information legal regimes reflect a balance between three types of interests. First, there is the interest of applicants, who would like a rapid and complete disclosure, effective penalties and sanctions applied to public authorities reluctant to implement the provisions of a Freedom of Information Act. Secondly, there are public authorities, which are interested in more time for complying with requests for public information and speculate every chance to refuse disclosure. Thirdly there are the third parties, interested at their turn in the procedure of consultation before disclosure. According to Article 8(2) of Regulation No. 1049/2001, the period of 15 working days foreseen for dealing with confirmatory applications for access to documents can, in 'exceptional cases' and provided that 'detailed reasons are given', be extended by another 15 working days.

The EO has found in his/her investigations that there are excessive delays[163] in answering requests for information, especially at the Commission. The intervention of the EO often led to apologies offered for delays.

In cases where the institution receives complex requests, the approach suggested by the EO would be to enter into informal agreements between the EU institution and applicants for a fair solution. The requester needs, however, to agree with the proposed solution. Extensions should be well grounded.[164] Often such complex requests end with the disclosure of a limited number of documents. In another case, the Commission explained that 'due to [its] concern to grant [the complainants] the widest possible access to the documents requested', it was carrying out a detailed individual examination of those documents and this constituted a good enough reason to delay the answer to a request for more than five months. The EO did not resonate with this attempt to rely on transparency concerns in order to disregard the deadlines for answering requests.[165]

The EO has opened an investigation regarding a constant malpractice of some institutions (especially the Commission) of exceeding the time limits

---

163 11 months for instance – see Case: 2058/2011/(BEH)JN.
164 Case: 1869/2013/AN.
165 Case: 339/2011/AN.

for answering requests. For instance, where the Commission's decision was taken some six weeks after the extended deadline foreseen by the Regulation.[166] The EO seemed to be satisfied with apologies for the delay. However, further remarks stated the fact that such practice might become an instance of institutional malpractice if not addressed in a structured manner. In cases when the Commission does not appear to have given the complainant an indication of how long it would take to deal with its application, the EO is of the view that it would be appropriate for the Commission to provide such an indication in future cases.[167]

As a general good practice, the EO has specified that institutions should give the complainant an indication of how long it would take to deal with the application, due to the fact that there is no sanction for not respecting the deadline for answering requests.[168]

In the same vein, failure to justify the extensions/delay – namely relevant circumstances that could constitute an 'exceptional case' within the meaning of Article 8(2), for instance when there is a need for consultation with other services of the same body, constitutes an instance of maladministration. Thus, the Commission was criticized by the EO for failing to indicate relevant circumstances that could constitute an 'exceptional case' within the meaning of Article 8(2) of Regulation No. 1049/2001, and that simple references, formulated in general terms, to the need to consult other Commission services cannot satisfy the requirement of 'detailed reasoning' provided in the same Article.[169] The EO came upon a case where the deadline for reply had been extended two times, but in the meantime the Commission had responded and apologized, so the EO considered the matter closed. However, it was a good opportunity to state that the extension of the deadline can be used only one time (Article 8(2) of Regulation No. 1049/2001 does not provide for a second extension of the deadline).[170]

As regards the deadlines for confirmatory application, the EO notes that, while an applicant is required to make a confirmatory application within 15 working days of any *express* refusal to grant public access under Article 7(2) and Article 7(3) of Regulation No. 1049/2001, no such deadline applies as regards a failure by an institution to respond to an initial application. Consequently, the EO is of the opinion that an applicant who becomes entitled under Article 7(4) of Regulation No. 1049/2001 to make a confirmatory application (because he/she has not received a reply within

166 Case: 1195/2010/OV.
167 Case: 1302/2009/TS.
168 Case: 339/2011/AN.
169 Case: 3163/2007/(BEH)KM.
170 Case: 1861/2009/(JF)AN.

the prescribed time limit) can thus introduce a confirmatory application at any time.[171]

In many instances in which EU bodies do not comply with the legal deadlines, oftentimes the intervention of the EO triggers a late response from the EU institutions. The reasons usually invoked for late response include: numerous documents, some of them old and in archives or in the possession of various bodies subordinated to the Commission to look into even if in the end the number of documents actually disclosed is rather small; third-party correspondence, thus the need to consult with them. In latter cases, the institutions should initiate such a consultation as soon as they ascertain the need for it, in order to be able to abide by the time limits stipulated in Regulation No. 1049/2001.[172]

5 The Role of the EO in Enhancing Access to Information

This section discusses in more detail the EO's contribution to the creation of a sound and independent body of norms of good administration in the area of free access to documents and transparency. We start this section by trying to answer a simple question, namely which are the principles of good administration mostly used by the EO in decisions pertaining to requests for access to documents.

Based on the categorization of the principles of good administration from part I, section 2, it can be argued that a first category of norms employed pertain to the category of rules of administrative practice in line with the idea of providing a good service to the public. Perhaps the most often invoked rule from this category refers to the obligation to act courteously. Other rules refer to language rights, recommendations on how to keep adequate records and how to handle requests erroneously addressed (transfer/redirect). These rules concern for the most part factual behaviour and organizational matters. The EO employs two very different approaches. On the one hand, the EO clearly indicates when he/she applies these norms and also explains what those norms imply in the particular circumstances of a case. This approach of the EO, used with regard to this category of extra-legal rules (rules which for the most part are not enshrined in legal texts), has the advantage that institutions clearly understand how they are expected to behave under certain circumstances. Clear indication of the norm employed is also useful in cases when the EO extends the scope of a certain duty – for example, Article 13 from the Code

171 Case: 465/2010/FOR.
172 Case: 1111/2012/AN.

comprises the obligation to respond to the applicant in his/her own language. The EO has, however, argued that it is also good practice to carry out surveys, which are meant to offer input for legislative changes in all languages of the Union. On the other hand, there are also situations when the EO employs more general norms of good administration, not limited to the specific circumstances of a case. The EO will simply state that 'the principles of good governance require a certain conduct', without actually mentioning which concrete principle he/she is referring to.

A second category of norms employed by the EO refers to procedural and substantive rights derived from Community law. From this category the most often used in the area of free access and transparency is the duty to state reasons. This obligation is encountered in cases where the institutions invoke the exceptions from Regulation No. 1049/2001 (Article 4(2)) in order to justify the refusal to grant access. The EO has, in numerous decisions, emphasized that it is good administrative practice to demonstrate that the requested documents fall within the categories listed in Article 4 of Regulation No. 1049/2001. Moreover, institutions need to offer detailed enough explanations regarding the grounds for refusal – explain in the context of each case how disclosure will undermine certain interests. The EO acknowledges that the institutions enjoy a wide discretion in determining whether certain documents are exempted and he/she usually accepts the explanation of the institutions as long as it is convincing and well-grounded. It is important to note that the EO has sometimes offered indications in his/her decisions on how EU institutions should conduct the test for the identification of an overriding public interest. In almost all of the cases regarding refusal due to exempted information, the EO seems to rely heavily on the case law of CJEU in order to justify his/her findings and the proposed solution. This is also in response to the legalistic arguments put forth by the EU institutions.

Another principle of good administration that occurs rather frequently in the EO's decisions deals with the timeliness of replying to requests for access. Regulation No. 1049/2001 sets strict time limits both for replying to the initial request and to confirmatory applications. In most cases the EO will make a decision along the following lines: 'It is good administrative practice to reply to confirmatory applications for access and to do so within the relevant deadlines foreseen in Regulation 1049/2001. The Commission's failure to do so in the present case constitutes an instance of maladministration.'[173] It is interesting to note that the EO does not limit his/her evaluation to simply observing if the time limits from the law are

[173] Case: 271/2010/GG.

complied with. In a small number of cases the EO performs a careful and in-depth examination of whether the long time necessary for processing the request is justified or not by the factual circumstances of the case (e.g., access to more than 300 documents). In one instance the EO found no maladministration despite the delay of the Commission (this decision will be further examined at the end of this section).[174]

Based on the empirical research, we were able to either identify or deduce some principles of good administration that were formulated by the EO in cases pertaining to free access to documents but which are not currently included in the European Code of Good Administrative Behaviour. Below, there is a short description and justification for the inclusion of these principles in the Code in the future.

- As already discussed in a previous research, the principle of transparency should perhaps be included in the Code as a free-standing principle. In several decisions in the area of free access to documents the EO makes reference to the fact that, as a general rule, EU institutions should be as open and transparent as possible. The EO mentions the duty of the institutions to provide information on their own initiative about procedures or activities that could be of relevance for the general public. This recommendation is particularly important with regard to highly sensitive information, which generally tends to be regarded by institutions as exempted from disclosure. Proactive disclosure and communication means that the institutions can in certain cases select the information that is suitable for publication thus opening to the public policy areas that in the past have been marked by secrecy (US–EU negotiations, trilogues, etc.). Other goals to be accomplished by greater transparency and proactive disclosure include greater legitimacy and public trust as well as a more significant contribution of the public to certain policy areas that have a broad societal impact. Currently, Article 22 from the Code refers only to the duty of institutions to provide information upon request. In the study by De Leeuw,[175] she argues in favour of the inclusion of the principle of active and adequate provision of information. This wording covers the proactive disclosure of information as well as the duty to act with care and precision.
- Partial disclosure and *ex officio* re-examination of the request once the circumstances of the case which have generated the refusal of

174 Case: 1869/2013/AN.
175 De Leeuw (note 11).

the institution change. In several cases the EO argued that the EU institutions should consider partial disclosure of certain documents that are otherwise covered by exceptions. This provision regarding partial disclosure is already enshrined in Regulation No. 1049/2001. However, a novelty concerns the recommendation of the EO that institutions should reconsider *ex officio* the individual application if, for example, a decision-making process or some international negotiations get finalized. In this case, the complainant should not be put in the position to reapply for information (it is debatable whether or not EU institutions are willing to implement this recommendation).

- Comprehensive examination of the circumstances of each case, especially when institutions need to decide if an exception from free access applies or in other cases which refer to exceptional circumstances which are to be applied strictly (discontinuance of correspondence if it is vexatious or repetitive). In a number of cases the EO has stated that before deciding if an exception applies, the institution needs to identify all the documents pertaining to that request. This cannot be done in the absence of a comprehensive and carefully conducted evaluation. In a previous research, De Leeuw argues in favour of a broader principle, namely active and adequate gathering of information.[176] This principle clearly includes elements pertaining to other principles such as the principle of objectivity as well as the principle of care.
- Article 22(5) of the Code, which contains the obligation to transfer the letter or complaint to the competent service of the institution, should also include, at least with regard to access to documents, the obligation to forward the request directly to the person responsible for such duties.

A final question that we try to answer in this section concerns the type of review performed by the EO, more specifically if he/she employs legal norms or principles of good administration, or a combination of both. Before answering this question, certain aspects need to be emphasized. First, free access to documents is not a highly legalized policy area and numerous complaints regard factual behaviour and organizational matters. This means that extra-legal principles forming the outer layer of good administration are likely to occur. Second, Regulation No. 1049/2001, which comprises the applicable rules for granting access to EU documents, is outdated and in need of serious revamping. This means

---

[176] De Leeuw (note 11) p. 31.

that with respect to certain aspects, the applicable norms need to be found elsewhere. Third, access to information and more generally transparency is a field benefiting from the contribution of best practices from other jurisdictions, both national and international. It is therefore normal to see, up to a certain extent, the EO's norms being infused with principles or interpretations of some principles from other jurisdictions.

In light of the findings from the research and based on these observations, we evaluate the review conducted by the EO in the area of free access as a review mostly based on principles of good administration.

As already discussed in part I of this chapter, it is rather clear that the EO does not envision good administration outside of the existing legal provisions. The following case[177] clearly expresses this situation. The inquiries concerned EPSO's refusal to provide an applicant in a staff selection procedure with a copy of her corrected test papers (also another applicant in a staff selection procedure with comments concerning her performance in a practical test). In view of recent cases before the EU Civil Service Tribunal, where EPSO's refusal to grant access to corrected tests and to practical test papers was deemed legal by the court, the EO concluded that no further inquiries were justified. Such a review would clearly be labelled as legalistic. However, even in this case, the EO made the remark that EPSO should now seek to maximize the amount of information it gives in the competency passport, which now is the only document by which applicants can understand precisely how they were assessed. With this remark, she applied the principle of transparency and proactive dissemination of information. There is, however, at least one decision made by the EO in which, in our opinion, the EO found no maladministration, despite the existence of contrary case law in that respect.[178] This could be interpreted as a step in the direction of what was labelled in the literature unlawful but proper behavior. In the cited case, the applicant requested a large volume of documents. The Commission took the view that in light of Article 6(3) of Regulation No. 1049/2001 it 'has the possibility to postpone the tight deadlines of the Regulation, provided it has explained the specific circumstances and proposed a reasonable time frame'. Based on the case law, the time limits from Regulation No. 1049/2001 cannot be changed and Article 6(3) concerns only the content or the number of documents applied for (Case C-127/13 P). The EO's assessment clarified that in the case at hand, in strictly legal terms, the Commission was not entitled to extend the time frame established in Regulation No. 1049/2001. The next paragraph (22)

---

[177] Case: 2006/2011/ER.
[178] Case: 1869/2013/AN.

from the EO's decision is however compelling and is therefore reproduced in its entirety:

> The Ombudsman's assessment of a complaint, however, goes beyond purely legal arguments and includes considerations of reasonableness, fairness and good faith. From this perspective, an applicant who agrees on a 'fair solution' with an institution accepts that it is not reasonable to expect a comprehensive decision within the statutory time limits. In these circumstances, the institution's failure to decide on access in relation to all of the requested documents within the statutory time limits cannot be regarded as maladministration. The question thus arises, whether, in cases in which there has not been any agreement on a 'fair solution', as in this case, an institution's failure to decide the access application within the statutory time limits, necessarily amounts to maladministration.

Based on our research we also identified cases in which illegal behaviour was also deemed as improper. In these cases, the EO conducted both a review based on legality as well as a review on the basis of principles of good administration. For example, in a case,[179] the European Parliament refused to provide information with regard to the allowances of specific MEPs to a journalist. The EO, after consulting with the European Data Protection Supervisor, came to the conclusion that 'the public had a right to be informed about the MEPs' behaviour. The European Parliament, following the investigation by the EO, agreed to provide some information about allowances on its website but refused to grant access to the requested information. The EO regretted that Parliament had chosen to justify its refusal fully to accept his draft recommendation by relying on a legal interpretation of Regulations 1049/2001 and 45/2001, which weakens the principle of transparency and which was rejected by the Court of First Instance. In conclusion, the EO maintained his finding of maladministration as regards most aspects of the case.

CONCLUSIONS

The EO is highly involved in the area of free access to documents and information and the institution's recent interventions (own inquiries) with regard to controversial topics such as increasing the transparency of TTIP or making the 'revolving door' review more robust in order to avoid conflict of interests can be regarded as instances of enhancing the understanding of what good administration means in this policy area.

---

[179] Case: 3643/2005/(GK)WP.

The contribution to the development of norms of good administration is made not so much through decisions in individual cases but mostly through own inquiries and reports drafted following visits to the agencies of the EU. However, the principles following from the EO's own inquiries and reports are often mentioned in individual cases. In other situations, individual complaints have triggered the other mechanisms for control that the EO can employ.

The review performed by the EO in cases pertaining to free access to documents is a legality review but often combined with principles of good administration. The so-called category of extra-legal principles of good administration is often invoked in the decisions pertaining to free access, especially the principle of courtesy, which is meant to ensure that institutions are service-minded and respectful in their interactions with the citizens. Other principles invoked quite frequently include the duty to make decisions within a reasonable time limit, the duty to state the grounds of decisions, language rights, etc. Other principles, closely connected with the ones already discussed have also been identified. A future version of the Code could consider at least the inclusion of a general principle of transparency.

6. Discretion and law in the EU administration: where the courts do not enter

Joana Mendes*

1 INTRODUCTION

The Court of Justice of the European Union endorsed a deferential approach to the significant expansion of the executive powers of the European Union (EU) institutions and of its agencies in, at least, two important instances, in the aftermath of the financial and sovereign debt crises. In the *ESMA* case, the Court dismissed the claim of the United Kingdom according to which the powers of the European Securities and Markets Authority (ESMA) breached the limits of delegation as defined in previous case law, most notably in *Meroni*. In doing so, it acknowledged that the EU legislator may attribute discretionary powers to EU agencies, as long as these are 'precisely delineated' and 'amenable to judicial review'.[1] In *Gauweiler*, the Court upheld the legality of the Outright Monetary Transactions (OMT) programme to the European Central Bank (ECB) by, *inter alia*, applying a rather deferent standard of judicial review of the ECB's discretion.[2] In a different way, both cases raise the question of how far may law reach when structuring the exercise of discretion of the EU executive actors. If the legality of the arguably far-reaching discretionary powers of the ESMA – to endorse here the view defended by

* I am grateful to the participants of the European Ombudsman 20th Anniversary Colloquium, *Democracy and Accountability in the EU: The Role of the European Ombudsman*, held in June 2015 where the ideas that led to this chapter were initially discussed. A version of this chapter was published in the *Common Market Law Review* in 2016. This research was funded by the Netherlands Organisation for Scientific Research (NWO), under the VENI grant scheme.

[1] Case C-270/12, *United Kingdom v European Parliament and Council* (*ESMA*), EU:C:2014:18, para. 53 (reasoning on paras. 43 to 52) and para. 105.

[2] Case C-62/14, *Gauweiler et al. v Deutscher Bundestag*, EU:C:2015:400, paras. 68 to 80, in particular para. 74.

the UK – is justified because, given the conditions defined in the enabling act, they are 'amenable to judicial review', how far may judicial review reach? If the lenient review of the OMT programme may be explained by the nature of this measure – an incomplete programme announced in a press release, lacking both the degree of specific regulation in a legal act and actual implementation[3] – how could legal tools operate in structuring the ECB's discretion if the programme were implemented?

The way in which the Court would review concrete manifestations of the exercise of discretion by the ESMA and by the ECB in these instances would be an exercise in hypothetical, if not speculative, reasoning. Yet, the more general question of how far legal tools may reach can be addressed by relying on existing case law. This is what this chapter sets out to do. After highlighting that judicial review of discretion is premised on the idea of limits (Section 2), the chapter moves on to show how far the deployment of legal principles and rules may allow the EU Courts to control discretionary choices (Section 3). The focus will be on two trends of the case law, where judicial review was tighter. The first regards the stringent standard of judicial review of administrative discretion as formulated in a merger control case (*Tetra-Laval*) and subsequently applied in other areas of EU law; the second, the scrutiny of compliance with the principle of careful and impartial examination. This case law thus provides a contrasting view to the impression of deference conveyed by *ESMA* (on the powers granted on a permanent basis to the financial agencies, as a result of the crisis) and *Gauweiler* (on the powers exercised by the ECB in exceptional circumstances).[4] The two trends of case law chosen indicate how far the EU Courts went in reviewing administrative discretion in the EU and, thereby, they also reveal where the Courts have not entered. They have closely scrutinized the way the Commission has conducted complex technical assessments, but have arguably refrained from entering public interest appraisals that also form the core of discretionary administrative decisions. This chapter argues that this emphasis of judicial review on the correctness of complex technical assessments excessively confines the role of law in structuring the exercise of discretion (Section 4). While the

---

[3] See Case C-62/14, *Gauweiler et al. v Deutscher Bundestag*, Opinion of A-G Villalón, EU:C:2015:7, para. 162.

[4] *ESMA* and *Gauweiler* are indicative of the scope of powers that EU executive bodies may have, because of deference to legislative choices (in the case of *ESMA*) or to an expansive view on a Treaty mandate (arguably the case in *Gauweiler*), not of deference to administrative decisions. How the CJEU reviews the exercise of discretion that executive actors have under EU law and what role law should have in relation to administrative discretion, is the question this article addresses.

limits of judicial review may be explained by institutional reasons, this chapter argues that they should not exhaust the role of law in structuring the exercise of discretion. In doing so, it contrasts the role of the Courts and the role of the European Ombudsman in structuring discretion (Section 5).

2 DISCRETION AND THE LIMITS OF LAW

It is the premise in rule of law systems that law both attributes discretionary powers and delimits the choices administrative actors make in fulfilling their functions. There are different layers to what law may mean in relation to discretion. Law are the formal legal texts generated by political processes that define and delimit the mandates of administrative actors (legislative acts and Treaty provisions). Law has also a deeper normative sense that transcends the legislative act. It is a normative order that binds public authority to fundamental political-legal values via constitutional provisions and general principles of law, which inform and limit political processes and which administrative action ought to concretize and respect.[5] Arguably, this premise ought to apply even in those areas of administrative action where legality is thinner (for instance, various forms of guidance that define the way market operators, citizens and Member States should comply with EU law).

But discretion strays clearly beyond law. Law defines more or less stringently the space within which administrative actors need to choose a course of action that best suits the public interest, also in view of the means and resources they are able to mobilize. Law has a role within this space, insofar as it defines criteria that ought to guide the decision. But what is the best or better option may have little to do with substantive legal determinations. It is influenced by policy choices that may not be straightforwardly supported by law, and are rather determined by political directions defined by the top decision-makers; it is governed by expert judgments, on the basis of which complex economic and technical assessments are made; it is fundamentally influenced by bureaucratic motivations, by the moral and ideological preferences of those involved in decision-making, by the specific contexts in which the decisions are made.[6] Arguably, all

---

[5] On the principle of legality in EU law, and on its difficulties, see Azoulai and Clément-Wilz, 'Le principe de légalité' in Auby and Dutheil de la Rochère (eds.) *Traité de Droit Administratif Européen* (Brussels, Bruylant 2014), 543–63, at 544–55.

[6] Baldwin, *Rules and Government* (Oxford, Clarendon 1995), at 25.

these elements come into play when deciding issues such as whether 'the possibility of default by any Member State or supra-national issuer' poses a threat to financial stability capable of justifying a prohibition of short-selling activities, or whether a threat to public health is serious enough to justify the suspension of imports of wild birds.[7] Decisions of this sort are discretionary insofar as they entail a choice, both to define the standards that should guide the final decision, in view of the legal criteria defined, and to determine what that decision will be.[8]

It follows that, as a matter of principle, judicial review of administrative discretion should be limited. If the role of the Court of Justice is, in essence, to ensure the observance of law (Article 19(1) of the Treaty on the European Union (TEU)) – so the principle goes – then, when faced with instances in which the institutions are given a 'wide margin of discretion', judicial review should be limited to verifying 'whether the rules on procedure and on the statement of reasons have been complied with, whether the facts have been accurately stated, and, whether there has been any manifest error of assessment or misuse of powers'.[9] Both given the nature of discretionary powers – enmeshed in complex technical assessments and in policy options (as well as in bureaucratic motivations) – and the institutional role of the EU Courts, judicial review ought not curtail the ability of the EU institutions and bodies to assess which solution best serves the public interests at stake in view of the concrete circumstances in which they need to decide. Judicial review of administrative discretion is thus premised on limits determined by separation of powers: law demarcates a space of discretion but does not command the choices made therein;

---

[7] Respectively, Art. 28(1)(a) of Regulation (EU) 236/2012 of the European Parliament and of the Council of 14 March 2012 on short selling and certain aspects of credit default swaps, OJ 2012, L 86/1, and Art. 24(3)(b) of Commission Delegated Regulation (EU) 918/2012 of 5 July 2012 supplementing Regulation (EU) 236/2012, OJ 2012, L 274/1; and Art. 18(1) of Council Directive 91/496/EEC of 15 July 1991 laying down the principles governing the organization of veterinary checks on animals entering the Community from third countries, OJ 1991, L 268/56.

[8] Galligan, *Discretionary Powers: A Legal Study of Official Discretion* (Oxford, Clarendon Press 1986), at 21; Mattarella, 'Discrezionalità Amministrativa' in Cassese et al. (ed.) *Dizionario di Diritto Pubblico*, Vol. III (Milano, Giuffrè 2006), 1993–2003, at 1994 (indicating that the specificity of the discretionary choice lies in the way taken to pursue the public interest); Venezia, *Le Pouvoir Discrétionnaire* (Paris, LGDJ 1959), at 20, 22. In a different sense, see Schmidt-Assmann, *La Teoria General del Derecho Administrativo como Sistema* (Madrid, Marcial Pons 1998), at 220 (emphasizing that discretion concretizes law in view of pre-determined ends).

[9] Among many other examples, see Case 42/84, *Remia and Others* v *Commission*, EU:C:1985:327, para. 34.

courts enforce the law but do not hamper discretionary choices that observe legal determinations.[10]

However, the premise according to which judicial review of discretionary powers should be limited has prevented neither the General Court from reviewing rather stringently the factual basis and the qualification of complex technical assessments, at least in relation to non-legislative acts, nor the Court of Justice from endorsing such stringent review.[11] While arguably such a review may be needed to enable a meaningful degree of judicial control over discretionary decisions, it may potentially encroach upon the space of decision-making of the institutions that were granted discretionary powers. This is, of course, the tension at the heart of judicial review of discretion.

But which scope for choice will Courts possibly restrict when performing a stringent review of complex technical assessments? According to the legal doctrine prevalent in some continental legal systems, technical complex assessments either do not entail discretion, as the term would only refer to choices that stem from assessing and weighing competing public interests, or entail a different kind of discretion.[12] Settling the technical aspects of a decision requires specialized technical knowledge. Once the technical questions are solved, they may leave no margin of choice: there may simply be no room for alternative decisions. The outcome is determined by the technical knowledge that the administrative authority has collected (whether produced by its own services or acquired externally). To the extent that technical assessments may entail a choice, because the specific expertise required does not settle the issue, this would leave the administrative authority a 'margin of appreciation', not, strictly

---

[10] See, e.g., Case T-13/99, *Pfizer Animal Health v Council*, EU:T:2002:209, para. 393: 'It is not for the Court to assess the merits of either of the scientific points of view argued before it and to substitute its assessment for that of the Community institutions, on which the Treaty confers sole responsibility in that regard . . . Since the Community institutions could reasonably take the view that they had a proper scientific basis for a possible link, the mere fact that there were scientific indications to the contrary does not establish that they exceeded the bounds of their discretion in finding that there was a risk to human health.'

[11] See Section 3 below.

[12] The distinction between administrative discretion ('*discrezionalità amministrativa*') and technical discretion ('*discrezionalità tecnica*') has prevailed, *inter alia*, in Italian administrative scholarship (see Mattarella, *supra* note 8, in particular at 1994, 1996, 2000).

speaking, the possibility to make a discretionary choice.[13] What appears to be a mere conceptual nicety may have a normative consequence: in performing a stringent review of complex technical assessments, the Courts would not encroach upon the discretion of the EU administrative actors; they would only verify whether the criteria set by law has been complied with by controlling the factual basis of the decision.[14] This is a matter of technical accuracy, not a matter of choice stemming from balancing the competing interests at stake.

The EU Courts do not distinguish between complex technical assessments and the appraisal of public interests that grounds a discretionary choice when called upon to review EU legal acts.[15] However, the distinction is far from being irrelevant in EU law. Most notably, it grounds the so-called *Meroni* doctrine, which the Court of Justice revisited and revised in the *ESMA* judgment. Arguably, it could provide an argument to justify the Court's position in this case: If the discretion of the ESMA merely stems from the complex technical assessments it needs to perform – if the decisions it needs to adopt are 'dictated' to it by the technical knowledge that it applies – then neither the fact that such discretion is attributed to the ESMA appears normatively problematic, nor would Courts restrict its discretion by performing in a future instance a stringent review of those assessments. It is noteworthy that the association between technical assessments relying on 'professional considerations' and 'clearly defined executive powers' – distinct from 'a wide margin of appreciation' that relies in the '[arbitration] between conflicting public interests' – is made in the allegations of the Parliament and the Commission and is visible in

---

[13] For a reflection of this position in EU legal studies, see Bailey, 'Scope of judicial review under Article 81 EC' 41(5) CML Rev. (2004), 1327–60, at 1339; Caranta, 'On Discretion' in Prechal and van Roermund (eds.) *The Coherence of EU Law: The Search for Unity in Divergent Concepts* (Oxford, Oxford University Press 2008), 185–215, at 198; Barbier de la Serre and Sibony, 'Expert Evidence before the EC Courts', 45(4) CML Rev. (2008), 941–85, at 956. Bouveresse, *Le Pouvoir Discrétionnaire dans l'Ordre Juridique Communautaire* (Brussels, Bruylant 2010), at 63–6, who stresses the difficulty of the distinction.

[14] See, e.g. Barbier de la Serre and Sibony, *supra* note 13, 958 and 984. See, however, Mattarella, *supra* note 8, at 2000, referring to Italian administrative law.

[15] Critical of the possibility to transpose this distinction to EU law, because the CJEU have not used it consistently, see Fritzsche, 'Discretion, Scope of Judicial Review and Institutional Balance in European Law', 47(2) CML Rev. (2010), 364. See also Bouveresse, *supra* note 13, 57–60. Schwarze, writing in 1992, warned that the EU Courts' use of concepts familiar to national jurists could be deluding (Schwarze, *European Administrative Law*, Sweet & Maxwell, 2006 [1992], 296–7).

the Court's reasoning.[16] The same view could also support, for different reasons, the way the Court of Justice approached the discretion of the ECB in *Gauweiler*. If, despite the controversial nature of monetary policy measures, their appropriateness depends essentially on technical assessments, then as long as the necessary expertise is deployed with 'care and accuracy' the fact that there may be competing views on the adequacy of a measure only means that the ECB (and the European System of Central Banks – ESCB) may make a *technical* choice, one in which, in this case, the Court could not detect a manifest error.[17]

The same distinction between 'technical discretion' and 'discretion proper' is also influential in legal commentary on judicial review of discretion in the EU.[18] Yet, one should strongly doubt its empirical and normative value. Given the nature of discretionary powers, both types of assessments may be enmeshed in such a way that holding on to such analytical distinctions would risk twisting the reality of administrative decision-making in a manner that is potentially detrimental to a proper understanding of what may be at stake. Returning again to the examples of *ESMA* and *Gauweiler*, denying that ESMA may conduct public interest appraisals in prohibiting or imposing conditions to short-selling activities (even if only in exceptional cases) does not appear realistic (it is noteworthy that the exercise of those powers depends also on the assessment of the possible responses by national authorities). It also seems excessively narrow, in view of the potential effects of its actions, to claim that the only thing one should expect from the ESCB when adopting measures of monetary policy would be to make an accurate and careful use of its technical expertise. Surely, the determination by ESMA of whether a competent national authority has taken measures that 'adequately address the threat', requires technical evaluations but these are also inexorably linked to weighing competing interests and, in this sense, involve policy choices; in this case, the verification of the conditions upon which the exercise of the discretionary power rests already entails a room for choice, given their indeterminacy.[19] The same

---

16 Case C-270/12, *ESMA*, *supra* note 1, paras. 35, 40, and 52 (cf. para. 53). Cf. the allegations of the United Kingdom at paras. 29 and 30.

17 Case C-62/14, *Gauweiler*, *supra* note 2, paras. 72 to 80.

18 See *supra* notes 13 and 15.

19 The ESMA may only adopt those measures if there is 'a threat to the orderly functioning and integrity of the financial markets or to the stability of the financial system of the Union' (Art. 28(2)(a) of Regulation (EU) 236/2012, *supra* note 7). What this means was defined by the Commission in a delegated regulation, which specifies that a threat shall mean, among other things, 'any threat of

arguably applies to the ECB when adopting measures that would guarantee price stability in the EU. In cases such as this, whether discretion emerges from policy judgments or from choices that technical expertise does not preclude (in the sense that it does not provide only one reasonable solution) may be a very thin line.[20] Ultimately, the emphasis on the accuracy of technical assessments may belittle the policy choices that such assessments entail. Not only the verification of the conditions that, according to the applicable legal norms, may trigger the power to adopt a discretionary decision, but also the indication of alternative courses of action delimit a space of decision-making where complex technical assessments and policy choices meet and, arguably, become intertwined.

One may question whether policy choices that are now legally attributed to administrative actors should be made by such actors, given their legitimacy assets, or inquiry whether legal mandates should be more demanding in framing spaces of discretion. Both issues pertain to the relation between legislators and bureaucracies, in particular to their respective powers and to the autonomy and legitimacy of the later. Notwithstanding their importance, this is not a discussion to be had here. The chapter rather focuses on the life of discretion after attribution, on how it relates to law once it has been given to administrative actors. Specifically, it inquires how far legal principles and rules allow the EU Courts to go when controlling the discretionary choices of the EU administration. The following section will examine this question by focusing on two lines of case law: the more stringent standard of review that the Courts have applied when reviewing complex technical assessments, and the way in which they have relied on one procedural guarantee – the principle of careful and impartial examination – as a means to compensate what would, in principle, be a minimal control of substantive matters. Both will indicate how far the EU Courts went in the cases where they have performed a strict review of discretion. Both have concerned mostly the administrative discretion of the European Commission, but they are arguably also applicable to other EU administrative actors.

---

serious financial, monetary or budgetary instability concerning a Member State . . .' or/and 'the possibility of default by any Member State or supra-national issuer' (Art. 24(3) of Commission Delegated Regulation (EU) 918/2012, *supra* note 7).

[20] See, further, Section 3 below.

3 DISCRETION: THE EMPIRE OF TECHNOCRACY?

3.1 A Stringent Standard of Review

The formal standard of judicial review of administrative discretion is well established in the EU Courts' case law. As mentioned above, in an instance where the EU institutions have wide discretion, judicial review is limited to examining whether procedural rules were complied with and whether an act contains a 'manifest error or constitutes a misuse of powers, or whether the authority did not clearly exceed the bounds of its discretion'.[21] While this formula has been relatively stable, it has enabled, over time and across sectors, a significant variation in the intensity of judicial review.[22] In an important tendency, which may be traced back to merger cases (specifically to *Tetra Laval*), the Courts have effectively performed a searching review of factual assessments, in a way that may '[potentially neutralize] de facto the very principle of the recognition of a margin of economic assessment'.[23] In *Tetra Laval*, the Court of Justice acknowledged that the applicable legal provisions '[conferred] on the Commission a certain discretion, especially with respect to assessments of an economic nature'.[24] However, it considered that the Commission's margin of discretion with regard to economic matters does not mean that 'the Community Courts must refrain from reviewing the Commission's interpretation of information of an economic nature'. The Court added:

> Not only must the Community Courts, inter alia, establish whether the evidence relied on is factually accurate, *reliable and consistent* but also whether that evidence contains all the information which must be taken into account in order to assess a complex situation and whether it is capable of substantiating the conclusions drawn from it.[25]

---

[21] For an earlier instance, see, e.g. Case 55/75, *Balkan-Import Export GmbH v Hauptzollamt Berlin-Packhof*, EU:C:1976:8, para. 8.

[22] On the varying degrees of deference, see Craig, *EU Administrative Law* (Oxford, Oxford University Press, 2012), at 409–29. See also Hofmann, Rowe, and Türk, *Administrative Law and Policy of the European Union* (Oxford, Oxford University Press, 2011), at 498–9. The creation of the General Court in 1999 marked an important shift in the CJEU's scope of review (e.g. Fritzsche, *supra* note 15, at 378).

[23] A view expressed in the Case C-382/12 P, *MasterCard Inc. and Others v Commission*, Opinion of A-G Mengozzi, para. 119.

[24] Case C-12/03, *Commission v Tetra Laval*, EU:C:2005:87, para. 38.

[25] Case C-12/03, *Tetra Laval*, *supra* note 24, para. 39, emphasis added.

The Courts have reiterated this line of reasoning in subsequent judgments, in cases relating to Commission decisions pertaining to the infringement of competition rules[26] and in state aids cases,[27] as well as to Council decisions in the field of anti-dumping.[28] They have also followed this standard of review in instances where the complexity of the assessment was not related (only or at all) to information of economic nature, as in cases regarding economic and financial sanctions directed at suspects of terrorist association,[29] or pertaining to the regulation of risks to public health and the environment.[30] The latter also indicate that this standard of review is not exclusive to decisions having a specified addressee or addressees. It may apply to non-legislative acts of general scope or to decisions that, having identified addressees, have nonetheless a general scope

---

[26] See, e.g., Case C-413/06 P, *Bertelsmann and Sony v Independent Music Publishers and Labels Association (Impala)*, EU:C:2008:392, paras. 144–5 (where the ECJ nevertheless found that the General Court had committed errors of law in using this standard of review – see paras. 146–50); Case C-272/09 P, *KME Germany and Others v Commission*, EU:C:2011:810, paras. 94, 102; Case C-386/10 P, *Chalkor AE Epexergasias Metallon v Commission*, ECLI:EU:C:2011:815, para. 62; Case C-382/12 P, *MasterCard Inc and Others v Commission*, EU:C:2014:2201, paras. 155–6 (considering that the General Court had not applied the correct standard of judicial review – paras. 157–60, 167, 169); Case T-471/11, *Éditions Odile Jacob SAS v Commission*, EU:T:2014:739, para. 136; Case T-90/11, *Ordre national des pharmaciens (ONP) and Others v Commission*, EU:T:2014:1049, para. 57.

[27] Case C-525/04 P, *Spain v Commission and Lenzing*, EU:C:2007:698, paras. 56 and 57; Case T-1/08, *Buczek Automotive v Commission*, EU:T:2011:216, para. 83, referring to review of the Commission's interpretation of economic or technical data to define what is state aid – the standard of judicial review was confirmed on appeal; see also Case C-73/11 P, *Frucona Košice v Commission*, EU:C:2013:32, paras. 73–6.

[28] Case T-528/09, *Hubei Xinyegang Steel Co. Ltd v Council*, EU:T:2014:35, para. 53.

[29] Case T-85/09, *Kadi v Commission*, EU:T:2010:418, para. 142, upheld on appeal: Joined Cases, C-584/10 P, C-593/10 P and C-595/10 P, *Commission and others v Kadi*, EU:C:2013:518, paras. 97, 119, 124. More recently, see, e.g., Case T-208/11 and T-508/11, *Liberation Tigers of Tamil Eelam (LTTE) v Council*, EU:T:2014:885, para. 163; Case T-348/11, *Safa Nicu Sepahan Co. v Council*, para. 66.

[30] See Case T-475/07, *Dow AgroSciences Ltd and Others v Commission*, EU:T:2011:445, paras. 150–53; Case T-257/07, *France v Commission*, EU:T:2011:444, para. 87; C-405/07 P, *Netherlands v Commission*, EU:C:2008:613, para. 55. For an instance where this standard of review applied to a decision of an EU agency, Case T-187/06, *Ralf Schräder v Community Plant Variety Office (CPVO)*, EU:T:2008:511, para. 61. In this case, the Court explicitly added that the same standard can apply in cases where the technical complexity stems from 'appraisals in other scientific domains, such as botany or genetics' (para. 62).

of application, as in the case of market authorizations (or the refusal to enter given products in the lists of those that may circulate in the internal market).[31]

The need to enable the detection of *manifest* errors of assessment and, thus, to avoid an undue limitation of judicial review, is arguably among the factors that may explain this evolution. This concern is well illustrated by the considerations of the referring court in *Technische Universität München*, by which it questioned the Court's 'practice of confining judicial review to the question whether the Commission's decision was vitiated by a manifest error of fact or law or misuse of power':[32]

> Limited review in accordance with the previous case law of the Court of Justice would mean that a legally incorrect decision of the Commission adversely affecting Community citizens would be upheld merely because the mistakes on the part of the Commission were not manifest. The more difficult the technical questions to be decided the more immune from challenge the Commission's decision would be. It is questionable whether such a restriction of the legal protection of Community citizens is compatible with the constitutional principle guaranteeing effective legal protection which is recognized by Community law.

The same preoccupation with a meaningful degree of judicial review is also present in the EU case law, where the Courts have stressed that they cannot use the Commission's margin of discretion 'as a basis for dispensing with the conduct of an in-depth review of the law and of the facts'.[33]

While the *Tetra Laval* standard of review does not cover the spectrum of possibly varying degrees of intensity of judicial scrutiny, it does indicate

---

[31] See, e.g., a Commission regulation amending the annexes of a legislative act (Case T-257/07, *France v Commission*, *supra* note 30); a Commission decision addressed at the Member States concerning the non-inclusion of a given substance in the list of authorized substances (Case T-475/07, *Dow AgroSciences and Others v Commission*, *supra* note 30); a Commission decision addressed to a Member State on the basis of Article 114(5) and (6) TFEU (ex 95 EC) (C-405/07 P, *Netherlands v Commission*, *supra* note 30).

[32] Case C-269/90, *Technische Universität München v Hauptzollamt München-Mitte*, EU:C:1991:317, Opinion of A-G Jacobs, paras. 10 to 16, regarding the possibility to review decisions of technical nature. Incidentally, the referring court was of a Member State (Germany) where the idea of a full control of the conditions upon which the exercise of discretion depends was widespread at the time of this reference (see, e.g. Kuhling, 'Kontrolle von Ermessungsentscheidungen in Deutschland' in Parisio (ed.) *Potere Discrezionale e Controllo Giudiziario* (Milano, Giuffrè 1988) 9–21, at 9 (with translation at 17).

[33] See Case C-389/10 P, *KME Germany and Others v Commission*, EU:C:2011:816, para. 129, and Case C-386/10 P, *Chalkor v Commission*, *supra* note 26, para. 62.

how far the EU Courts may go when applying the test of 'manifest error of assessment' to review the merits of discretionary decisions. It reveals a quite hands-on judicial approach, which, provided that other legal rules and principles are complied with, nevertheless appears to be restricted to a control over complex assessments that ground the legal qualification of facts and, hence, constitute the basis of discretionary decisions.[34] This impression is borne out if one also considers another line of case law, where the Courts assessed whether in exercising discretion the EU institutions have complied with the principle of care.

3.2 Discretion and Care

The duty of careful and impartial examination has entered EU law as a result of a 'dynamic interaction between litigants and the Courts'.[35] It has allowed the Courts to achieve a compromise between, on the one hand, meeting the expectations of litigants and national courts about improved judicial protection against discretion of the EU administration, and, on the other hand, leaving enough space to the EU institutions to define issues of economic policy.[36] The famous formulation of *Technische Universität München* has been often reiterated in the case law:

> where the [Union] institutions have such a power of appraisal [entailing *complex technical evaluations*], respect for the rights guaranteed by the [Union] legal order in administrative procedures is of even more fundamental importance. Those guarantees include, in particular, the duty of the competent institution to examine carefully and impartially all the relevant aspects of the individual case . . . Only in this way can the Court verify whether the factual and legal elements upon which the exercise of the power of appraisal depends were present.[37]

A cursory analysis of the Courts' case law indicates that the duty of care is essentially a tool to revise the factual bases of administrative decisions. It concerns the process of collecting the information needed to appraise

---

[34] There are doubts regarding the exact scope of application of the *Tetra-Laval* standard. A-G Mengozzi, in his opinion on *Master Card*, indicates that in competition cases the standard seems to be limited to *facts*, not to their assessment (Case C-382/12 P, *MasterCard*, Opinion of A-G Mengozzi, *supra* note 23, para. 119). Yet, the fact that it refers to the Commission's *interpretation* of factual information indicates that its scope is potentially broader.

[35] Nehl, *Principles of Administrative Procedure in EC Law* (Oxford, Hart 1999), at 11.

[36] Nehl, *Principles of Administrative Procedure*, *supra* note 35, at 105.

[37] Case C-269/90, *Technische Universität München v Hauptzollamt München-Mitte*, EU:C:1991:438, para. 14.

the relevant factual and legal aspects of a given situation, and the manner in which such information is assessed. The General Court refers to a duty to 'examine carefully and impartially *all relevant evidence* in the case in question',[38] to a 'sufficiently thorough analysis of the file',[39] to 'the duty of the Commission to gather, in a diligent manner, *the factual elements necessary* for the exercise of its broad discretion',[40] to the requirement that the institutions take 'account of all the relevant circumstances and [*appraise*] *the facts* of the matter *with all due care*'.[41] The Court of Justice has confirmed that the duty to conduct a diligent and impartial examination is a means to ensure that 'when adopting the final decision, [the Commission has] *the most complete and reliable information* possible'.[42] These observations seem to apply irrespective of the individual or general scope of the act under review, but all refer to instances where the duty of care either generated an individual right – because of the way it affected the persons concerned – or, in the given instance, could not have such an effect.

In fact, as it stands in current case law, the duty of care mainly allows the EU Courts to enhance the individual protection of plaintiffs affected by administrative acts that were adopted on the basis of insufficient or inadequate information.[43] This feature does not mean that the duty applies only to procedures leading up to the adoption of individual decisions, but rather to cases where the individual protection of the persons concerned is justified in view of the effects of the acts adopted.[44]

---

[38] Case T-369/03, *Arizona Chemical and Others v Commission*, EU:T:2005:458, para. 85 (emphasis added).

[39] Case T-210/02, *British Aggregates v Commission*, EU:T:2006:253, para. 178.

[40] Case T-333/10, *Animal Trading Company (ATC) BV and Others v Commission*, EU:T:2013:451, para. 84 (emphasis added).

[41] Case T-443/11, *Gold East Paper and Gold Huasheng Paper v Council*, EU:T:2014:774, para. 164 (emphasis added).

[42] Case C-290/07 P, *Commission v Scott*, EU:C:2010:480, para. 90 (emphasis added).

[43] Two hallmark judgments delivered in 1991 establish the principle of care as standard of procedural legality and individual protection: Case C-16/90, *Eugene Nölle v Hauptzollamt Bremen-Freihafen*, EU:C:1991:402 (anti-dumping); Case C-269/90, *Technische Universität München v Hauptzollamt München-Mitte*, *supra* note 32 (customs). The same protective dimension of the principle of care applies to Member States: Case T-263/07, *Estonia v Commission*, EU:T:2009:351, paras. 109–12.

[44] For an instance in which the duty of care applied to a general administrative act (a decision to suspend imports of products in view of a serious threat to health), see Case T-333/10, *Animal Trading Company (ATC)*, *supra* note 40, paras. 84 to 94. This was an action for non-contractual liability where the Court implicitly admitted that the duty of care functioned as an individual procedural guarantee of

Yet, because of this protective dimension, the EU Courts have acknowledged the limits of extending the duty of care beyond the limits of adjudicatory procedures. The General Court has held that, in procedures leading up to acts of general application, 'the duty of diligence is essentially an objective procedural guarantee arising from an absolute and unconditional obligation on the [EU] institution relating to the drafting of [the act] and not the exercise of any individual right'.[45] It is 'imposed in the public interest'.[46] One would concur with this stance. The legal protection of individual positions that one may derive from a duty of careful and impartial examination ought not to operate in the same terms in relation to acts of general application. Irrespective of the way in which they may affect the legal position of the persons concerned, the fact that such acts apply to instances delimited by objective criteria and entail general legal effects (which is also the case in state aids decisions) indicates that public interest considerations ought to prevail when individual protection could hinder the suitable pursuance of the public interests at stake.[47] Also within adjudicatory procedures the Court has limited the attempts of plaintiffs to extend the reach of the duty of care (in its guise of individual guarantee) in a way that could potentially damage the efficiency of the administrative process. In particular, the General Court has denied that the duty of care could be a procedural guarantee invoked by complainants in state aid procedures, to avoid that the protection of the interests of third parties to the procedure would constrain the discretion of the Commission. In the Court's view, the diligent and impartial examination of the complaints in the context of the preliminary procedure of Article 108(3) of the Treaty on the Functioning of the European Union (TFEU) (ex 88 EC) is carried out 'in the interests of sound administration of the fundamental rules of the Treaty relating to state aid'.[48] In a similar vein, Advocate-General Poiares Maduro defended in *T-Mobile* that 'the requisite diligent and impartial examination is not carried out in relation to [the persons concerned], but first of all by reference to the general interest in sound administration and the proper application of the rules of the

---

the companies that had been affected by a general decision addressed at Member States.

[45] Case T-369/03, *Arizona Chemical, supra* note 38, paras. 86 and 89, concerning the adaptation of a directive to technical progress.

[46] Case T-369/03, *Arizona Chemical, supra* note 38, para. 88.

[47] The way these considerations ought to play out in relation to procedural rights is a different issue (see Mendes, *Participation in EU Rule-making: A Rights-based Approach* (Oxford, Oxford University Press 2011), Chapters 4 and 5.

[48] See, e.g., Case T-210/02, *British Aggregates, supra* note 39, para. 177.

Treaty'.[49] In *T-Mobile*, the Court of Justice reverted the judgment of the General Court that had annulled a Commission decision refusing to investigate a complaint of breach of competition law applicable to public undertakings under Article 106 TFEU. Thereby, it strongly opposed the view of the General Court according to which the Commission's obligation to undertake a diligent and impartial examination of a complaint would arise from the 'right to sound administration of individual situations'.[50]

In these cases, while fencing out the protective dimension of the duty of care, the Courts have emphasized an objective dimension of this duty. Even where it does not generate any individual right, the duty of careful and impartial examination needs to be observed as part of a proper administrative conduct (sound administration).[51] In the area of risk regulation, this objective dimension has been translated into the principles of excellence, transparency and independence that ought to guide scientific assessments of the Commission, the breach of which may be invoked in Court by individuals directly and individually concerned.[52] But beyond this precision, in the cases where the Courts singled out this objective dimension they did not elaborate further on what care could otherwise mean.[53] It remains, nevertheless, a tool to revise the factual bases of administrative decisions. As the General Court has explicitly recognized:

> the obligation for the competent institution to examine carefully and impartially all the relevant elements of the individual case *is a necessary prerequisite* to enable the European Union Courts to ascertain whether the elements of fact and of law on which the exercise of . . . broad discretion depends were present.[54]

In the Court's view, compliance with this duty is all the more important in view of the 'limited judicial review of the merits, confined to examining whether a manifest error has been committed'.[55] Nevertheless, despite the emphasis on limited judicial review, the verification

---

[49] Case C-141/02 P, *Commission v T-Mobile Austria GmbH*, Opinion of A-G Poiares Maduro, EU:C:2004:646.

[50] See para. 48 of the judgment at first instance (Case T-54/99, *T-Mobile Austria GmbH v Commission*, EU:T:2002:20) and para. 72 of the judgement in appeal (Case C-141/02 P *Commission v T-Mobile Austria GmbH*, EU:C:2005:98).

[51] Case T-210/02, *British Aggregates*, *supra* note 39, para. 177; Case T-369/03, *Arizona Chemical*, *supra* note 38, para. 88.

[52] See, e.g., Case T-369/03, *Arizona Chemical*, *supra* note 38, para. 88.

[53] At least not in the cases analysed in this chapter.

[54] Case T-333/10, *Animal Trading Company (ATC)*, *supra* note 40, para. 84 (emphasis added).

[55] Case T-333/10, *Animal Trading Company (ATC)*, *supra* note 40, para. 84.

of whether the duty of care has been complied with may lead the Court to ascertain in some detail what the Commission ought to have investigated and did not, in order to be able to take the decision at stake, as well as what the Commission may or may not invoke in support for its decision in view of the factual information it has been able to gauge.[56] Such an examination may allow the Court to conclude for the lack of 'specific factual evidence substantiated by sufficient data' as well as of enquiries that 'would have vindicated the [Commission's] overall approach'.[57]

At this point, the duty of care converges with the line of case law initiated with *Tetra-Laval*. Both enable the Court to scrutinize the information on the basis of which the act was adopted, the way the decision-maker has collected and treated that information and to assess the plausibility of the conclusions it took therefrom. On this basis, the reviewing court is capable of assessing the plausibility of the decisions in view of the facts that grounded the choices ultimately made. Whether this control still preserves the space of discretion of administrative actors may be discussed.[58] The judicial inquiries that follow from this case law appear to confine the range of choices available to the decision-maker, or at least, the spectrum of what could be considered reasonable or plausible choices in view of the filters that the Courts apply. In this sense, at least, they narrow down the scope of discretion. While the Courts do not always perform or endorse such a searching review, the above indicates the possibility of a potentially far-reaching control of discretion. It indicates also an approach to judicial review that structures the exercise of discretion in a specific way, as will be explained next.

3.3 The Reach of Judicial Review vs. the Reach of Law

The picture that emerges from the above account is one in which the Courts may go quite far in controlling the exercise of discretion. But just how far do the EU Courts go? The *Tetra-Laval* standard of review and the case law on the duty of careful and impartial examination both indicate that the Courts have not shunned examining in detail the way the EU institutions have conducted complex technical assessments and the ways

---

[56] Case T-333/10, *Animal Trading Company (ATC)*, *supra* note 40, paras. 90 and 92.

[57] Case T-333/10, *Animal Trading Company (ATC)*, *supra* note 40, para. 91.

[58] Such an assessment will at least in part depend on the concept of discretion that one endorses (see Section 2).

in which they collect the information that bases such assessments.[59] Both lines of case law refer to the assessment of facts. The standard of review defined in *Tetra Laval* applies to the review of 'the Commission's interpretation of information of economic [or other] nature', to evidence that must be 'factually accurate, reliable[,] consistent', complete and 'capable of substantiating the conclusions drawn from it'.[60] The duty of care has the same focus on factual assessments.[61] Within that space of decision-making that relies on policy considerations and complex technical assessments, the Courts thus seem to isolate the latter. Both lines of case law seem to have a similar purpose: by controlling the factual basis of the decisions, the Courts would not interfere with policy choices (whether only apparently is another matter). Thus, the duty of care limited to complex factual assessments ensures a meaningful review (that is, one that is capable of detecting *manifest* errors of assessment) without risking a too far-reaching incursion in the space of *choice* of the EU decision-makers. Of course, verification of compliance with the duty of care enables an additional step in assessing the correct exercise of discretion. But this step is still about verifying the correctness of the factual basis of the discretionary decisions and ensuring that all steps were taken to that end – not, arguably, the correctness of the decisions themselves. The stress placed in the objective dimension of the duty of care, which emerged to limit the potential reach of the individual protection that litigants sought when invoking it, did not change the core of this duty: it is a legal tool to review the factual assessments underlying decisions of the EU administration. The 'sound administration of the fundamental rules of the Treaty' thus seems to be ensured by full reliance on technical accuracy and completeness of the information that grounds the exercise of discretion.

Both the *Tetra-Laval* standard of review and the principle of care seem to filter out considerations of public interest. They enable the Courts to scrutinize those choices that follow logically from factual assessments – as a matter of cognition – not the choices that stem from balancing the public interests that ought to be pursued against those that may be forfeited in the given circumstances – a matter of volition. The scrutiny of such choices remains outside the scope of these two techniques. It would fall under the realm of proportionality, which is often invoked to control

[59] The General Court does so while examining the facts before it, the ECJ when reviewing on appeal the General Court's assessment regarding compliance with the duty of care (e.g. Case C-290/07 P, *Commission v Scott*, *supra* note 42, para. 62).

[60] See notes 25 and 34 *supra*.

[61] See references in notes 38 to 42 *supra*.

whether discretion was exercised in a proper manner within its respective legal limits. But also a proportionality review – and, with it, the review of public interest appraisals – may be done through the filter of the accuracy of technical assessments. When assessing whether the decision adopted is proportional, the Courts may simply rely on the careful and impartial examination of the facts (or lack thereof) to determine whether the decision-maker proved that all relevant matters were taken into account and that there were less restrictive measures available.[62] This was the stance the Court took in *Gauweiler*, where 'care and accuracy' were considered the attributes of technical assessments necessary and sufficient not only to safeguard the ESCB against manifest errors of assessment but also to judge the appropriateness of the OMT decision.[63]

This approach arguably reinforces the technocratic thinking underlying EU regulation. This effect may be reinforced by the likely impact of judicial review on the way the EU administrative bodies exercise discretion. The Courts' approach, as revealed by the above case law, appears to convey a specific message. As long as the decision-maker is able to demonstrate that, first, it relied on factually accurate, reliable and consistent information, covering all the facts that must be taken into account, secondly, that all these elements were examined carefully and impartially, and thirdly, that this information substantiates the conclusions drawn from it in a reasoned way, the discretionary choice will most likely be considered lawful (provided, of course, that other applicable legal rules and principles have been complied with).[64] One may argue that this is how far courts should indeed go. But it is important to point out that this line of case law has an important side effect: it narrows down the reach of law in structuring the exercise of discretion insofar as it explicitly avoids any judgment on the specific composition of possibly competing public interests that the decision entails. One should critically reflect on whether these are the terms in which law – in the broader sense of a normative order that

---

[62] Case T-333/10, *Animal Trade Company (ATC)*, *supra* note 40, para. 103, where the Court relies on the same reasoning as compliance with the duty of care, concluding that no compliance with care means no compliance with proportionality.

[63] Case C-62/14, *Gauweiler*, *supra* note 1, paras. 74 to 80, in particular, para. 75.

[64] Case T-257/07, *France v Commission*, *supra* note 30, para. 88, where the General Court explicitly brings together the standard of review established in *Tetra Laval* and the duty of careful and impartial examination. In this case, these tools served to assess whether the Commission was entitled to consider that a given level of risk did not exceed the level of risk deemed acceptable for society – clearly, a political decision.

binds public authority to legal-political values – ought to structure the exercise of discretion.

4 DISCRETION, CARE AND LAW: A PUBLIC INTEREST PERSPECTIVE

The Courts' focus on complex technical assessments – and, as a result, possibly also the Commission's as the main institution thus far concerned by the case law mentioned – arguably neglects an important feature of discretionary decision-making. The processes of collecting the information that is needed to assess the relevant factual and legal aspects of a given situation are guided by a specific purpose: the pursuance of the public interests that decision-makers are bound to fulfil under their legal mandate. Administrative decision-makers do not choose these public interests. They are identified in the applicable legal norms, even if at a high level of generality – e.g., the protection of public health, the international competitiveness of a given industry, financial stability, etc. Legal norms also define the conditions that, once verified, can trigger the exercise of discretion. Such conditions both delimit the scope of discretion and concretize the public interests that decision-makers ought to be pursuing when making discretionary decisions.[65] Thus, for example, when defining the power of the ESMA to temporarily prohibit or restrict short-selling activities, the legislator indicates that those measures are adopted to ensure the 'orderly functioning and integrity of financial markets' and financial stability within the EU; it also indicates that, when adopting such measures, the ESMA needs to consider, *inter alia*, the efficiency of financial markets and the certainty of market participants.[66] These are the public interests that the ESMA needs to balance, protect and pursue. They have arguably a broader relevance than the one the Court stressed in its judgment: more than just one of the factors that circumscribe the powers of the ESMA,[67] they constitute the yardstick against which the decisions of the ESMA should be assessed, as explained next.

---

[65] Soares, *Interesse Público, Legalidade e Mérito* (Atlântida, 1955), at 150, according to whom the conditions of action defined by the legislator guide the decision-maker in identifying the public interests at stake in each given situation.

[66] Art. 9(5) of Regulation (EU) 1095/2010 of the European Parliament and of the Council of 24 November 2010 establishing a European Supervisory Authority, OJ 2010, L 331/84 and Art. 28(3)(a) and (c) of Regulation (EU) 236/2012, *supra* note 7.

[67] Case C-270/12, *ESMA*, *supra* note 1, paras. 47 and 48.

The public interests thus incorporated in a legal mandate define not only the purpose of the granting of discretion but also its scope, and ought, as such, to guide the exercise of discretion. In this sense, complex technical assessments cannot be – or, at least, ought not to be – isolated or dissociated from the pursuance of the public interests that are, at the same time, the core and goal of administrative decision-making. More deeply, there is a dialectical relationship between the assessment of facts and the appraisal of public interests that discretionary decisions presuppose.[68] It is during the process of assessing the circumstances that may require administrative action that the public interests envisaged in the abstract scheme of the enabling legal norms acquire significance: those circumstances unveil the interests that need to be protected. Should the efficiency of financial markets be disrupted by an administrative decision intended to counter a threat to financial stability, within the limits legally defined? What does the protection of financial stability require? These are questions that can only be answered in view of the factual circumstances that the decision-maker confronts. It is otherwise difficult to indicate, in substantive terms, what the powers of the ESMA to ensure financial stability may mean. Also one only knows the type of measures that should be adopted – to the extent that the legislator provides a choice – after a factual assessment of those circumstances. Should it be a notification, an order of disclosure, a prohibition or imposition of conditions to given financial transactions?[69] At the same time, this process occurs in relation to, and is hence co-determined by, the legal provisions that defined the interests the administration ought to be pursuing in the first place (in this case, the functioning and integrity of financial markets, financial stability, the efficiency of financial markets, but also the interests of Member States and of the various financial markets' participants).[70] Arguably, it is this assessment of the circumstances (eventually, complex technical assessments) in relation to the interpretation – and construction – of the public interests envisaged by law that ought to guide the substantive choices of the administrative decision-maker.[71]

---

[68] See also Mendes, 'Law, Public Interest and Interpretation: Prolegomena of a Normative Framework on Administrative Discretion in the EU', *Yale Law & Economics Research Paper* No. 519 (2014), at 26–8, available at https://papers.ssrn.com/sol3/papers2.cfm?abstract_id=2539068 (last visited 20 February 2017).

[69] Article 28(1) of Regulation (EU) 236/2012, *supra* note 7.

[70] Soares, *supra* note 65, refers to 'circular inter-relations'. On the example, see note 66 *supra* and recital 11 of Regulation (EU) 1095/2010, *supra* note 66.

[71] There are areas where it may be particularly doubtful whether there are predetermined public interests grounding the activity of the Commission, or, at least

The dialectical link between complex technical assessment and public interest appraisals may be obvious.[72] Yet, it entails two consequences that the case law examined above overlooks. Firstly, the duty of careful and impartial examination of *factual information* is not self-standing; rather, it is intertwined with a duty to pursue public interests and to carefully balance competing public interests. While the duty of care may function as an individual procedural guarantee of legally affected persons, when placed in this perspective, its centre of gravity ought to lie elsewhere: in the objective dimension that has remained relatively silenced or unclear in the Courts' case law. Secondly, the processes through which the EU decision-makers collect information and conduct complex technical assessments shape, directly, the weighing of competing public interests that are involved in the exercise of discretion. In this sense, they are also political.

The duty of care, in the broader normative sense proposed, is a legal duty that derives from the attribution of administrative discretion to act in a certain way. A duty of care that serves the 'sound administration of the rules of the Treaty' would require discretionary decisions to be – apart from technically accurate – inclusive and fair, insofar as they should reflect a balanced composition of the protected interests that, by law, ought to be part of the assessments that lead to their adoption. This duty is therefore grounded in the respective enabling legal norms and in the normative legal order of which they are part.[73] Undoubtedly, the assessment of whether the protection of public interests requires action, when that action is due, what it should consist of, and how it should be pursued entails complex technical assessments, which ought to be grounded on a careful and impartial examination of facts. But in view of the dialectical relationship stressed above, these can hardly be analytically dissected from the accommodation

---

whether the heteronomous character of the ends of its action seems prima facie implausible. One example is the pursuance of complaints of infringement of competition rules, of Member State infringement of the Treaty, where the Commission purports to act in the 'Union interest', but where it is unclear how it defines that 'Union interest'.

[72] Even if the *ESMA* judgment would indicate otherwise. Here, by highlighting the public interests that ESMA needs to take into consideration, the Court preferred to single out the limb of technical factual assessments (Case C-270/12, *ESMA*, *supra* note 1, paras. 45 and 52) to set aside the claim of the UK that the regulation actually attributed wide discretionary powers entailing the weighing of competing interests and, hence, policy choices (cf. para. 29). The Court's concern – and yardstick – was its ability to perform judicial review, which 'precisely delineated' powers would enable.

[73] Soares, *supra* note 65, 200.

of competing public interests that a discretionary choice also entails. It is the intertwinement between expertise and policy choices that will ultimately determine the adequacy and propriety of the course of action chosen in view of the public interests that the legislator determined ought to be fulfilled in that instance. The processes through which EU decision-makers make public interests appraisals is only partially captured by legal reasoning, general principles of law and legal norms. Nevertheless, normatively, the public interests defined by law remain the source of the authority of administrative decision-makers and the source of their duty to pursue them. They are, together with the factual technical assessments, the yardsticks to assess a correct – and lawful – exercise of discretion.

In addition, as indicated, the processes and structures that ensure the accuracy, completeness and a sufficiently thorough analysis of the facts condition, by their very configuration, the public interest appraisals that are eventually made. They determine the type of public interest considerations that weigh on the final assessments, even if they are set up to ensure the impartiality and quality of the specialized knowledge used in EU decision-making without which the ensuing decisions would lack credibility and legitimacy. The most obvious example is perhaps the composition of expert groups.[74] But many others could be invoked. Comitology committees, in addition to expertise, enable the consideration of the possible competing interests of Member States and shape the final decision accordingly. Also the way in which procedures are designed is influential. The bilateral structure of competition law procedures – in essence opposing the Commission and the undertakings investigated – arguably places the economic interests of consumers, arguably one of the core public interests that competition law protects, in a secondary place in the public enforcement of competition law.[75] From this perspective, stressing the accuracy, completeness, reliability of the information gathered and the thoroughness and diligence of the assessments made both endorses and reinforces an objectivity that, depending on the way in which the underlying processes and structures were designed and

---

[74] See, in this regard, the issues raised in the European Ombudsman's own-initiative inquiry OI/6/2014/NF concerning the composition of Commission expert groups (Letter to the European Commission requesting an opinion in the European Ombudsman's own-initiative inquiry OI/6/2014/NF concerning the composition of Commission expert groups, available at www.ombudsman.europa.eu/en/cases/correspondence.faces/en/58861/html.bookmark (last visited 20 February 2017).

[75] Cseres and Mendes, 'Consumers' Access to EU Competition Law Procedures: Outer and Inner Limits', 51(2) CML Rev. (2014), 483–521, at 489–91, 520.

implemented, may only be apparent. More strongly, it may dress with the veneer of legality decisions that, *because* they are technically accurate, favour a composition of public interests to the detriment of other interests that, by force of law, should have been taken into consideration and may have been excluded from the deliberations that underlay the choice ultimately made. The discretionary decision may be considered rational and objective while falling short of ensuring an inclusive and fair treatment of the competing public interests involved, the balance and pursuance of which law would require. The duty of care would embody and ensure the normative demands of law that are not exhausted in the verification of the technical soundness and accuracy of a decision. Those normative demands entail fairness in the way administrative actors assess and balance legally protected public interests, as a means to ensure the concretization of political, economic, social and cultural values that the EU legal order protects.[76] The current focus of judicial review of discretion, as indicated by the case law analysed, relinquishes one of the essential functions of law in relation to discretionary powers. The granting of authority is done by reference to the pursuance of public interests. Its exercise postulates a duty to act in a way that ensures, in substance, the realization of those interests, insofar as they ought to be duly considered. This legal duty – in addition to other non-legal considerations – ought to structure the policy choices that derive from weighing competing public interests. Understanding care in the broader normative sense proposed would require that discretionary decisions, apart from technically accurate, ought also to be informed by, and ultimately concretize, the values and principles of the legal order that ground and bind the authority to adopt them. In this sense, the discretionary decision that would resist the 'manifest error' test would be not only the decision that is reasonable by technically rational patterns (because it is well supported by all the relevant elements of fact), but also the one that stems from a balanced consideration of the competing legally protected public interests – a decision that, in this way, would be valid by legally rational patterns.

---

[76] On the mutual intertwinement between form and matter, see Gomes Canotilho, *Direito Constitucional e Teoria da Constituição*, 7th edn. (Coimbra, Almedina 2003), at 243–4.

5 DISCRETION, CARE, AND PUBLIC INTEREST: AN INSTITUTIONAL PERSPECTIVE

5.1 The Courts

Pointing out a broader meaning of the legal duty of care may entail the risk of breaching the fragile balance that the Courts may have sought to achieve by restricting the duty of care to a requirement of diligent and impartial examination of facts. We have seen above that both the *Tetra-Laval* standard of review and the duty of care, as established by the Courts, have arguably preserved the autonomy of the EU institutions and bodies to make policy choices.[77] In particular, care, just as the duty to give reasons, is not purely a procedural guarantee. There is often only a very fine line between reviewing the way decisions are made and the merits of the decisions at stake. Verification of compliance with the duty of care stands in this fine line.[78] Importantly, it is also a means to ensure the very possibility of judicial review, as the EU Courts have stressed. Broadening the meaning of care, in the sense indicated above, and assuming that this duty would be justiciable, could annul the space of discretion that, in view of the allocation of powers under the Treaty, ought to be preserved.

From this perspective, there would seem to be little point in stressing the dialectical relationship between, on the one hand, care in conducting an investigation that grounds complex technical assessments and, on the other, care in duly regarding the competing public interests that, in view of the applicable legal norms, should be accommodated in a given instance. Such a view would unnecessarily mingle and confuse two different operations: the assessment of facts, governed by a duty of careful and impartial examination, as established in the case law; and the appraisal of public interests, which, institutionally, is a matter where the Courts ought not enter (except via the principle of proportionality). Blurring the already difficult borderline between reviewing factual assessments and controlling the balancing of interests would potentially enable the Court to enter squarely in the domain of discretion.

This is the conclusion one could reach when approaching discretion from the perspective of judicial review and overshadowing the perspective

---

77 In this sense, on the duty of care, see Nehl, *supra* note 35, at 105.

78 See Tiili and Vanhamme, 'The "Power of Appraisal" (*Pouvoir d'Appreciation*) of the Commission of the European Communities vis-à-vis the Powers of Judicial Review of the Communities' Court of Justice and Court of First Instance', 22 Fordham Int'l L.J. (1999), 885–901, suggesting that the Commission's obligation to investigate must be separated from its assessments (at 895).

of the administrative process and its relation to law. This conclusion is both suggested and supported by separation of powers' considerations: in ensuring that the law is observed, the Courts should not stray beyond legality. When assessing facts, the Courts are checking whether the basis for exercising a legally attributed power are fulfilled; when assessing the way public interests have been balanced, they would be entering the core of discretion. Even if one would share a holistic view on discretion, capable of better grasping the role of law in discretionary decision-making and of avoiding an unjustified technocratic characterization thereof, one would accept that judicial review ought not stray beyond the limits of the *Tetra-Laval* standard of review. If by now it is fairly established in the case law that 'the technical nature of a case should not cause [the Court] to forsake its duty . . . to ensure that the law is observed',[79] the Court cannot transpose the limit of substituting the decision of the administrative decision-maker for its own opinion. If the conception of discretion and the role of law defended here would be reflected in judicial review, the Courts could risk breaching this last frontier. This may explain why the objective dimension of the principle of care has remained, in general, rather elusive in the case law.

These considerations suggest that the legal categories with which courts (and public lawyers) work distort, for institutional reasons of separation of powers, the role that law ought to have in structuring the exercise of discretion. Institutional reasons could justify a 'twist' in what would otherwise be a normatively desirable account of discretion and the role of law within it.

Yet, the above conception of the duty of care has the merit of underlining that the spaces of discretion that the legal order attributes to the decision-maker are spaces within which choices are made not only in view of what is technically sound or of what may be politically determined. Discretionary choices are also guided by *legal* criteria. These are found in the enabling legal norms, in the general mandate of the decision-maker and in the values and principles which underpin the EU legal order and which administrative decision-makers ought to concretize when exercising their authority. Beyond the generally accepted postulate that discretionary decisions ought to respect general principles of law as well as fundamental rights – which often delimit the space of judicial review – what the proposed duty of care underlines is also the legal character of discretionary power. This perspective highlights that, also from a legal point of view,

[79] Case C-269/90, *Technische Universität München v Hauptzollamt München-Mitte*, Opinion of A-G Jacobs, *supra* note 32, para. 11.

technically accurate decisions should not be legally valid if they favour certain public interests to the detriment of others as a result of a process which was not inclusive insofar as not all relevant legally protected public interests may have been duly considered. This effect may be caused not by lack of care in collecting the necessary information, but rather by the way in which the structures of collecting information have been conceived or by administrative processes that may escape judicial review. In essence, the broader duty of care endorsed above contradicts the conclusion that 'nothing more can be required' of the holder of discretion other than that 'it use its . . . expertise and the necessary technical means at its disposal to carry out [a reasonable] analysis with all care and accuracy'.[80] Whether the political or otherwise potentially controversial character of the measures adopted is or is not within the reach of the courts is debatable in view of the conception of the duty of care defended above, which stresses the legal character of discretion. In any event, those measures are not outside the reach of law, more specifically, of the legal duty to pursue and duly consider legally protected public interests. In particular when the executive powers of the EU institutions have extended in an unprecedented way, it is important to stress this broader reach of law, which the case law of the EU Courts currently hides (if not denies).

5.2 The Ombudsman

While the intrinsic links between complex assessments and public interest appraisals may reveal an uneasy space for Courts, the Ombudsman would, prima facie, not face the same constraints. Her mandate, institutional position and means of action stress the distinct complementary role that the Ombudsman may have in ensuring the legality of discretionary decisions. The mandate of the Ombudsman to act upon instances of maladministration extends beyond legality, understood as compliance both with legal provisions and with general principles of law.[81] This mandate facilitates a broader understanding of discretion, insofar as the Ombudsman's decisions are not a priori formatted to set apart the legal from the non-legal aspects of a given decision. More importantly, for our purposes,

---

80 Case C-62/14, *Gauweiler*, *supra* note 2, para. 75.

81 See, e.g., 'Legality and Good Administration: Is There a Difference?', Speech by the European Ombudsman, P. Nikiforos Diamandouros, at the Sixth Seminar of National Ombudsmen of EU Member States and Candidate Countries on 'Rethinking Good Administration in the European Union', Strasbourg, France, 15 October 2007, Point 4, available at www.ombudsman.europa.eu/speeches/en/2007-10-15.htm (last visited 20 February 2017).

the Ombudsman has a specific institutional position quite different from that of the Courts, given its constitutive link to the European Parliament and the possibility to report directly to the Parliament on instances of maladministration.[82] In addition, and accordingly, the Ombudsman also has tools and means of action that enable inquiries that are not specifically directed at controlling whether the EU institution has complied with the law and with general legal principles, or at determining what the rights of the complainant are and whether they have been respected.[83] The Ombudsman's main goal when dealing with a complaint is to settle the dispute by seeking a friendly solution. The purpose here is not to adjudicate a dispute according to a binary logic of legality/illegality, but to ensure that there is a middle ground on which the institution or body concerned and the complainant can agree that there is not a problem, or, to the extent that there is one, the decision-maker will undertake to solve it and the complainant is satisfied with this commitment – one which, importantly, the Ombudsman is able to monitor actively. Arguably, this setting may be better suited to address questions regarding whether public interests are being properly pursued – whether all relevant considerations are being taken into account in view of the public interests that should be pursued – than a judicial setting, where the issue of whether the institution behaved legally necessarily frames the dispute, and where the understanding of legality may not encompass the dimensions of law pointed out in the previous section.[84]

At the same time, the Ombudsman has shaped its review of discretion along the lines of judicial review. The Ombudsman has used, in abstract, the same standard as the Courts, limited to ascertaining compliance with procedural rules, accuracy in fact-finding and scrutinizing discretion in view of a possible manifest error of assessment or misuse of powers.[85] The Ombudsman has stressed that when the office 'investigates whether

---

[82] Art. 228 TFEU (ex 195 EC) and Art. 3(4), (7) and (8), 6(1) of the Statute. See Harden, 'When Europeans Complain: The Work of the European Ombudsman', 3 Cambridge Yearbook of European Law (2000), 199–237, at 209–14. Tsadiras, 'Unravelling Ariadne's Thread: The European Ombudsman's Investigative Powers', 45 CML Rev. (2008), at 758–9. This 'symbiotic link' can be problematic regarding the powers of the Ombudsman vis-à-vis acts of Parliament (see Tsadiras, at 770).

[83] See Harlow and Rawlings, *Process and Procedure in EU Administration* (Oxford, Hart 2014), at 80–4; Tsadiras, *supra* note 82, at 757–70.

[84] Cf. Diamandouros, *supra* note 81, point 4, in fine.

[85] At this general level, this observation hides possible differences in the approaches of the CJEU and of the Ombudsman when using the same standard of review.

a [Union] institution or body has acted in accordance with the rules and principles which are binding upon it' – the core of maladministration – the Ombudsman's 'first and most essential task must be to establish whether it has acted lawfully'.[86] Beyond compliance with rules and principles that are binding on the EU administration, and as long as the limits of the legal authority conferred are complied with, the Ombudsman will also not review the merits of discretionary decisions.[87] Also in this respect, the Ombudsman clearly does not seek to demarcate its role from that of the Courts: the 'general limits' of the conferred authority are those 'established by the jurisprudence of the Court of Justice'.[88]

Notwithstanding this approximation to judicial review, in the dialogue that the Ombudsman establishes (and mediates) between the EU institution and the citizens, she has been able to identify ways in which competing public interests should be adequately regarded in the making of discretionary decisions, explicitly addressing the link between the processes of collection of information that underlie and influence policy choices, on the one hand, and the public interests that ought to be pursued, on the other. Instances where the Ombudsman assesses the impartiality, independence and objectivity of the decisions of the EU institutions and bodies appear to be particularly suitable to this effect. Some of the claims the Ombudsman receives explicitly refer to the defence and consideration of public interests that the EU institutions may have overlooked.

A decision concerning the information structures that underlie the policy choices of the Commission in the area of biofuels illustrates the distinctive contribution of the European Ombudsman in structuring administrative discretion of the EU institutions along the lines defended in this chapter.[89] Reacting against the predominance of commercial interests in an advisory group – the European Biofuels Technology Platform – in particular from the automotive and oil industries, the complainant claimed that the public

---

[86] *Annual Report*, 1997, at 24, where maladministration was defined as occurring 'when a public body fails to act in accordance with a rule or principle which is binding upon it' (at 23). On the sources used by the Ombudsman, see Harden, *supra* note 82, at 223.

[87] *Annual Report*, 1997, at 26, according to which '[t]he Ombudsman does not seek to question discretionary administrative decisions, provided that the institution or body concerned has acted within the limits of its legal authority'.

[88] *Annual Report*, 1997, at 26. Harden, *supra* note 82, 224, explicitly indicates that 'the Ombudsman is not an appellate tribunal' that could review the merits of discretionary decisions.

[89] Decision of the European Ombudsman closing its inquiry into complaint 1151/2008/(DK)ANA against the European Commission, 9 July 2013 ('Biofuels Decision').

interests of 'environmental sustainability' and the 'human rights of local communities of agro-fuel producing countries' were not sufficiently taken into account in the Commission's energy policy, thus jeopardizing the objectivity of the advice given and the impartiality of the Commission's decisions, from the level of policy definition to its implementation.

In his assessment, the Ombudsman started by recalling that, *according to the applicable directive*, decisions regarding the desirability to promote the use of biofuels should be based on 'a detailed analysis' of environmental, economic and social impacts.[90] In his view, an assessment of the objectivity of the decisions at issue required considering the 'technical content and quality of the output and *the basis on which it is formulated*'.[91] While the Commission should ensure the plurality of sources of advice, representing different interests, it was within its discretion to decide 'how to achieve the necessary overall balance'.[92] The Ombudsman considered reasonable the Commission's explanations on why the European Biofuels Technology Platform was industry-dominated, but this was not sufficient to placate the complainant's concerns regarding the objectivity of the recommendations, which, irrespective of their binding or non-binding nature, were liable to influence the Commission's decisions.[93] The Ombudsman thus asked for further explanations. He suggested that the Commission would specifically indicate, firstly, whether there are any mechanisms that ensure the objectivity of the opinions on which the Commission relies to make policy choices; secondly, whether the public consultations and advisory groups are 'intended to, and actually [do] ensure that sufficient attention is given to the issues of public interest raised by the complainant'; and, thirdly, the extent to which the Commission takes into account various external inputs into decision-making.[94] In doing so, the Ombudsman arguably did not interfere with the Commission's discretion on how to ensure pluralism in the information gathering structures that underlie its decisions. At the same time, safeguarding the Commission's discretion in this regard did not prevent him from addressing possible biases, which could deny the values that the EU legal order protects, as explicitly indicated in the applicable directive. He did so by simply asking the Commission to explain in a detailed manner how it ensures the proper consideration of the

---

[90] Biofuels Decision, *supra* note 89, point 27.

[91] Biofuels Decision, *supra* note 89, point 30, emphasis added.

[92] Biofuels Decision, *supra* note 89, point 34, in line with other cases. Discretion, in this instance, did not refer to the merits of given decisions but to the basis of the Commission's substantive choices.

[93] Biofuels Decision, *supra* note 89, points 35–6, 31, and 79.

[94] Biofuels Decision, *supra* note 89, point 40.

public interests that, according to the directive, ought to be balanced in the Commission's decisions.

In this case, the Ombudsman brought to the fore the dialectic link between the factual assessments of a given matter – for which the Commission relies, at least in part, on the input of an external expert group – and the public interests that ought to be pursued in this instance, as determined in the applicable directive. The connection, in his view, is clear: by force of the applicable law, 'every choice in the field of research policy, however technical in nature or narrow in scope, cannot be dissociated from numerous other environmental, social and economic considerations'.[95] Without questioning the discretion of the Commission to organize the decision-making structures (i.e., to choose from various 'input sources' in the process of collecting information), the Ombudsman thus recalled the public interests that, *by legal determination*, needed to be pursued in this field.[96] 'Technological neutrality' and 'openness to a wide spectrum of technological options' (invoked by the Commission) were not enough. According to the Ombudsman, the public interest appraisals that necessarily underlined technical choices prevented the Commission from downplaying the political importance of the decisions at stake by invoking the lack of 'technological bias'. Specifically,

> for the Platform's recommendations to meet the objectivity requirement in the areas of research and technological development policy, to which it has a direct input, *the Platform must take into account all relevant considerations*. If the Commission measures the objectivity of the Platform's recommendations in the field of biofuels research policy by the lack of technological bias, then it adopts too narrow a perspective.[97]

Acting objectively is not only a matter of carefully analysing the expertise and technical means available. As mentioned, the Ombudsman anchored this broader view on what it means to act objectively on the applicable legal provisions that identified the legally protected interests relevant in this case. The Commission eventually agreed that it should enhance the objectivity of the Platform's recommendations and committed to doing so.[98]

This case was not about whether a specific decision was biased or

---

[95] Biofuels Decision, *supra* note 89, point 78 (building on point 36, where the Ombudsman referred to the recital of the Directive that indicated the importance of taking into account 'environmental, social and economic considerations').

[96] Biofuels Decision, *supra* note 89, point 36.

[97] Biofuels Decision, *supra* note 89, point 78 (emphasis added).

[98] Biofuels Decision, *supra* note 89, point 112.

whether it properly considered the broader range of public interests at stake. It was about the structures on the basis of which the Commission makes substantive discretionary choices, which may decisively influence the direction these may take. It illustrates how the Ombudsman may pierce the Commission's informal practices and structures that underlie its technical assessments and link them back to the political considerations that, in view of the applicable legislation, should inform the exercise of discretion. Arguably, the fact that the Ombudsman decides via friendly dispute resolution and non-binding decisions allows her to preserve the space of discretion that the Commission should retain. The risks of overstepping that space, while indicating the relevant public interests that the Commission needs to take into account and ensure, are perhaps smaller when the control performed need not be translated in a binding binary result of legality/illegality. The Ombudsman may point out that what is not legally imposed is 'not legally barred' and may be followed as a matter of care in ensuring the proper consideration of competing legally protected interests (public and private) when conducting factual assessments.[99] As much as the review performed by the Ombudsman also needs to preserve the space for substantive discretionary choices, the institutional position of her office – in particular the constitutive link to the European Parliament – arguably entails fewer institutional constraints when recalling and acting upon the range of public interests that ought to be considered in decision-making.

The other side of the coin is, of course, the non-legally binding nature of the decisions of the Ombudsman. However, while from the perspective of the complainant this feature may amount to a weaker form of remedy, the collaboration with the EU institutions that the Ombudsman seeks to ensure may lead to structural changes in the ways in which they exercise their discretion. The Ombudsman's ability to report resistances and persistent problems to the European Parliament may considerably weigh on the targeted institutions.

6 CONCLUSION

In the cases in which the EU Courts went further in the review of administrative discretion, they made the lawfulness of the exercise of discretion depend mostly on the accuracy, completeness, reliability of the informa-

[99] Decision of the European Ombudsman closing his inquiry into complaint 846/2010/PB against the European Commission, points 78 and 79.

tion gathered and the thoroughness and diligence of the complex assessments that the Commission, as other executive bodies, need to make in the performance of their functions. Such an approach seems to confine the role of law in structuring discretion to issues that are (or appear to be) procedural in nature, while still performing a meaningful degree of review. By way of two principles of law – effective judicial protection, and careful and impartial examination – the EU Courts have been able to check the legality of decisions that ultimately rely on 'questions that only [an expert] can answer'.[100] This could be as much as one may expect from courts, for institutional and material reasons. Separation of powers would recommend judicial restraint over political choices, in particular if these concern controversial matters. If courts may compensate (at least in part) their lack of technical expertise via various procedural means, their role is not to second-guess choices that should be autonomously defined by an administrative body within the limits of law. These considerations may explain – and, for some, justify – the deference of the Court of Justice to the powers attributed to the ESMA and to the OMT decision of the ECB, in a context of particular turbulence. In addition, the stringent way in which the EU Courts have reviewed administrative discretion following the two lines of case law analysed in this chapter would placate concerns regarding the role of law in controlling the exercise of those powers, should they ever be concretized and subject to judicial challenge.

Yet, this chapter has argued that the EU Courts have struck the balance between the need to preserve a room for choice (the essence of discretionary powers) and a sufficient judicial control in a specific way. The EU Courts have dissected technical complex assessments (which they review) from public interest appraisals (which they tend to leave outside the scope of review). There are normative consequences to this approach, which should be critically assessed. Namely, it emphasizes the technical nature of the acts under review, potentially leading to label as 'technical' decisions that are far from being only that, and reinforcing the correctness of technical assessments as the prevalent criterion to assess discretion and its exercise. This effect is well illustrated by the Court's rulings in *ESMA*, where the Court implicitly downplayed the policy considerations entailed in the powers of ESMA, and in *Gauweiler*, where it emphatically stressed, when reviewing the proportionality of the OMT decision, that 'nothing

---

[100] Case C-269/90, *Technische Universität München v Hauptzollamt München-Mitte*, Opinion of A-G Jacobs, *supra* note 32, para. 15 (see also para. 13: 'the technical nature of a case should not cause the Court to forsake its duty . . . to ensure that the law is observed. The Court cannot shy away from technical questions').

more can be required of the ESCB apart from that it use its . . . expertise and the necessary technical means at its disposal to carry out [a reasonable] analysis with all care and accuracy'.[101]

The chapter contended that, in general, by focusing judicial review of discretion on whether the EU executive has acted competently – i.e., whether they collected all the information that could be available and carefully examined it – the EU Courts fail to assess the legality of discretionary decisions against a fundamental normative yardstick: whether the decisions have sufficiently considered public interests that by force of legal norms should be pursued in a given instance. Given that the authority of administrative decision-makers to make discretionary decisions is delimited by reference to such public interests, how these are weighed in a given instance is an important aspect of the legal legitimacy of administrative action that the EU Courts seem to relinquish. Straying this far may lead the Courts to venture into areas where institutional and material reasons would recommend restraint. Nevertheless, the limits of judicial review of discretion as currently defined in the EU Courts case law ought not to obscure the dialectical link between complex assessments and public interest appraisals, which discretionary decisions entail. They can hardly be analytically dissected, as they appear in the case law analysed. Such intertwinement postulates a duty of care, which is broader and normatively more demanding that the one enshrined in the EU Courts' case law. From a public interest perspective, care requires, in addition to factually accurate assessments, the due consideration *in these assessments* of the legally protected public interests that, by force of law, ought to be balanced, protected and pursued. Care would postulate fairness and inclusiveness in such public interest appraisals. As a result, law would validate discretionary decisions that, apart from technically accurate, would also respect and concretize the political, economic, social and cultural values that the EU legal order protects. Duty of care, in this sense, unveils the broader role of law in structuring discretion that judicial review on discretion currently hides.

The way the European Ombudsman has acted upon complaints of lack of objectivity and impartiality illustrates this broader role of law. Without prejudice to a different judicial approach to the review of discretion, which the duty of care (in the broader sense defended here) would suggest, the article has highlighted the distinct contribution that the Ombudsman may give to ensuring the legality of discretionary powers. Because of the specific institutional role of the Ombudsman, of her mandate and

101 Case C-62/14, *Gauweiler*, *supra* note 2, para. 75.

means of action to assess the soundness of administrative processes, the Ombudsman seems to be particularly well placed to structure the exercise of discretion in a way that stresses the intrinsic link between pursuing public interests and making accurate and careful factual assessments. Like the Courts, the Ombudsman can investigate the factual basis of EU legal acts. But, arguably, the distinct institutional position of the office enables the scrutiny of aspects that, if controlled by the Courts, could be perceived as overstepping the limits of their jurisdiction – e.g., whether the very structures of gathering information are fashioned in a way that ensure a suitable balancing of the public interests that, by legal determination, ought to be considered in each instance. In addition, the setting of friendly dispute resolution may be, in given instances, more heedful of the space of discretion that administrative actors should preserve, while still both controlling and enabling change in the way discretion is exercised. Unlike the Courts, the Ombudsman may suggest *ways* in which the public interests that the EU institutions should pursue, by force of the applicable legislation, could be adequately balanced in an inclusive and fair way.

7. New perspectives for the European Ombudsman opened by the Lisbon Treaty*

Roberto Mastroianni

1 INTRODUCTION

The purpose of this chapter is to highlight the impact of the Treaty of Lisbon on the role and activities of the European Ombudsman (hereinafter, the EO), in the light of recent practice. If it is true that the above-mentioned Treaty did not formally increase or modify the powers and competences of the EO, it clearly improved its importance and responsibility in two different ways.[1] On one side, it broadened its mandate by adding 'agencies and offices' in the list of European administrations potentially covered by its inquiries, as well as by extending its competence to the former second pillar (Common Foreign and Security Policy). On the other side, it improved the rights of European citizens by recognizing the legal binding force to the Charter of Fundamental Rights, which expressly qualifies recourse to the EO (Article 43) and the right to a good administration (Article 41) – as well as the right to access to documents (Article 42) – as fundamental rights of the European Union. A few observations will follow, from a procedural point of view, concerning the relationship between EO investigations and judicial review proceedings.

Given this basic framework, as an example of the EO's proactive approach in the application of the existing rules, the chapter will then

* This chapter, as the whole volume, is part of a publication in the framework of PRIN project 2012 (2012SAM3KM) on Codification of EU Administrative Procedures, financed by the Ministero dell'Istruzione, dell'Università e della Ricerca, Italy.

[1] See N. Diamandouros, 'The European Ombudsman and Good Administration post-Lisbon', in D. Ashiagbor, N. Countouris and I. Lianos (eds.), *European Union after the Treaty of Lisbon*, Cambridge University Press, 2012, 210 *et seq.*

focus on the EO recent inquiry on the functioning and possible revision of the European Citizens' Initiative (ECI). On 5 March 2015, the EO concluded its analysis by adopting a decision including a list of suggestions and guidelines for a more citizen-friendly functioning of the ECI.

2 THE IMPACT OF THE LISBON TREATY ON THE ROLE AND SCOPE OF ACTION OF THE EO

The main provision dealing with the role and the mandate of the EO is Article 228 of the Treaty on the Functioning of the European Union (TFEU). Even though such provision appears in Chapter I of the Treaty, devoted to 'The institutions', the Lisbon Treaty reform neither appointed the EO as an independent institution nor changed its *status* otherwise. For this reason, Article 228 TFEU still remains in the context of section I of the chapter, which refers to the European Parliament (EP), as the EO continues to be appointed by the EP, and the activities of the two are still tightly linked.

As previously indicated, the Lisbon Treaty did not vest any new competence in the EO. Nevertheless the latter's mandate has been broadened, first of all by specific provisions of Article 228 TFEU, whose implications arise mainly from an institutional point of view.

In fact, according to the current version of that article of the Treaty, the EO's competence covers 'maladministration in the activities of the Union institutions, bodies, offices or agencies', while since its establishment and until the Lisbon reform it was limited to the activities 'of the Community institutions or bodies' (Article 195 of the Treaty of the European Community (TEC)). Such novelty is not without practical consequences.[2]

First of all, it must be underlined that according to the list of EU institutions provided by Article 13 of the Treaty on European Union (TEU), the EO's mandate now reaches the activities of the European Council. I will deal with this further below. In contrast, there is no definition or authoritative list of Union 'bodies, offices and agencies'. Those terms must be interpreted in the sense of including bodies, offices and agencies established by the Treaties, even though a broader interpretation may be

[2] It should be noted that the text of Article 43 of the Charter of Fundamental rights of the European Union, as modified at Strasbourg in 2007, reflects this evolution by adding to the previous text a reference to 'offices or agencies' of the European Union.

allowed in order to extend the control on other entities, whose activity is capable of affecting individuals.[3]

In this context, the activities of such entities may be examined by the EO in case of alleged maladministration, notwithstanding the source of their appointment (secondary law, as in the case of the European Chemicals Agency and the European Union Agency for Fundamental Rights; or international treaties).

Concerning 'bodies', the EO has conducted inquiries and adopted decisions with regards, for instance, to BEREC (Body of European Regulators for Electronic Communications),[4] which replaced, in 2010, the European Regulators group for electronic communications networks and services.[5] It is interesting to note, though, that its predecessor was investigated in 2007 (and the case closed in 2009) for breach of duties related to requests of information, when it was a 'European group', and still not formally a 'body'. This confirms the EO's approach, as it seems to have never limited the scope of its mandate exclusively in relation to the *formal* denomination of the subject concerned, so conducting its inquiries on the widest possible framework of entities.

Concerning 'agencies', some inquiries have been conducted about this new category as well. For example, regarding the new agencies set up after Lisbon,[6] in 2011 the EO investigated by its own initiative the European Securities and Markets Authority (ESMA) in relation to an alleged breach of duties for incorrect application of substantive and/or procedural rules in competition and selection procedures, since the latter adopted a decision to reject the complainant's application on the basis of criteria that were not set out in the notice of vacancy.[7] Moreover, in 2014, another case was opened against it, assuming that ESMA's decision on the composition of its 30-member Securities and Markets Stakeholders Group failed

---

[3] For similar considerations in relation to Article 263, para. 1, TFEU, see Opinion of Advocate General Jääskinen, 4 December 2014, case C-439/13P, *Elitaliana v Eulex Kosovo*, para. 45 *et seq.*

[4] Own-initiative inquiry OI/4/2013/CK. concerning the EU Agencies. It is interesting to note that in this inquiry the OE qualifies BEREC as an 'agency'.

[5] BEREC was established by Regulation (EC) No. 1211/2009 of the European Parliament and of the Council of 25 November 2009.

[6] On the EU agencies regulatory framework post-Lisbon see H. M. Ekelund, 'Making Sense of the 'Agency Programme' in post-Lisbon Europe: Mapping European Agencies', *Central European Journal of Public Policy*, 2012, 26 *et seq.* In general, note that in 2014 inquiries conducted by the EO concerned new agencies were 13.7 %, following the European Commission, which has been implied in 59.6 % of cases (in 2013 those percentages were respectively 24% and 64.3%).

[7] Case 1167/2011/MMN.

to do justice to the requirement to ensure a balanced representation of stakeholders across the Union, since, among other things, it provided the inclusion of only one representative of small and medium-sized enterprises (SMEs) and two employee representatives, who apparently could not properly represent the interests of SMEs.[8]

Regarding the European Banking Authority (EBA), it was investigated because of the manner in which its key advisory body, the Banking Stakeholder Group, was selected.[9] Another procedure was opened against the EBA since information on its website was available only in English, and that circumstance could have impeded citizens to access information. Violations of multilingualism – especially on websites – seem to be among the most popular grounds for complaints before the EO. On that specific occasion, a petition was presented to the EP Committee on Petitions, but then, since it concerned a possible instance of maladministration, the Committee decided to transmit it to the EO, who dealt with it as a complaint. It is worth noting, in that regard, how on that occasion the concrete interrelation between the EO and the EP – or its internal committees – has demonstrated to work in a very effective manner.

Concerning 'offices', the Office for Harmonization in the Internal Market (OHMI) was the subject of an inquiry for the first time in 2006.[10] At that time the provision in force was Article 138 TEC, according to which EO's competence covered only institutions or bodies, with no specific mention of offices. Nevertheless, the EO found the complaint admissible without investigating if the office's activity was out of the scope of its powers. Such an approach does seem to confirm, as in the aforementioned case of bodies, that the number of entities falling within EO's mandate has always been as wide as possible, with the aim to guaranteeing the respect of the principle of good administration. Similar considerations bring to the conclusion that, in substance, the scope of application of the EO's mandate has not been broadened as a consequence of the Lisbon reform: rather, the new Treaty has codified the existing practice consisting in comprising entities different from 'institutions and bodies'[11] within the EO's purview.

---

[8] Case 545/2014/LP.

[9] Case 1876/2011/LP.

[10] Case 366/2006/ID.

[11] See G. Carella and I. Ingravallo, 'Article 228 TFEU', in A. Tizzano (ed.), *Trattati dell'Unione Europea*, Milano, Giuffré, 2014. It will be interesting to verify the EO's approach in relation to a recent complaint on *judicial transparency*, more in particular on the 'refusal of the Council to publish opinions regarding nominations for the Court of Justice and the General Court'. In that case, in fact, even though the inquiry regards the Council, it is related to the (activity of the) panel

As already mentioned, not only the specific provisions of the Treaty devoted to the EO have contributed, to a certain extent, to broaden the EO's mandate, but also other provisions have played a role in this process, by affecting the EO's mandate 'from the side'.

First of all, in relation to entities whose activity is subject to the EO's control, an increase in their number derives from the new framework of EU institutions as established at Lisbon. On that regard, the European Council acquired the *status* of an institution and, therefore, its activity now falls in full within the scope of the EO's mandate. Together with other revisions put forward by the Lisbon Treaty, this increased considerably the legal accountability of the European Council,[12] in particular where its activity cannot be subject to jurisdictional scrutiny, i.e. the Common Foreign and Security Policy (CFSP) and the Common Security and Defence Policy (CSDP) (on which see further below). In fact, in addition to some inquiries concerning the European Council's handling of the citizens' requests for access to documents, a complaint recently closed concerned the use of service cars by its President. In particular, the aspect related to the use of service cars was overtaken by that related to the dismissive replies of the European Council (when the complaints were not completely ignored).[13]

As to the increase of the material scope of the EO's scrutiny, the Lisbon reform has abolished the pillars system, which broadened the EO's material scope of action, hence encompassing complaints falling under the CFSP and the CSDP. In particular, concerning the CFSP, at the end of 2010 the EO opened an own inquiry concerning the Council of the European Union, the European Commission and the High Representative/European External Action Service.[14] The case, closed in 2013, concerned the issue of accountability for instances of maladministration in the activities of missions carried out within the context of the CSDP: since the right to good administration is a fundamental one, it has to be protected also as regards the activities of CSDP civilian and military missions. Furthermore, an own-initiative inquiry was opened – and closed as well – in 2014, in relation to the way in which the European External Action Service (EEAS)

---

established by Article 255 of the TFEU, whose task is to give opinions on candidates' suitability to perform the duties of Judges and Advocates-General.

[12] Understood as the supervision of the observance of the EU rule of law (see N. Vogiatzis, 'Exploring the European Council's Legal Accountability: Court of Justice and European Ombudsman', *German Law Journal*, 2013, at 2661).

[13] The case was solved by a friendly solution and with the apologies of the European Council to the complainant.

[14] Case OI/12/2010/(BEH)MMN.

handled allegations of serious irregularities involving the EU Rule of Law Mission (EULEX) in Kosovo.[15] On that occasion, the EO noted that EULEX had failed to comply with its own standard procedure in investigating such allegations. The EO also found that the way in which the external prosecutor was recruited needed to be examined. However, given that the expert recently appointed by the EU High Representative has made it clear that these issues will form part of his future review, the EO considered that there was no need for further action on her part.

This aspect, in connection with the inclusion of agencies and offices, implies a potentially significant increase of admissible complaints and new inquiries on the action of all these entities falling within the CFSP field. Indeed, this is confirmed by the fact that since its creation – via the Lisbon Treaty – and launch, the EEAS has been the subject of 3 to 4 per cent of the EO's total number of inquiries during the last year.

It is important to highlight how, also in this context, the extension of the EO's mandate may have positive – although indirect – consequences for the protection of individuals, so to at least partially counterweight the exclusion of the Court of Justice of the EU jurisdiction in the same field. It is widely accepted that the notion of 'maladministration' is very broad, as it goes beyond cases where the rule or principle is legally binding, but still it encompasses the violation of prescriptive rules. From that point of view, the activities or omissions of institutions, bodies, agencies and offices, which could not be in question in actions brought before the Court of Justice of the European Union (CJEU), may be scrutinized by the EO from the viewpoint of acts of 'maladministration'. If it is true that, in general, recourse to the EO does not provide the same advantages for individuals' rights as direct access to Courts, it is also true that, for instance, the decision of the European Council not to disclose a document in the CFSP (in violation of the principle of transparency) may be 'attacked' only via an inquiry of the EO. The same conclusion applies in other fields which are not excluded from the CJEU jurisdiction but where access to the Court is limited by the latter's rather strict interpretation of the Treaty provision concerning challenge of acts from private individuals.[16]

In conclusion, as a consequence of the increased responsibilities entrusted to the EO by the Treaties, it seems that (almost) no aspect of EU institutional life can escape some sort of accountability.

---

15 Case OI/15/2014/PMC.

16 CJEU 28 April 2015, C-456/13 P, *T & L Sugars and Sidul Açúcares v Commission.*

Nevertheless, I am not totally convinced that the CJEU and the EO complement each other:[17] the CJEU's judicial review in the former 'II Pillar' still needs to be improved, since there should be no entity in the European institutional framework exempted from the rule of law (Article 2 TEU).

The rules concerning *legislative procedures* may also extend the scope of intervention of the EO. This is the case, for instance, of the EO's inquiries concerning transparency of the 'Trilogues' procedures and more in particular, the disclosure of documents adopted by the main institutions in that context.[18] In our view, this represents a very delicate step forward, as the Treaty only refers to 'good administration' as the goal of the EO's intervention and it is not obvious that the trilogues, being a part of the law-making process, falls into this category. The EO herself, in the letter opening the inquiry sent to the institutions involved, states that 'transparency as regards the *law-making process* is vital for building trust in the EU. Trilogues are now an established feature of the *ordinary legislative procedure*.'[19] Nevertheless, the EO's decision to investigate has probably been influenced by the greater importance that the principle of transparency acquired after the Lisbon reform, since it is codified both in the Treaties and in the Charter. Also on that regard, practice represents the most important answer to the possibility, for the EO, to broaden the interpretation of 'maladministration', so to encompass even legislative (or, at least, para-legislative) activities.

3 THE RIGHT TO REFER TO THE EO AS A FUNDAMENTAL RIGHT

One of the most important results of the Lisbon Treaty revision is the legally binding character conferred to the EU Charter of Fundamental Rights (henceforth, 'Charter'). In particular, Article 43 of the Charter recognizes the right to refer to the EO as a 'citizens' right', in Title V – which deals with European citizenship. Therefore, the right to refer to the EO acquires the status of 'fundamental right'. In any event, even when the Charter's provisions were not legally binding, EU institutions' and bodies'

---

[17] N. Vogiatzis, *supra*, note 12, 1661.

[18] Case OI/8/2015/JAS (Own-initiative inquiry, opened on 26 May 2015, concerning 'Disclosure, by the European Parliament, Council of the EU and European Commission, of documents relating to trilogues and transparency of trilogues in general').

[19] Emphasis added.

behaviour by not complying with it was considered maladministration, and therefore inquired into by the EO.[20]

One may wonder, though, how 'fundamental' this right is if a complainant has little chance to directly challenge the EO decisions or omissions, but this would bring us too far here.[21] Nevertheless, such innovation clearly has a positive effect on citizens' awareness of their right to refer to the EO.

The same is true for the right to good administration (Article 41 of the Charter), which is the main 'substantial' point of reference in the EO's activity, and includes the right to be heard and receive reasoned decisions as well as the right to transparency. On that regard, it is worth underlining that transparency and openness of the EU institutions are by definition a prerequisite for good administration within the EU. Not surprisingly, the Charter consecrates a specific provision to the right of access to documents (Article 42). The EO contributes in a concrete fashion to achieve that goal: not only citizens' complaints grounded on the refusal of access to documents are certainly the most common, as results from the annual reports,[22] but as a general rule the EO does not limit its investigations on an eventual breach of specific normative rules on access to document,[23] but encompasses 'simple' cases of maladministration.

That said, it is undeniable that the general tasks performed by the EO, in challenging maladministration, contribute to implementation of those fundamental rights. A few more observations, though, are necessary in order to determine the material scope of the fundamental right to refer to the EO, from two different standpoints, a subjective and an objective one.

Concerning the material scope of Article 43 of the Charter, it is interesting to note some limitations from a *subjective* point of view, namely on the

---

[20] I. Harden, 'Article 43 (European Ombudsman)', in S. Peers, T. Hervey, J. Kenner and A. Ward (eds.), *The EU Charter of Fundamental Rights – A Commentary*, London, Beck/Hart/Nomos, 2014, 1121 *et seq.*

[21] On that regard, see further below, Section 4.

[22] See, for instance, annual reports of the EO for 2008 and 2014.

[23] Right to access to documents and competence of the EO in case of violation are provided not only by Regulation 1049/2001 (of the European Parliament and of the Council of 30 May 2001 regarding public access to European Parliament, Council and Commission documents, OJ L 145, 31.5.2001), but also by specific acts setting up and regulating single bodies, offices and agencies. See, for instance, Decision of the Court of Justice of the European Union of 11 December 2012 concerning public access to documents held by the Court of Justice of the European Union in the exercise of its administrative functions (2013/C 38/02); Regulation (EU) 1095/2010 of the European Parliament and of the Council of 24 November 2010 establishing a European Supervisory Authority (European Securities and Markets Authority), amending Decision No. 716/2009/EC and repealing Commission Decision 2009/77/EC, OJ L 331, 15.12.2010.

nationality of the complainant. In the light of Articles 20 and 24 TFEU, access to the EO is still considered as part of European citizenship, therefore recognized to European citizens. Both Article 228 TFEU and Article 43 of the Charter extend the right to refer to the EO to natural persons residing in the EU as well as to legal persons having their registered office in the EU. In sum, these provisions and the Statute of the EO[24] exclude that its inquiry might be formally triggered by an extra-EU national or by a company not established in the EU, although those subjects can be negatively affected by 'maladministration', as confirmed by the fact that according to Article 42 of the Charter 'every person', and not every citizen, enjoys a right to good administration. It is true, on the other hand, that – if I understand correctly their implementation in practice – the Treaty rules as well as the EO Statute do not require a 'personal' interest to file a complaint. In other words, the limitation provided by the above-mentioned rules may be interpreted as to concern only the natural or legal person that actually files the complaint, which in principle could involve the situation of a different person suffering maladministration, including a third country national or a company registered outside the Union.

In any event, the EO is probably conscious of this problem since it decided to give a very broad interpretation to the notions of 'residence' in a Member State and of 'legal person'. On that regard, it is worth underlining its approach in opening at its own-initiative inquiries following complaints declared inadmissible due to the rules just mentioned.[25] Nonetheless, because of such 'subjective' limitation, there may be cases of maladministration that may never come to the attention of the EO. Given the importance of the EO activity in the general context of the protection of individual's rights – as practice shows, the institution or body concerned normally accepts and implements the EO's conclusions and proposals for better quality administrative activities – a textual extension of this 'fundamental right' to everyone appears to be the right solution. This obviously requires a Treaty revision.

---

[24] See Article 2, para. 2, of Decision of the European Parliament on the regulations and general conditions governing the performance of the Ombudsman's duties, adopted by Parliament on 9 March 1994 (OJ L 113, 4.5.1994, p. 15) and amended by its decisions of 14 March 2002 (OJ L 92, 9.4.2002, p. 13) and 18 June 2008 (OJ L 189, 17.7.2008, p. 25).

[25] See Case OI/11/2010/AN, *Reimbursement of a subcontractor's expenses*. Since the complainant was not an EU national or resident, the complaint fell outside the EO's mandate. However, the latter considered that it was in the general interest to clarify the facts reported by the complainant by means of an own-initiative inquiry. See on this point J. Dupont-Lassalle, 'La pratique du Médiateur européen: un succès d'estime?', *Revue des affaires européennes*, 2-2013, 280 *et seq.*

Concerning the material scope of the fundamental right to refer to the EO from an *objective* point of view, I would like to draw attention to the possibility of extending the EO's scrutiny to national administrations. It is well known that the administrative implementation of EU law is largely the responsibility of Member States. It has been suggested that Article 43 should be interpreted in the light of Article 51 of the Charter, so as to cover also cases of maladministration when *national bodies* apply EU law. Such an approach may appear more in line with the general scope of the rules of the Charter (Article 51),[26] but contrary to the wording of Article 43, according to which the EO deals with 'cases of maladministration in the activities of the institutions, bodies, offices or agencies of the Union'. The CJEU adopted this literal interpretation in recent judgments concerning Article 41 of the Charter.[27]

In that context, the problem remains on how to foster uniform interpretation of 'good quality' administration in cases where national bodies act as the *longa manus* of the EU. The unwritten *general principles* of EU law lying behind Article 41 of the Charter applies also in 'domestic' situations, therefore in 'parallel' cases it should be the task of national or regional ombudspersons to intervene in compliance with such European principles.[28] Unfortunately, their tasks and powers vary from Member State to Member State and might not be as 'effective' as recourse to the EO (for instance, Italy

---

[26] 'The provisions of this Charter are addressed to the institutions and bodies of the Union with due regard for the principle of subsidiarity *and to the Member States only when they are implementing Union law*' (emphasis added).

[27] CJEU 17 July 2014, joined cases C-141/12 and C-372/12, *YS and Others and M and S*, paras. 67 to 69. On the substance of the questions referred, YS, M and S as well as the Greek Government argued that the applicant for a resident permit may take Article 41(2)(b) of the Charter as a basis for a right of access to the file, given that, in the context of the procedure for granting such a permit, the national authorities apply the asylum directives. By contrast, the Netherlands, Czech, French, Austrian and Portuguese Governments and the Commission considered that Article 41 of the Charter covers exclusively EU institutions and cannot, therefore, establish a right of access to a file in the context of a national procedure. The Court stated that 'It is clear from the wording of Article 41 of the Charter that it is addressed not to the Member States but solely to the institutions, bodies, offices and agencies of the European Union (see, to that effect, the judgment in Cicala, C-482/10, EU:C:2011:868, paragraph 28). Consequently, an applicant for a resident permit cannot derive from Article 41(2)(b) of the Charter a right to access the national file relating to his application' (para. 69).

[28] For acknowledgement of the right to good administration, enshrined in Article 41 of the Charter, as a general principle of EU law see *inter alia* CJEU 8 May 2014, case C-604/12, *NH*, para. 49, as well as *YS and Others and M and S*, para. 68.

does not have any 'national' ombudsman office). A possible solution to that problem could be to reinforce the European Network of Ombudsmen, drawing upon the experience of the European Competition network.

4 AN ANALYSIS FROM THE POINT OF VIEW OF EU PROCEDURAL LAW

The nature of the EO's tasks is not a judicial one, nevertheless it may produce positive – if not similar – effects on individuals, especially in cases where access to EU Courts is made difficult due to Treaty rules on *locus standi*.

Article 263 TFEU, para. 4, partially modifies the rules for private individuals' access to EU Courts, with the intention to improve their ability to challenge EU acts. Still such access remains rather problematic, as made clear by the recent case-law of the Court,[29] due to the interpretation given by the CJEU to the Treaty rules, in particular when they require 'direct and individual concern'. The limited improvement of individuals' access to EU Courts highlights the importance and effectiveness of recourse to the EO in situations where application to the CJEU is considered inadmissible.

Even though the EO's decisions are not legally binding (they never had this character, nor did the Lisbon Treaty modify it), this instrument could perhaps be seen – at least in some circumstances – as an efficient alternative to access to Courts, or, to some extent, as a complementary tool. On that regard, long before the Lisbon revision, the General Court stated that 'in the institution of the Ombudsman, the Treaty has given citizens of the Union, and more particularly officials and other servants of the Community, an alternative remedy to that of an action before the Community Court in order to protect their interests. That alternative non-judicial remedy meets specific criteria and does not necessarily have the same objective as judicial proceedings.'[30]

The first ground for such a conclusion is the fact that no particular condition must be fulfilled in order for an individual to address the EO: the 'individual concern' test, in particular, does not apply. Second, the scope

---

[29] See R. Mastroianni and A. Pezza, 'Striking the Right Balance: Limits on the Right to Bring an Action under Article 263(4) of the Treaty on the Functioning of the European Union', *Am. Univ. Int'l L. Rev.*, 2015, at 743. In the recent case-law see ECJ, judgment of 28 April 2015, case C-456/13 P, *T & L Sugars Ltd.*

[30] Court of First Instance, judgment of 10 April 2002, case T-209/00, *Lamberts v Ombudsman*, II-02203, para. 65.

of the EO's investigations is wider than the jurisdiction of the EU Courts, since it targets activities of the EU institutions also when they do not bring to a formal 'act' (while CJEU competence is limited to acts). Third, in terms of content, the EO's scrutiny does not only deal with the lawfulness of a certain activity but goes beyond it. 'Maladministration' may be interpreted in different ways; nonetheless such a notion certainly covers rules, values and standards whose violation does not constitute illegality *stricto sensu*, in particular obligations voluntarily assumed by an institution or ethical standards. In similar cases, institutions' conducts may fall within the scope of the EO's scrutiny even if no *unlawful* activity is carried out (see, for example, the aforementioned case of civilian and military missions in Third Countries in the context of the CSDP). Therefore, recourse to the EO becomes the only possible means of 'redress' when no other form of protection is allowed.

At this juncture, a further question arises, concerning the possibility to challenge, via a judicial remedy, acts or failures to act of the EO itself. Such a remedy is normally excluded by the EU Courts.[31] As to actions of annulments, the Court has normally – even in a very recent case – excluded such possibility, on the ground that the EO's decision are not intended to produce legal effects *vis-à-vis* third parties[32] (moreover, they are neither legal acts nor are they adopted by an EU institution, body, office or organization[33]). The Court has adopted the same approach – of

[31] It is the case of actions brought on the basis of Article 263 TFEU, nevertheless some activities not related to the EO's inquiry powers may be reviewed before the CJEU, such as decisions concerning its officials (see, for instance, Civil Service Tribunal 17 July 2012, case F-54/11, *BG v European Ombudsman*, even though the action was dismissed in its entirety).

[32] General Court (order) 19 November 2014, case T-430/14 *Mirelta Ingatlanhasznosító v Commission*, paras. 9 and 10. On that regard the Court stated that '. . . *selon la jurisprudence, le Médiateur n'a pas le pouvoir de prendre des mesures contraignantes et le rapport qu'il transmet au Parlement, lorsqu'il relève un cas de mauvaise administration, se limite à constater l'existence d'un tel cas dans l'action d'une institution et, le cas échéant, à formuler des recommandations (voir ordonnance du 3 novembre 2008, Srinivasan/Médiateur, T:196/08, EU:T:2008:470, point 11 et jurisprudence citée). En conséquence, le rapport du Médiateur ne produit, par définition, aucun effet juridique à l'égard des tiers, au sens de l'article 263 TFUE, et ne lie pas non plus le Parlement qui est libre de décider, dans le cadre de l'exercice des pouvoirs qui lui sont conférés par le traité, de la suite à y donner (voir ordonnance Srinivasan/Médiateur, précitée, EU:T:2008:470, point 11 et jurisprudence citée)*'.

[33] ECJ 25 October 2007, C-167/06 P, *Komninou and Others v Commission*, ECR I-00141 (Summary publication), para. 44; Court of First Instance (order) 3 November 2008, T-196/08, *Srinivasan v European Ombudsman*. In that judgment

inadmissibility – on ground of the same considerations in relation to actions for failure to act.[34] In contrast, an action for damages is – in principle – admissible.[35]

In sum, according to the EU Courts, the EO's decisions would not produce legal effects on the complainants: if the former finds a case of maladministration, it must simply inform them of the outcome of the inquiries, of the opinion expressed by the institution or body concerned and of any recommendations made to it.[36] If it is true that no binding effects may formally derive from the EO's inquiries to the entities involved, I am not completely convinced that the reports of maladministration are deprived of legal effects with regards to the complainants. In practice, such a report normally is the basis of a change of behaviour from the entity involved. In addition, as previously mentioned, the strict attitude of EU Courts appears at odds with the inclusion of the right to refer to the EO as a 'fundamental' one, now enshrined in a primary law provision (Article 43 of the Charter).

The Court's approach with regard to judicial review of EO activity is not unanimously approved. Some authors suggest that, to give effectiveness to the principle of good administration, the EO acts and decisions should be challengeable before the CJEU, especially considering the discretional powers recognized to it with regards to private individuals' complaints.[37] This approach stems from the CJEU case-law on the EP Petitions Committee's decision rejecting petitions proposed by citizens as

---

the Court stated: 'By definition . . . the Ombudsman's report does not produce legal effects vis-à-vis third parties within the meaning of Article 230 EC, and is furthermore not binding on the Parliament, which is free to decide, within the framework of the powers conferred on it by the Treaty, what steps are to be taken in relation to it' (para. 11). The Court also added that the Ombudsman 'is not amongst the institutions and bodies whose acts are referred to by the first paragraph of Article 230 EC . . . he does not therefore have the capacity to be made defendant to a challenge' (para. 13).

[34] Court of First Instance (Order) 22 May 2000, case T-103/99, *Associazione delle Cantine Sociali Venete v European Ombudsman and Parliament*, ECR II-04165, paras. 45 and 46.

[35] CJEU 23 March 2004, case C-234/02 P, *Mediator v Lamberts*, I-02803, paras. 50 to 52.

[36] See Decision 94/262/ECSC, EC, Euratom of the European Parliament of 9 March 1994 on the regulations and general conditions governing the performance of the Ombudsman's duties (OJ 1994 L 113, p. 15), and related *dispositions d'exécution*.

[37] See I. Harden (*supra*, note 20), at 1142 *et seq.*; A. Peters, 'The European Ombudsman and the European Constitution', in *Common Market Law Review*, 2005, 697–743.

inadmissible, according to which such decisions may be reviewed as to the respect of the obligation to state reasons.[38]

5 THE 'NEW COURSE' OF THE EO: THE EXAMPLE OF THE ECI

The increase in number and in quality of the own-initiative inquiries shows that the EO is playing an increasingly particularly 'proactive' role, aiming not only to remedy single cases of maladministration but also to ensure in advance the realization of the fundamental right to 'good governance'. This takes place via the conduct of inquiries on general questions that, as recently noted by Ms O'Reilly, 'are intended to be helpful to the institutions concerned by promoting good administrative practice'.[39] This approach is consistent with the EO's mission which, as announced in the strategy adopted in 2014, is to serve democracy by working with EU institutions to create a more effective, accountable, transparent and ethical administration.

If it is true that such an 'alternative' mission does not appear clearly in the Treaty provisions,[40] it is indisputable that such an extensive interpretation of Article 228 TFEU is fully accepted in practice.

However, the role of the EO as the 'promoter' of new practices more in line with the good administration requirements is not entirely new. In fact, even before the entry into force of the Lisbon Treaty, some of the EO's intervention formed the basis for further initiatives by the Community legislator or for the amendment of certain practices of EU institutions to the point where some scholars have qualified the EO's acts as a new source of soft law.[41]

The own-initiative inquiry on the right to public access to documents of the EU institutions, the subsequent special report to the EP[42] and the further initiative of the EO[43] are a first example, dated back to 1996, of

---

[38] See General Court, 14 September 2011, case T-308/07, *Ingo-Jens Tegebauer v European Parliament*, II-00279 (Summary publication); see also CJ, 9 December 2014, case C-261/13 P, *Schönberger v Parliament*, paras. 22 to 26.

[39] Letter of 26 May 2015 to the Commission President starting the inquiry OI/8/2015/JAS on transparency of trilogues.

[40] Article 3 of the EO's Statute is more clear in this respect.

[41] P. Bonnor, 'The European Ombudsman: A Novel Source of Soft Law in the European Union', *Eur. Law Rev.*, 2000, 39.

[42] 616/PUBAC/F/IJH, OJ of 10 February 1998, C 44, p. 9.

[43] Draft recommendation to the European institutions, bodies and agencies in the own initiative inquiry OI/1/98/OV.

such an approach. In fact, the EO's initiative has strongly contributed to the adoption of Regulation 1049/2001 regarding public access to EP, Council and Commission documents.[44]

A second example is the own initiative concerning the possibilities for improving the quality of the Commission's administrative procedures when dealing with complaints concerning Member States' alleged infringement of EC law. The result of this inquiry, opened following a great number of complaints, was the adoption of the Commission communication to the EP and the EO in relation with the complainant in respect of infringements of Community law.[45]

A further example is the inquiry opened in 1998 concerning the existence and the public accessibility, in the different Community institutions and bodies, of a Code of good administrative behaviour that, starting from the information supplied, has led to the elaboration of a model of code.[46] Moreover, with the same aim various initiatives have been launched[47] to explore the possibility, relying upon the available legal bases,[48] of developing a Code that would unify, simplify and improve EU administrative procedures, through the adoption of a legally binding act.[49]

However, after the entry into force of the Lisbon Treaty, one may note

---

44 Regulation (EC) 1049/2001 of the European Parliament and of the Council of 30 May 2001 regarding public access to European Parliament, Council and Commission documents, OJ of 31 May 2001, L 45, p. 43.

45 Commission communication to the European Parliament and the European Ombudsman on relations with the complainant in respect of infringements of Community law (COM) (2002) 141 final, OJ of 10 October 2002, C 244, p. 5.

46 See www.ombudsman.europa.eu/shortcuts/document.faces/en/3806/pdf.bookmark, accessed 6 January 2017.

47 European Parliament resolution of 15 January 2013 with recommendations to the Commission on a Law of Administrative Procedure of the European Union (2012/2024(INL)).

48 Article 298 TFEU, inserted by the Treaty of Lisbon, is generally regarded as a suitable legal basis for the codification of EU administrative procedure.

49 In this connection, regard must be had to the European ReNEUAL (Research Network on EU Administrative Law) Project, which has drafted model rules on EU administrative procedure, and to the Italian Project of National Interest 'The codification of European administrative procedure', which has carried out additional research in that area. Moreover, the EP has established its own Working Group on European administrative law and has adopted a resolution, based on Article 225 TFEU, with recommendations to the Commission on EU administrative procedure (European Parliament resolution of 15 January 2013 with recommendations to the Commission on a Law of Administrative Procedure of the European Union (2012/2024(INL)).

a change of approach. While at the base of the previous investigations at the EO's own initiative there were a significant number of complaints for alleged maladministration, recent initiatives show the tendency of the EO to open inquiries[50] regardless of (but still in connection with) complaints against actions of the institutions.[51]

Some of these recent own-initiative inquiries deserve a high degree of attention. Among them, the inquiry OI/10/2014/MMN, concerning transparency and public participation in relation to the Transatlantic Trade and Investment Partnership (TTIP) negotiations; the – just opened – second inquiry on timeliness of payments by the European Commission OI/11/2015/EIS and the already mentioned own-initiative inquiry OI/8/2015/FOR concerning transparency of trilogues.

Emblematic of the described 'new approach' is the recent own inquiry concerning the ECI.[52] In fact, even though, in principle, the Treaty rules and the ECI Regulation implementing them[53] do not provide for a formal role of the EO, the latter has strongly contributed to promote a more citizen-friendly procedure.[54] Indeed, the idea of public participation is one of the key features of the ECI, as it allows at least one million EU citizens to request the Commission to bring forward new legislative proposals. Therefore, it is quite natural that the rules governing its functioning, including those related to the administrative procedure, are caught in the realm of the EO's mandate.

It is not surprising, then, that the EO was and still is active in that respect, both in the moment of drafting the rules of this new instrument and in checking its application.

In 2010, the EO contributed to the Commission's public consultation

---

50 This approach is confirmed by the initiative on access to documents of the institutions, in which the EO states that '[o]ne of the reasons for this own initiative inquiry was that during my time in office, I received numerous complaints which brought to my attention instances of maladministration which could have been avoided if clear information had been available about the administrative duties of Community staff towards the citizens'.

51 In her letters to the EP and the Commission opening own-initiative inquiry into the functioning of ECI, the EO affirms that '[t]he objective of the inquiry is to encourage and support efforts to improve the citizens' initiative procedure'.

52 Own-initiative inquiry OI/9/2013/TN into the functioning of the ECI procedure. The ECI was put in place by the Article 11 of the Lisbon Treaty, which has assigned to a specific regulation, adopted in 2011, the establishment of the rules and conditions for the exercise of this new instrument of participatory democracy.

53 Regulation (EU) 211/2011 of the European Parliament and of the Council of 16 February 2011 on the citizens' initiative, OJ of 11 March 2011, L 65.

54 Diamandouros, *supra*, note 1, 217.

on the ECI by focusing on the registration process (for instance, requiring that admissibility and merits of the request had to be separately considered), on the possible complaints concerning the transparency of initiatives, on the time-limits and on the Commission's role as 'supervisor'.[55]

After the entry to force of Regulation 211/2011, in view of its possible revision, the own-initiative inquiry opened 'to encourage and support efforts to improve the citizens' initiative procedure'[56] had – as emphasized by Ms O'Reilly[57] – two objectives: to ensure that the current ECI Regulation is applied correctly and in the most citizen-friendly possible way as well as to provide inputs in order to review the ECI Regulation.

It is worth noting that, with regards to the ECI, before its own-initiative inquiry, the EO has received a single complaint,[58] closed without recognition of any 'maladministration', which demonstrates the autonomy of the EO's investigation from actual 'infringements'. This is confirmed by the approach used. In fact, in the own-initiative inquiry, the EO tried to engage the largest number of stakeholders: initially,[59] the invitation to submit comments was addressed only to citizens' committees of the various ECI opened, closed or withdrawn; subsequently, it was extended to other groups in civil society, only potentially interested in the ECI proceedings.[60]

Having analysed 19 feedbacks from Members of ECI and stakeholders, in January 2014 the EO invited the Commission to submit observations

---

55 See http://ec.europa.eu/dgs/secretariat_general/citizens_initiative/docs/european_ombudsman_en.pdf, accessed 6 January 2017.

56 Letter to the European Parliament opening own-initiative inquiry OI/9/2013/TN into the functioning of the European citizens' initiative (ECI) procedure available on www.ombudsman.europa.eu/it/cases/correspondence.faces/en/53106/html.bookmark, accessed 6 January 2017.

57 Presentation of the own-initiative inquiry into the ECI procedure, Brussels, Belgium, 13 April 2015, ECI Day 2015.

58 Case 2071/2013/EIS of 02.12.2013. It is a complaint brought by a representative of the citizens' committee of ECI 'Stop Vivisection'. The grievance concerned the Commission's refusal to allow an extension of the period for the collection of subscriptions due to certain problems in obtaining the necessary certification of the collection system.

59 The inquiry was opened on 18 December 2013.

60 See the Invitation to submit comments on the functioning of the European citizens' initiative (ECI) procedure of 1 March 2014, www.ombudsman.europa.eu/it/cases/correspondence.faces/en/53239/html.bookmark, accessed 6 January 2017.

on the basis of a number of key points.[61] In its reply,[62] the Commission highlighted that, with reference to the preliminary registration of ECI, it had made available to the public the information service carried out by the Europe Direct Centre; showed that certain difficulties related to the existence of different requirements in different Member States for the collection of subscriptions were a result of the legislation applicable;[63] underlined that the software, available for free, had already been implemented and is subject to constant amendments; finally, took note that the lack of legal status for the committees could cause problems for the organizers of the ECI.

Having received the Commission's response, the EO adopted a decision by which it suggested 11 guidelines for further improvement of the procedure set out by Regulation 211/2011.[64]

Regardless of the merit of those suggestions, which fall beyond the scope of this chapter, it is useful to note how, by its own inquiry, the EO suggested an intervention of the EU legislator in order to improve the

---

[61] Letter to the European Commission requesting an opinion in the European Ombudsman's own-initiative inquiry OI/9/2013/TN into the functioning of the European citizens' initiative (ECI), of 15 July 2014.

[62] The Commission reply of 6 October 2014 is available on www.ombudsman.europa.eu/en/cases/correspondence.faces/it/59067/html.bookmark#, accessed 6 January 2017.

[63] The Commission argued that on this point there has been a compromise between the co-legislators under pressure of the Council.

[64] In particular, with regard to the preparation stage, the EO, with the aim of avoiding that an ECI being rejected for formal reasons, including an insufficient information on how to draft its text, emphasized the importance of the Commission's engagement with citizens who show an interest in shaping a new ECI, asking to provide as much as possible collaboration via the Europe Direct Contact Centre. With regard to the admissibility stage, the EO, moved by the feedback received on the restrictive approach of the Commission in the interpretation of the admissibility criteria of the Article 4(2) of Regulation 2011/2011 – rather than assess whether the proposal is not manifestly outside the framework of its powers, it seems that the Commission evaluates that it clearly fall in them – called on the EU institution to provide sufficient and consistent reasoning for its decision to refuse to register an ECI, so that citizens can understand and scrutinize its position and possibly exercise their right to contest it. With regard to the examination stage, the EO invited the Commission to articulate more clearly for citizens its political evaluation as distinct from the legal evaluation and to enhance (during all stages of the procedure) the public debate generated through the ECI procedure. Finally, with regard to the collection of supports, the EO asked to improve the software in order to facilitate EU citizens wishing to sign an ECI and proposed to simplify and standardize for all Member States the requirements in terms of the personal data to be provided when signing a statement of support.

functioning of ECI as an instrument of participatory democracy able, if properly used, to empower citizens to 'shape the Union'.[65]

However, in its Report on the application of Regulation (EU) 211/2011 on the citizens' initiative of March 2015, while stating to take into account the feedbacks received from stakeholders, directly or via the EO's own-initiative, the Commission considered that the ECI had been fully implemented and that it was still too early to assess the long-term impacts of the ECI on the EU institutional and legislative process.[66]

The example cited is indicative of the new course played by the EO and of its key role in the dialectic between citizens and institutions. It also highlights the limits of its powers: the report of the Commission, in fact, while formally taking into account the issues raised by the EO, failed to put them in place.

6 CONCLUDING REMARKS

As noted in the previous paragraphs, the right to apply to the EO represents one of the core citizens' rights and is an appropriate instrument for a direct participation in the life of the EU.

In this respect, the principle of participatory democracy has witnessed a significant impulse by the adoption of the Lisbon Treaty with, on the one hand, the introduction of the possibility for a million of citizens to ask the Commission to present a legislative proposal, and, on the other, the extension of the EO's powers.

In the light of the examples cited above, new developments may be envisaged in order to further improve the described EO's proactive approach in

---

65 In the decision closing the own-initiative inquiry OI/9/2013/TN concerning the European Commission, the EO noted that 'citizens may expect and demand policy and legislation from the EU that the EU and its institutions may not have had the intention of considering. This, however, constitutes the very essence of this new instrument of participatory democracy: it empowers citizens to shape the Union. If public political debate is facilitated properly in the context of the ECI tool, this debate can give the desired effect to this new democratic right for citizens.'

66 It is also important to underline that the Commissions' 'administration' of the ECI is currently under scrutiny also at the level of EU Courts. See pending case T-646/13, *Minority SafePack v Commission*, where the Citizens' Committee challenges under Article 263 TFEU the Commission's refusal to register an initiative as manifestly outside EU competences; and pending case T-561/14 *One of Us and Others v Parliament and Others*, concerning the Commission's decision not to give a positive outcome to the ECI in the legislative process.

implementing, in general, good administration. Actually, more than from the provisions of the Treaty, the real increase of the EO's powers comes from a number of other elements able to improve not only the protection of citizens' rights but also the functioning of the EU as a whole.

In fact, the exercise of their rights (political, democratic, etc.) by an increasing number of citizens may establish a virtuous circle promoting an improved functioning of the institutions and, consequently, an increase in public trust in the EU. Those circumstances, in turn, would contribute to intensifying the importance and responsibility of the EO.

In conclusion, in the light of these reflections, it may be stressed that the EO's action, after the adoption of the Lisbon Treaty, has become even more effective and, in particular, more focused on preventing cases of maladministration rather than 'sanctioning' them.

The inquiry concerning the ECI, just like the one on 'trilogues', represents, in my opinion, a clear proof of this new approach, which is influenced by the legally binding character of citizens' rights provided by the Charter. In fact, it is decisive, for the protection of those rights, to act in advance in order not only to avoid single cases of maladministration, but also to positively influence all EU public bodies at the moment of shaping new general rules concerning citizens' rights.

In other terms, this is the new concept of 'good administration', and these are the new relevant perspectives for the EO. It is important that such an approach is coherently accepted and promoted by other public bodies, including the main political and judicial institutions of the EU.

8. The European Ombudsman's role in promoting good governance

Ian Harden

During its first twenty years of operation, the European Ombudsman developed a significant role in promoting and monitoring aspects of good governance of the EU institutions. In setting out the European Ombudsman's powers and functions, neither the Treaty nor the other relevant texts[1] refer to governance. The present chapter will argue that the concept is nonetheless useful in understanding the Ombudsman's contribution to the functioning of the European Union and its relationship with citizens.

An explanation of the standpoint from which the chapter is written may be useful. The author, currently an honorary professor of law, joined the Ombudsman's office in 1996, becoming successively head of the legal department and secretary general. Whilst trying to be objective, the chapter is thus written from the perspective of a participant with an academic background, rather than constituting an academic analysis. However, the conceptual framework it puts forward was not part of the self-understanding of the Ombudsman's office during the author's time.

The chapter begins (Section 1) with a brief explanation of how the terms governance and good governance are used in the chapter, as well as the relevant organizational context in which the Ombudsman functions. It then explains, in Section 2, how potential obstacles to the Ombudsman's role in promoting good governance were avoided or overcome. Section 3 examines the range of instruments used to establish the governance role. Section 4 explores the contours and limits of that role at the end of the Ombudsman's first two decades of operation and Section 5 sketches the

---

1 See in particular the Statute of the Ombudsman: i.e., Decision of the European Parliament 94/262/ECSC, EC, Euratom of 9 March 1994 on the regulations and general conditions governing the performance of the Ombudsman's duties, 1994 OJ L 113 p. 15, as last amended by Decision of the European Parliament 2008/587/EC, Euratom of 18 June 2008, 2008 OJ L 189 p. 25.

prospects for further development, as they appeared at the time when the author left the office.

1 GOVERNANCE AND GOOD GOVERNANCE

There is a rich academic literature on governance and the word is also widely used by practitioners in a variety of contexts. For present purposes, it is useful to think of governance in terms of questions that one may ask about organizations of different kinds, in particular:

- Who decides what is to be done and how do they decide?
- How are people made accountable for what they decide and do?
- How are disputes resolved?

The answers to these questions, and indeed the precise questions themselves, depend on the context. That is to say, they differ according to the kind and level of organization that is involved. One may focus on the internal workings of particular organizations such as business corporations, voluntary associations or government agencies. More abstractly, the focus may be social, political and economic organizations at different levels (e.g., global, regional, national, local, multilevel).[2] Studies of governance usually concern themselves not only with formal structures, which typically follow the logic of hierarchy, but also the contribution of market mechanisms and informal arrangements such as networks. A key theme in the literature is that to focus only on traditional institutions of government is too narrow an approach, whether the aim is to understand the world as it is, to change it for the better through effective policies, or both.

Adding 'good' to 'governance' focuses attention on questions of organizational design to achieve desired results. The word 'results' here refers to process values that enhance legitimacy such as, for example, transparency and public participation. It also refers to substantive outcomes, but rarely in the sense that a concern for good governance may legitimately include seeking to bring about predetermined outcomes. Rather, the point is that, when designing rules, institutions and procedures, it is important to

---

[2] 'Institution' has a similar range of meanings. The word may be used to refer to specific bodies, such as the governing institutions of a State, or the institutions of the European Union, but also, more broadly, to social, economic and political phenomena understood as systems.

address issues that may distort organizational behaviour, including, for example, collective action problems, externalities, perverse incentives such as moral hazard, as well as the dangers of free-riding, regulatory capture and the pursuit of bureaucratic self-interest.[3]

It should be obvious from the above that the academic analysis of good governance requires an inter-disciplinary approach involving not just law, but also economics and political science in particular. From a practitioner's perspective, making a worthwhile contribution to good governance requires a focus on what is feasible with available resources, and coordination with others in the same business in order, at a minimum, to avoid conflict and duplication and, ideally, to produce synergies. Sections 3 and 4 of this chapter will examine what the Ombudsman has done in this regard.

Article 228 of the Treaty on the Functioning of the European Union (TFEU) sets the context of the Ombudsman's work by empowering the Ombudsman to conduct inquiries into complaints against the *institutions, bodies, offices and agencies of the Union, with the exception of the Court of Justice acting in its judicial role.* Article 2(1) of the Statute of the Ombudsman provides that no action by any other authority or person may be the subject of a complaint to the Ombudsman. Both the Treaty and the Statute refer explicitly to complaints, but the Ombudsman has understood the power to conduct own-initiative inquiries as being similarly limited. As a result, organizations established by international agreements other than the Union Treaties fall outside the mandate. Furthermore, the Ombudsman did not take up suggestions made by some complainants and commentators that public authorities of the Member States should be considered to be Union bodies when they are applying EU law, thus avoiding overlap and potential conflict with the role of national ombudsmen and similar bodies in the Member States.[4]

---

[3] The Commission's White Paper *European Governance – A White Paper* COM (2001) 428 final, 25 July 2001, defined governance as 'rules, processes and behaviour that affect the way in which powers are exercised at European level, particularly as regards openness, participation, accountability, effectiveness and coherence'. From the current author's perspective, the White Paper sets out a conception of good governance in the context of the EU as a multilevel entity.

[4] For a more detailed legal analysis of the organizational limits on the Ombudsman's mandate to deal with complaints, see Ian Harden's chapter on Article 43 in Steve Peers, Tamara Hervey, Jeff Kenner and Angela Ward (eds.) *The EU Charter of Fundamental Rights: A Commentary*, Hart/Beck 2014.

2 FROM MALADMINISTRATION TO GOOD ADMINISTRATION

Article 228 TFEU and the Statute empower the Ombudsman to inquire into 'maladministration'. Neither text defines or explains the term, thus leaving open the question of the subject matter of the Ombudsman's inquiries and the criteria applied in them.

The Ombudsman's first Annual Report (for 1995, published in 1996) addressed the question of what constitutes maladministration by making three points: (i) maladministration includes failure to act in accordance with the Treaties, or with rules and principles of law; (ii) other things may also amount to maladministration; (iii) *the open ended nature of the term is one of the things that distinguishes the role of the Ombudsman from that of a judge.*[5] These points were made against the background of the Ombudsman's decision to open inquiries into certain complaints directed against the Commission in its role as 'Guardian of the Treaties', acting under what is now Article 258 TFEU. That Article empowers the Commission to investigate possible infringements of EU law by Member States and, eventually, to bring the matter before the Court of Justice. The relevant complaints to the Ombudsman questioned the Commission's findings in an infringement procedure concerning a particular road construction project (the Newbury Bypass in the United Kingdom). The Commission closed the procedure without bringing the matter to the Court, on the grounds that the Environmental Impact Directive 85/337 did not apply and that no infringement therefore existed.[6]

The Ombudsman's decision to open an inquiry into the Commission's handling of the matter caused concern to a number of actors, including (obviously) the Commission, but also the Committee on Petitions of the European Parliament, which was examining certain petitions about the Newbury Bypass. The right to petition the European Parliament, like the right to complain to the Ombudsman, is a fundamental right of citizenship of the Union. Most petitions are, in substance, directed against Member States for failure properly to carry out their obligations under EU law. In practice, the Committee on Petitions forward such petitions to the Commission for an opinion. The Ombudsman's inquiry was thus seen as having a potential impact on the handling of petitions to Parliament,

---

[5] Pages 8-9 of the 1995 Report. The Ombudsman's Annual Reports are available on the website: www.ombudsman.europa.eu, accessed 9 January 2017.

[6] The Ombudsman's decision closing the inquiry into the complaints is available on the website: www.ombudsman.europa.eu/cases/decision.faces/en/573/html.bookmark, accessed 9 January 2017.

both in the specific case and more generally. Moreover, the case law rejects as inadmissible attempts by natural or legal persons to bring court proceedings against the Commission about its handling of infringements. In the context of the EU, so the argument goes, confidential negotiations between the Commission and a Member State allow infringements to be discussed alongside other matters, thereby facilitating trade-offs across policy fields and enhancing the Commission's ability to push forward the general EU interest. Unsurprisingly, many people in the Commission saw the Ombudsman's inquiry as unwarranted and potentially disruptive interference in an area in which the Commission enjoyed wide discretion in negotiating with Member States.

The European Parliament was thus prompted to express concerns about the possible effects on the institutional balance and, reversing the position it had taken in relation to the Ombudsman's 1995 Annual Report, to call for a 'clear definition' of maladministration. The Report of the Committee on Petitions even went so far as to invite the *Commission* to define maladministration and to opine on whether procedural rights in the infringement procedure are the responsibility of the Ombudsman.[7] In response, the Ombudsman took the initiative to offer a definition in the 1997 Annual Report: *maladministration occurs when a public body fails to act in accordance with a rule or principle which is binding upon it*. As the accompanying explanation made clear, this was a succinct encapsulation of the three points made in the 1995 Annual Report. In particular, the fact that the Ombudsman's inquiries take into account the principles of good administration means that findings of maladministration are not limited to violation of rules and principles that are *legally* binding. The European Parliament subsequently accepted this approach and the Committee on Petitions[8] helped steer the debate away from abstract questions of definition towards a question that remains a live issue at the time of writing: what concrete rules and principles of good administration should bind the Commission and other EU institutions?

2.1 Administration and Administrative Activity

Successful avoidance of the potential pitfalls involved in defining *mal*administration helped pave the way for the Ombudsman to focus on what constitutes *good* administration. However, whilst facilitating development

---

[7] See point 4 of the EP Resolution on the Ombudsman's activities in 1996, 1997 OJ C 286, p. 41 and paragraph 16 of the Report, PE 221.948/fin, A4-0211/97.

[8] PE 226.262/fin; A4-0258/98.

of the Ombudsman's governance role, that shift of emphasis involved a further risk: i.e., that the Ombudsman would become trapped in the quicksand of attempting to define 'administration' or 'administrative act'. The risk did not eventuate, probably because Article 228 TFEU refers to the activities of the EU institutions, with the exception of the Court of Justice of the European Union *acting in its judicial role*. The inclusion of the latter exception suggests that the legislator did not envisage that the Ombudsman should decide whether to open inquiries by reference to a general concept of administration, or of administrative activity. Nor has the Ombudsman found it useful to engage in such theorizing. Matters that do not involve possible maladministration have instead been identified piecemeal and *in concreto*, in discussion with complainants and with the institutions. These discussions have rarely involved a theoretical analysis of the nature of the activity involved.[9]

The only general category of exclusion that the Ombudsman formulated is for the *political work of the European Parliament*, including all the work of parliamentary Committees. Here principle and pragmatism pushed in the same direction. Procedurally, the final step that the Ombudsman may take if an institution rejects a draft recommendation is a special report to Parliament. Such a report puts the matter into the political domain and it is for Parliament to decide whether and how to pursue the matter. If Parliament as a political institution has already taken a position on the matter, presenting a special report would be tantamount to questioning its political choice. That would be a recipe for conflict, probably leading after a few years to politicization of the Ombudsman institution. Furthermore, the exclusion of Committee work enabled the Ombudsman to draw a clear line as regards possible maladministration in the handling of petitions to the European Parliament. For Parliament's services simply to neglect a petition or other correspondence could be maladministration. Once, however, a petition was registered and acknowledged as such, its further handling was deemed to be part of Parliament's political work. This approach avoided the Ombudsman becoming involved in Parliament's internal political discussions about particular petitions, or about processes and the level of resources for handling petitions in general.

Excluding the *political* work of Parliament made it unnecessary to deal separately with *legislative* activity, which could have had implications

[9] The author remembers one discussion in which the then director of the anti-fraud office (OLAF) sought unsuccessfully to convince the Ombudsman that OLAF fell outside the mandate because its investigations are judicial in nature. The Council has also sometimes expressed the view that certain Ombudsman inquiries fell outside the mandate because the activities concerned were not administrative.

for inquiries concerning the Commission and the Council. Moreover, the exclusion was confined to *Parliament's* political work, both as a matter of principle and in order to avoid the risk that the Commission and Council might seek to take advantage of more general wording. In practice, rather than claiming an explicit political role separate from its administrative activities, the Commission sought to rely on the concept of discretion to limit the scope of the Ombudsman's inquiries, particularly into the infringement procedure. The Ombudsman accepted that administrative law gave the Commission certain discretionary powers and that review of the exercise of discretion should not amount to substituting the Ombudsman's judgment for that of the Commission. Furthermore, the Commission never argued that discretionary powers are absolute and unreviewable. In these circumstances, the Ombudsman's inquiries tended to focus on whether there was maladministration in the concrete circumstances of the case, rather than whether there should be an inquiry at all. As regards the latter question, the Ombudsman exercised discretion by evaluating whether there are grounds for an inquiry, again with reference to the concrete elements available rather than abstract categorization.

2.2 The Development of a Systemic Approach

Article 228 TFEU refers to *instance(s)* of maladministration, as do certain key provisions of the Statute. However, to the best of the present author's recollection, there has never been any suggestion that the European Ombudsman's role in identifying maladministration and seeking solutions is confined to seeking redress in specific cases. Even if that had been the case, the general experience of ombudsmen is that the internal logic of such a role leads it to expand over time. Considerations of efficiency and effectiveness, as well as concern for the interests of individuals who might otherwise find themselves in similar circumstances, lead ombudsmen to try to ensure that general lessons are learnt when particular cases of maladministration are identified.[10] An ombudsman thus naturally tends to become forward-looking as well as backward-looking.

In turn, a focus on preventing maladministration in the future encourages a *systemic* approach: i.e., one that looks at an overall system, such as an organization as a whole, or an administrative process or procedure in general. Systemic maladministration could result from problems that

---

[10] See, for example, A. Abraham, 'Making Sense of the Muddle: The Ombudsman and Administrative Justice, 2002 – 2011' (2012) 34(1) *Journal of Social Welfare and Family Law*, 91.

affect the overall functioning of an organization, or from widespread deficiencies in applying rules or policies.[11] It might also be the result of defects in the relevant rules or policies. In fact, the distinction between poor application and poor rules or policies is not clear-cut, since good rule-making and good policy-making should anticipate and take into account possible difficulties of application, including lack of capacity among those who are supposed to follow, apply, or enforce them.

For ombudsman systems in general, therefore, a systemic approach to preventing maladministration can be described with equal validity as promoting *good* administration. Moreover, in the case of the European Ombudsman, the inclusion of the right to good administration in the Charter of Fundamental Rights of the European Union (Article 41) suggests that the Ombudsman should help to secure that right proactively, through a forward-looking systemic approach, rather than merely helping to pick up the pieces when it is not respected.[12] The following section examines the relevant instruments available to the Ombudsman to fulfil this role.

3 FROM GOOD ADMINISTRATION TO GOOD GOVERNANCE

3.1 Inquiries

The only powers specifically conferred on the European Ombudsman by the Treaty and Statute are to conduct inquiries, to report and to make recommendations. These powers may be exercised either following a complaint, or on the Ombudsman's own initiative. It would be natural to assume that most of the inquiries relevant for the governance role would be the latter kind. Whilst own-initiatives are indeed important, however, the contribution of complaints to the governance role should not be

---

[11] Compare the case law of the Court on infringements: an administrative practice can be the subject-matter of an action for failure to fulfil obligations when it is, to some degree, of a consistent and general nature. For an example of a case where the Court explicitly found a 'systemic' failure by a Member State, see Case C-494/01, *Commission v Ireland* 2005 ECR I-3331.

[12] The sequence in the text is an ideal-typical model of the logic of the ombudsman institution rather than a chronological schema of the development of the European Ombudsman. In practice, the latter developed forward-looking, systemic own-initiative inquiries at an early stage, whereas a mechanism to monitor and encourage learning from maladministration was only put in place a decade later, in 2006.

underestimated. Although many complainants seek redress for harm to their private interests, the Ombudsman's inquiries are not necessarily confined to the complainant's arguments and claims. Systemic issues may be identified and pursued in the public interest, either during an inquiry into a complaint, or through a separate own-initiative inquiry.[13] Furthermore, neither the Treaty nor the Statute makes the right to complain conditional on having a specific interest in alleged maladministration, nor has interpretation added any such requirement. On the contrary, *actio popularis* complaints are possible.[14] In other words, complainants themselves may seek to advance their conception of the public interest, including as regards systemic issues, rather than (or as well as) individual redress. In practice, however, it is unusual, for a complainant to formulate public interest arguments in a way that makes it appropriate for the Ombudsman to focus an inquiry on a systemic issue as defined by the complainant.[15] Normally, the Ombudsman's aim in dealing with such complaints is limited to ensuring that the institution concerned engages in an appropriate level of genuine dialogue with the complainant. The Ombudsman thus avoids being drawn too far into discussion of the merits of substantive policy choices.

To sum up, complaints are not just individual cases; they also provide a mechanism for the Ombudsman to harvest dispersed knowledge relevant to systemic issues. Furthermore, since it is hard to construct a plausible argument that the scope for the Ombudsman's own-initiative inquiries should be narrower than the right to complain, the potential scope of the latter supports the view that the Ombudsman has a broad mandate to be proactive on behalf of the public interest through own-initiative inquiries. Whether the subject was originally identified through complaints or came to the Ombudsman's attention in other ways, the own-initiative power gives the Ombudsman control over timing and the opportunity to research the subject matter fully.

Two of the Ombudsman's earliest attempts to bring about horizontal systemic changes at the EU level took the form of own-initiative

---

[13] Case T-209/00, *Lamberts v Ombudsman* [2002] ECR II-2203 para. 57; Case T-217/11, *Staelen v Ombudsman*, judgment of the General Court of 29 April 2015, ECLI:EU:T:2015:238, para. 156.

[14] On this point, see the opinion of Advocate General Trstenjak in Case C-331/05 P *Internationaler Hilfsfonds v Commission*, [2007] ECR I-5475, para. 59 and Case C-331/05 P, *Internationaler Hilfsfonds v Commission*, 2007 ECR I-05475 para. 26.

[15] For an example of a case where it was found to be appropriate to do so, see www.ombudsman.europa.eu/en/cases/specialreport.faces/en/386/html.bookmark, accessed 9 January 2017.

inquiries. The first succeeded in persuading most of the institutions and bodies, as well as the small number of agencies that existed at the time, to establish rules on public access to documents. The second inquiry led to the European Parliament's approval of the European Code of Good Administrative Behaviour (ECGAB), which was drafted by the Ombudsman. The ECGAB was widely adopted, or proved a source of inspiration, not only at the EU level, but also in the Member States and elsewhere. In both cases, the opening of the own-initiative inquiry was tied to possible maladministration through the suggestion that the absence of clear rules and principles to confine administrative discretion was inefficient and could lead to inconsistency. At the same time, the inquiries were also presented as part of a more ambitious agenda of cultural change towards openness and service to citizens as core elements of good administration. In formulating subsequent own-initiative inquiries, the Ombudsman also tried to strike a balance between these two approaches. In doing so, the guiding idea was that whilst potential criticism of maladministration may encourage institutions to accept specific concrete suggestions, it may also provoke a defensive reaction rather than cooperation in a broader search for greater legitimacy of the EU institutions.

In recent years, given that most institutions are disposed to cooperate, it seemed artificial and unnecessary to frame certain initiatives as formal inquiries. Instead, the Ombudsman took the role of a critical friend, trying to help the institution to improve its legitimacy in the eyes of citizens. This was the case, for example, with the programme of 'visits' to EU agencies, initiated in 2011. The first visits were not originally framed as inquiries and the explanation for them avoided mention of maladministration. Subsequently, however, the visits were classified as own-initiative inquiries, so as to be able to guarantee the security of documents or information provided in confidence by an agency at the Ombudsman's request.

The own-initiative inquiry remains a core instrument of the Ombudsman. In recent years, the office has put increased emphasis on such inquiries, through re-structuring and additional resources. Other instruments are available, however, and also helped the Ombudsman to develop the governance role.

3.2 Other Instruments

Compared to the inquiry, which is expressly foreseen by the Treaty, the Statute and the Ombudsman's implementing provisions, the other instruments that contribute to the governance role are relatively informal and unstructured. The inquiry has a definite procedure, which may include the exercise of powers to inspect documents and take testimony from officials. An inquiry ends with a closing decision and may also involve a draft recommendation and a special report. Since 2006, the Ombudsman has published a report on the follow-up given by the institutions concerned to recommendations and remarks made in closing decisions. From an organizational rather than a strictly legal perspective, one may distinguish between, on the one hand, the *methods* used to carry out an inquiry (analysis of submissions, inspections, taking testimony etc.) and, on the other hand, the *outputs* of the inquiry, which take a specific written form (draft recommendations, special reports, closing decisions, follow-up reports). In turn, methods and outputs both need to be clearly distinguished from *impact*; i.e., concrete changes that result from the inquiry.

Identifying and evaluating the impact of institutions and actions is a notoriously difficult problem in policy analysis and social science. An attempt will be made in Section 4 to identify areas where, arguably, the Ombudsman has had an impact on EU governance. The remainder of this section analyses the instruments, other than inquiries, used by the Ombudsman for this purpose. In doing so, it is important to distinguish (as for inquiries) between *methods* and *outputs*. A fourfold classification of outputs will be suggested below. As regards methods, it would be tiresome and even misleading to attempt to provide a taxonomy. For the purposes of the present analysis, it is sufficient to identify a single broad category of *outreach to other EU and international institutions* and to give some examples.

Outreach is essentially a form of networking. Its strategic purpose is to facilitate cooperation and coordination with other institutions, in order to maximize the effectiveness of the Ombudsman's activities. Concretely, a key component is the exchange of information and ideas (sometimes described as benchmarking or best practice). Some examples of outreach by the Ombudsman to non-EU institutions include contacts with and participation in meetings organized by the Organization for Economic Cooperation and Development (OECD) (especially its work on transparency and integrity in lobbying); the Aarhus Convention secretariat; the Council of Europe; the UN High Commissioner for Human Rights; and the Independent Accountability Mechanisms of international financial institutions. Examples of outreach to EU institutions will emerge from the classification of outputs that follows.

By analogy with inquiries, the relevant outputs are those that take a *specific written form*. Most such outputs can be found on the Ombudsman's website, although often with difficulty since they are not as visible as outputs from inquiries, nor are they easily searchable. The following classification seems useful, although there is inevitably a degree of overlap:

- interventions in public debate,
- statements of principle,
- cooperation agreements,
- advice.

Given that the focus of interest is the substantive impact of these and other outputs in terms of governance (dealt with in Section 4), it will suffice for present purposes to provide a brief sketch of each of the four categories.

Interventions in public debate include contributions to the Conventions on the Charter and the Constitution (1999–2000 and 2002–2003 respectively) and to the reflection group on the future of the European Union (2007–2010), as well as written responses to public consultations organized by the Commission with a view to the preparation of legislative proposals. Examples of the latter include the European Citizens' Initiative (ECI), the review of the Financial Regulation and the Stakeholder Consultation guidelines. The Ombudsman also commented publicly on legislative proposals, in particular on access to documents, as well as seeking to put EU administrative procedures on the legislative agenda.

The best known of the Ombudsman's *statements of principle* and arguably the most influential, has already been mentioned: the ECGAB. The ECGAB was drafted as part of an own-initiative inquiry, which provided a useful means to involve the European Parliament in the process through a special report. Two other significant statements of principle, however, were developed without using the inquiry framework: the Statement of the European Network of Ombudsmen in 2007 and the Public Service Principles of 2013. The Network Statement was a rather remarkable achievement: after months of negotiation, all the national ombudsmen agreed the basic principles of their own relationship to EU law, including the Charter of Fundamental Rights. The Public Service Principles were the Ombudsman's first venture into using public consultation as a mechanism for enhancing both the legitimacy and the potential impact of the Ombudsman's own outputs.

The third category of instrument is the *formal cooperation agreement*, of which there exist three somewhat different instances. The Memorandum of Understanding (MoU) with the European Data Protection Supervisor avoids potential duplication and conflict. It recognizes the special expertise of the European Data Protection Supervisor (EDPS) in data protection matters and allows the Ombudsman to draw on that expertise when carrying out inquiries. The Ombudsman's participation in the EU 'Article 33(2) framework' under the UN Convention on the Rights of Persons with Disabilities was formalized in an exchange of letters with the other partners in the framework.[16] The MoU with the European Investment Bank (EIB) differs from that with the EDPS by covering, among other things, the institutional framework for handling complaints against the EIB.

The fourth and final category is *advice*, which may be provided after inter-service consultations between the Ombudsman's staff and those of the institution, or offered unsolicited, usually in the form of a letter from the Ombudsman.

The above categories constitute only one possible framework for analysis of the Ombudsman's non-inquiry outputs. Furthermore, it would be a mistake to overemphasize the distinction between inquiries and other instruments. The fact that inquiries do not lead to legally binding decisions permits a high degree of flexibility and informality in the way they are conducted. As a result, there is no one-to-one relationship between methods and outputs. Informal methods may be used during inquiries and inquiries may result in, or contribute to, outputs additional to those specifically foreseen for them. In recent years, for example, the Ombudsman has begun to conclude certain inquiries by issuing statements of principle, in the form of guidelines.[17]

4 THE SCOPE AND LIMITS OF THE OMBUDSMAN'S GOVERNANCE ROLE

As the preceding analysis has shown, what may appear at first sight to be a weakness – the absence of power to make legally enforceable decisions – is also a source of strength. Precisely because inquiries do not lead to enforceable decisions, the Ombudsman has wide room for manoeuvre in deciding what, and how, to investigate. The potential range of non-inquiry methods and outputs is even greater. The provisions of the Statute that (i) require the Ombudsman's duties to be performed in accordance with the powers conferred on the EU institutions and bodies by the Treaties, and (ii) exclude complaints about the actions of any other person or body do not significantly curtail the Ombudsman's freedom of action with regard to governance of the EU institutions.

Limits to the Ombudsman's governance role necessarily exist, however.

---

[16] At the time of the exchange of letters, the other partners were the European Parliament, the Commission, the Fundamental Rights Agency and the European Disability Forum.

[17] See, for example, OI/4/2013/CK and OI/8/2014/AN.

As the first European Ombudsman put it: the Ombudsman is not Batman, Robin Hood, Zorro or Asterix.[18] Given the absence of enforcement powers, the Ombudsman's impact depends crucially on perceptions of the *legitimacy* of the office, not only in the eyes of the public, but also among the EU institutions and others whose activities constitute the social reality in which impacts might occur. Legitimacy depends partly on institutional history. Here, there is a certain element of what might be called the Saint Denis principle: it is the first step that matters. In other words, once the Ombudsman has dealt convincingly with a particular subject, further interventions on the same subject, or one that is closely related, are unlikely to occasion surprise. Over time, however, legitimacy based on past practice comes increasingly to depend on the emergence of a coherent pattern that gives meaning and context to the discrete steps. After two decades of operation, it is reasonable to ask whether such a coherent pattern can be found for the Ombudsman's governance role. In the present author's view, the answer is yes, as regards both its conceptual basis and its scope.

The *conceptual basis* depends on three elements that are distinct but mutually supporting: complaints, law and citizenship of the Union. Arguably, the Ombudsman's impact on governance has been greatest when all three elements combine, as with the initiative towards rules on access to documents, which blended the avoidance of complaints, a passage in a Court judgment suggesting a legal obligation to adopt such rules and the idea of accountability to citizens. The link to complaints associates the subject matter to the powers and functions of the Ombudsman that are explicitly set out in the Treaty and Statute. The invocation of law, and the rule of law, is persuasive for EU institutions, which are highly sensitized to respect for legal rights and obligations. Citizenship ties the package together because it has an important legal aspect and complaint to the Ombudsman is one of the fundamental rights of Union citizenship, alongside access to documents and good administration. At the same time, citizenship has a political dimension that provides a channel for the Ombudsman to move through law and good administration into the area of good governance.

The multi-faceted nature of citizenship also contributes to a successful relationship with the European Parliament. The two institutions' relationships with citizens are separate, different in kind and complementary. Citizenship thus provides a conceptual space in which Parliament and the

---

18 Press release No. 12/99, 1 October 1999, 'I'm not Santa Claus says European Ombudsman', available at www.ombudsman.europa.eu/en/press/release.faces/en/85/html.bookmark, accessed 9 January 2017.

Ombudsman can cooperate in relation to governance issues whilst remaining independent of each other. In practice, for example, many of the Ombudsman's interventions in public debate have been at the invitation of the European Parliament, which also, for example, played a key role in the development of the ECGAB and encouraged the Ombudsman and the EIB to agree the MoU.

The *scope* of the Ombudsman's governance role as it has developed over two decades can also best be understood in terms of working out the implications of citizenship of the Union and helping to make it a reality. Central to this approach is the idea that the Union level of governance cannot rely on national traditions or identity as a source of legitimacy. The EU institutions must, therefore, make sustained efforts to win and retain the trust of citizens. This explains the central role that transparency plays in the Ombudsman's governance agenda.

As an aspect of governance, *transparency* cannot be reduced to the right of access to documents, still less to disputes over particular documents. Nor does it mean that the Ombudsman always takes the side of transparency in disputes where other principles are also relevant. On the contrary, the Ombudsman has consistently recognized that transparency needs to be balanced against other public interests, as well as against private rights of data protection, commercial confidentiality and privacy. The present author's view is that, so far and in cooperation with other actors, the Ombudsman has made two major horizontal contributions to transparency in EU governance. The first was to help put and keep transparency on the agendas of the EU institutions through interventions in public debates. The second was to establish an excellent working relationship with the EDPS, so as to avoid diverging approaches to balancing the fundamental rights of public access to documents and data protection. As regards transparency in particular institutions, the Ombudsman has had a positive influence on the EIB and, though perhaps to a lesser extent, the European Medicines Agency. The Ombudsman's impact through these contributions does not mean that all is well with transparency at EU level from a governance perspective. It remains the case that transparency is too often understood merely in terms of responding to public access requests and as a distraction from core business rather than an essential element of the culture of the EU institutions requiring a proactive approach. The Commission's negative and defensive response to the Ombudsman's advice to engage with the Open Government Partnership was particularly significant in this context.[19]

---

[19] See www.ombudsman.europa.eu/activities/cooperation.faces/en/59078/html.bookmark, accessed 9 January 2017.

The need for the EU institutions to win and retain the trust of citizens also justifies the Ombudsman's focus on the adequacy of arrangements for ensuring *ethical conduct*. It is important to emphasize that the Ombudsman's task is not to investigate allegations of individual wrongdoing. Furthermore, although the Ombudsman has a legitimate part to play in ensuring that the institutions themselves deal properly with individuals, including whistle-blowers, this role is of limited relevance from a governance perspective. Individual cases may or may not be indicative of systemic problems and, among other things, the Ombudsman should aim to ensure that institutions avoid both complacency in the absence of scandal and over-reaction when scandal occurs. Again in the personal view of the present author, the Ombudsman's main horizontal impact so far on the ethical aspect of good governance has been to gain a degree of acceptance for three ideas: (i) ethical conduct cannot be reduced to following rules; (ii) the key element required is active leadership by example towards an institutional culture of ethical behaviour; and (iii) the EU institutions are responsible for identifying and managing conflicts of interest – getting individuals to sign declarations does not relieve the institutions themselves of this responsibility. As regards particular institutions, the Ombudsman's positive influence in relation to ethics has been greatest on the European Central Bank and the Commission.

Citizenship also provides the organizing framework for the Ombudsman's focus on *public participation*. This constitutes a key process value that should be hard-wired into EU governance structures, both to protect legitimate private interests, and also as a way of improving the quality of EU policy-making by harvesting dispersed knowledge. The Ombudsman paid particular attention to the ECI by intervening in public debate as part of the legislative process and offering advice following an own-initiative inquiry. As regards impact, it is difficult to disentangle the effects of the Ombudsman's work from the overall results of the ECI, which are disappointing. On the other hand, the MoU with the EIB has proved effective. It committed the Bank to setting up an internal complaints mechanism as part of a different way of doing business that involves greater engagement with stakeholders. The complaints mechanism was therefore intended to have, and has achieved, knock-on effects on other aspects of EIB governance. The EIB has internalized the value of public participation and won praise from the Ombudsman for the procedure that it used for reviewing its transparency policy.

Finally, the three elements that constitute the *conceptual basis* of the Ombudsman's governance role – complaints, law and citizenship – combine in the field where the Ombudsman touches directly on multilevel governance; that is, the implementation and application of EU law in the

Member States. As regards the infringement procedure, the Ombudsman sought to balance the prevailing realist narrative of political bargaining by emphasizing its role as a mechanism for public participation in maintaining the rule of law. This approach bore fruit in the Commission's 2002 Communication on relations with the complainant in respect of infringements of Community law and, later, in the design of the 'EU Pilot' procedure. In parallel, the European Ombudsman also supported and encouraged the role of national ombudsmen in ensuring that EU law is correctly applied in the Member States through the European network of Ombudsmen. The overall impact of the Network is difficult to assess, although it is certainly uneven across the Member States. The key variable, which the European Ombudsman has little possibility to influence, is the extent of the powers accorded to the national ombudsmen within the various national constitutional and legal orders. The European Ombudsman's proposal that the EU Treaties should include a citizens' right to a non-judicial remedy was not taken up in the abortive Constitution, or the subsequent Lisbon Treaty.

The overall picture that emerges is of a governance role that emerges naturally from the European Ombudsman's work with complaints and concern for good administration. The conceptual basis and coherence of this role, focused on complaints, law and citizenship, also creates natural limits to its scope and thus avoids the risks to legitimacy that might otherwise arise. One might encapsulate this by saying that, without taking a substantive view of the public interest in particular policy fields, the Ombudsman promotes a conception of how the EU institutions should determine and safeguard the public interest. At the same time, the Ombudsman carries out the governance role against the background of an understanding of EU policies and a commitment to the EU and its citizens, so that the institutions understand that the Ombudsman is a friendly critic and that the purpose of criticism is to help them to win and maintain citizens' trust.

5 THE FUTURE OF THE GOVERNANCE ROLE

It seems unlikely that the legitimacy problems of the EU and its institutions are going to disappear any time soon. It is in the general EU interest, therefore, that the Ombudsman should be active as regards EU governance in order to help the institutions to enhance trust in their structure and functioning. Two aspects of how the Ombudsman works facilitate this role and provide a foundation for its further development in the future.

The first has already been mentioned. The Ombudsman does not just deal with problems that arrive piecemeal through complaints. The internal logic of a concern for good administration leads to a direct focus on systemic issues and organizational design in order to structure discretion. To be clear, this is not a question of either/or. On the contrary, the synergy between complaints and *ex officio* analysis gives special value to the Ombudsman's work on governance. There is scope to exploit this synergy further by systematic scanning of the legislative agenda, in particular the Commission's work programme, to identify relevant items, focus resources on the most important areas and prepare the Ombudsman's contributions in a timely way.

The second helpful aspect of the Ombudsman's way of working follows from the first. The Ombudsman can follow up on issues to monitor whether agreed actions are being implemented, whether intended results are being achieved, and whether additional or revised measures would be useful. In other words, the Ombudsman can complete the office's own policy cycle and help the other institutions to complete theirs. As noted above, one of the Ombudsman's outputs does indeed focus on the follow-up to certain decisions closing inquiries. There is undoubtedly ample scope to develop additional outputs and more effective instruments for following up the Ombudsman's governance contributions more generally.

As regards the scope of the governance role, the analysis in this chapter identifies three conceptual pillars that support a trio of subjects. It is possible, indeed probable, that this framework should evolve over time. At present, however, what might be labelled the two 'three-packs' (complaints-law-citizenship and transparency-ethical conduct-participation) continue to provide, in the author's view, a sound basis for the Ombudsman to achieve a lasting and significant impact on EU governance. In order to avoid potential misunderstanding, some further explanation may be needed at this point about the term citizenship. As part of the Ombudsman's conceptual 'three-pack', citizenship of the Union cannot be reduced to a strict legal analysis of the rights set out in the Treaty and Charter of Fundamental Rights. Nor does it imply that non-citizens are excluded or relegated to second-class status. The significance of citizenship of the Union for the Ombudsman's contribution to good governance of the EU is constitutional. From this perspective, citizenship implies the right to know and the right to participate. Both rights apply not only *vis-à-vis* EU institutions and actors, but also *vis-à-vis* national authorities and national actors when they are dealing with EU matters. It is true that the concrete legal expression of these rights is currently limited, especially as regards national authorities and actors. That is why the European Ombudsman, for whom law is only one tool in the box, has an essential role to play in making a reality of those rights. It is also true that the European Ombudsman cannot inquire into the activities of national authorities or actors. That simply adds to the importance of the Ombudsman's non-inquiry instruments and outputs.

In conclusion, it seems useful to raise a question about the visibility of the Ombudsman's governance role. As was already mentioned, the Ombudsman's non-inquiry outputs, which are so important for the governance role, are not prominently displayed on the website, nor are they easily searchable. Perhaps the time may be right to re-think the presentation of the overall range of outputs in order to reflect more accurately the scope of the Ombudsman's work.

9. From maladministration to good administration: retrospective reflections on a ten-year journey

P. Nikiforos Diamandouros

One of the best-known and memorable poems by Constantine P. Cavafy, the well-known Greek poet from Alexandria, is entitled 'Ithaka'. Its central theme is that life should be conceptualized as a long journey full of adventure, whose value ultimately resides not so much in reaching the final destination but, instead, in the wisdom the traveller derives from the rich and varied experiences accumulated along the way.

The ten years (2003–2013) that I was fortunate enough to spend as European Ombudsman were for me a memorable journey, full of rich experiences, both personal and professional, which I greatly treasure and regard as a major part of my own Ithaka.

The invitation to contribute to this anniversary volume, which the editors have generously extended to me, affords me the welcome opportunity to pursue two goals. First, to record some of the more salient experiences of the 'European' moment of my journey, when, as European Ombudsman, I endeavoured to situate good administration and the commitment to serve citizens that it pre-eminently implies at the very centre of the European Union's (EU's) administrative culture. My second goal is to complement this account with some brief, general reflections concerning the nature of the European Ombudsman institution and the broader, *systemic* challenges and dilemmas, which, in my view, it faces diachronically, and which transcend individual incumbents.

1 THE BACKGROUND: A BROAD OUTLINE

I wish to begin my account by acknowledging three background factors or sets of parameters, which, in various but important ways, were to affect my choices in leading the institution of the European Ombudsman forward. The first concerns the 'prior learning' associated with my academic background as a university professor of comparative politics specializing for nearly three decades in the study of democracy and of the rule of law. The *theoretical* training associated with this field of study equipped me with the knowledge necessary for appreciating, *inter alia,* the critical importance of institutions in shaping the conditions and settings necessary for enabling citizens meaningfully to participate in the democratic game and, in the memorable formulation of a quintessential document of the Enlightenment, to engage in 'the pursuit of happiness'.[1]

The second set of background factors, which was to play a major role in shaping my strategy for the future of the ombudsman institution in the EU, was intimately linked with my prior experience as the founding Ombudsman of Greece in the five years (1998–2003) immediately preceding my initial election as European Ombudsman. This experience entailed an abrupt and challenging transition from the sedate role of an academic theorist of democracy to that of a practitioner/applied social scientist called upon to engage in an experiment in institution building. The goal of such an experiment was to foster the creation of an administrative culture expressive of the logic of consensus, compromise, suasion and, ultimately, trust – a logic quintessentially associated with democracy in the contemporary world – which would self-consciously be focused on how to enable the Greek civil service best to serve and to benefit citizens and, more generally, users. Succinctly put, this is a logic which seeks to promote the notion that the state exists to serve the citizen and not vice versa. I note that such a logic was intrinsically alien to the highly conflictual culture which informs both society and state in the country in which the ideas associated with this experiment were introduced. A logic also which self-consciously sought to elevate the notion of 'best practices' into a central and guiding principle of Greek administrative culture. The experience derived from this experiment was of inestimable value to me in my years at the European level of governance.

The third set of background factors which significantly influenced my initial steps as European Ombudsman was the intellectual legacy bequeathed to me by my predecessor, Jacob Söderman, the founding European Ombudsman, who imaginatively and creatively established the institution and sagaciously led it during its critical formative years. His major achievements were, in my view, four: first and foremost, he convincingly succeeded in squarely positioning what for the EU legal order was a novel institution in the intellectual tradition of what is generally known as the 'classical ombudsman model'. In the contemporary world,

---

1 See the American Declaration of Independence, Preamble.

this model is firmly embedded in the rule of law, democracy and human rights and has its historical, cultural and political roots in the Nordic and Anglo-Saxon political and constitutional traditions. Secondly, he elevated the principle of serving citizens into a major, if not paramount, concern for the new institution. In practical terms, doing so implied a systematic commitment to administrative practices designed to maximize the capacity of citizens to seek *redress* in their dealings with the European public administration, thereby injecting the notion of European citizenship, entirely novel at the time, with tangible meaning and substance. Thirdly, he ensured the inclusion of an article concerning the right to good administration in the Charter of Fundamental Rights of the European Union (henceforth, 'the Charter'), which the European Commission (henceforth 'the Commission'), the Council of the European Union (henceforth 'the Council'), and the European Parliament (henceforth 'the Parliament') adopted as a non-binding document in Nice in 2000. The Charter was to acquire legal value equal to the Treaties with the adoption of the Treaty of Lisbon in 2009. The article on good administration was greatly to benefit European citizens and, over the years, commensurately to enhance the capacity of the European Ombudsman to promote good administration within the EU institutions. Finally, he bequeathed to me a well-functioning and efficient office, staffed with knowledgeable, intelligent and highly motivated professionals, who were to serve me loyally and creatively throughout my ten years in office, and were to prove ready to respond with imagination, resolve, enthusiasm, and commitment to the various challenges which inevitably arose along the way.

Early on, Söderman's efforts to serve citizens took the form of defining the central mission of the new institution as that of combating maladministration. I hasten to add that the Maastricht Treaty establishing the ombudsman institution did not define maladministration. It was thus left to the Ombudsman to do so and then to put it into practice. Responding to an invitation by the Parliament to do so, Söderman proceeded, in his *Annual Report* for 1997, to put forward a definition of maladministration, which, he argued, 'occurs when a public body fails to act in accordance with a rule or principle which is binding upon it'.[2]

Armed with this definition, Söderman went on to explore ways of expanding its application and of bringing it to the attention of both citizens and the EU public administration. To that effect, he produced in 2001 a code of good administrative behaviour, which the Parliament swiftly

[2] European Ombudsman. *Annual Report for 1997* (Luxembourg: The Publications Office, 1998), p. 23.

adopted. Formally known as the European Code of Good Administrative Behaviour, it was to serve as the basis for similar codes adopted subsequently by the Commission and the Council. It was also to prove a most useful and powerful weapon which added to the effectiveness of my efforts systematically to promote best practices not only within the EU public administration but also in a number of Member States, where it was, over the years, adopted.[3]

The final set of background factors which helped shape the broader context for many of the initiatives I was to undertake during my years as European Ombudsman, was a series of developments, which occurred in the period 1999–2001, that were to have a direct and lasting impact on the evolution of the institution. To appreciate their significance, it is necessary to recall that the provision for the establishment of the Ombudsman formed part of the chapter on citizenship which the Treaty of Maastricht introduced in the European legal order as part of a deliberate, more general effort by the Member States firmly to link the EU with democracy. In turn, the concern with, and focus on, democracy reflected the *Zeitgeist* of a particular historical moment, when, in the wake of the elimination of communism as a credible competing paradigm for the political organization of national entities, this form of government had acquired virtually uncontested legitimacy around the world. In these circumstances, the legitimacy to be conferred upon the EU, the happy product of top-down, inter-governmental arrangements relying primarily on indirect sources of legitimation, such as the rule of law and 'permissive consensus', through explicit association with democracy constituted an opportunity of momentous significance which the leaders of the Union could hardly afford to miss.[4]

Together with the notion of citizenship, the emergence of the logic of democracy in the EU brought along novel concepts, such as transparency and accountability. These concepts had long been associated with administrative best practices championed by, among others, ombudsman institutions in the Nordic and Anglo-Saxon parts of Europe (and in states that were the political and cultural heirs of the former British Empire) and used systematically to combat maladministration. In many ways, these concepts were dissonant with, if not alien to, the administrative culture, which, in the four decades following the founding of the

---

[3] The Code is available on the Ombudsman's website www.ombudsman.europa.eu/en/resources/code.faces#, accessed 9 January 2017.

[4] For the citizenship of the Union, see now Treaty on European Union, especially Articles 9–11 and Treaty on the Functioning of the Union (TFEU), especially Articles 20–25.

European Coal and Steel Community (1951) and, subsequently, of the European Economic Community (1957) that was to become the EU, had gradually become the dominant paradigm for the European public administration's *modus operandi.* This administrative culture bore the indelible imprint of the principles governing the French public administration in the critical formative years of the European institutions. Most noticeable in this respect was the influence exercised by the highly prestigious École Normale Supérieure. Established in the late eighteenth century, this august institution represents *par excellence* the values of expertise, meritocracy, authority, and top-down organization based on seniority that, since Napoleonic times, have been the distinguishing trait of French public administration. These values and principles became an integral part of the incipient European public administration through the decisive influence exercised over its development by towering figures, such as Robert Marjolin and Émile Noel. The former was one of the first French Commissioners to serve with distinction in the critical early years of the Hallstein Commission (1958–1967), while the latter held the post of Secretary General of the European Commission for 30 years (1957–1987) and, in many ways, decisively shaped its administrative ethos.

During these long, formative decades, this ethos and the administrative culture that it gave rise to served as a firm underpinning upon which the Commission gradually constructed its identity and role as the locomotive for, and 'strategic planner' of, the European integration project that the Founding Fathers of that initiative had from the very start far-sightedly assigned to it. This was a role which the Commission pursued diligently, with imagination and determination, in the process reshaping and reconceptualising its own understanding of its role and of the optimal means to be utilized in order to fulfil its mission of pushing that project ever forward. In many ways, the Delors Commission (1985–1994) represented the high point of this conceptualization of the role of the Commission and exemplified the ethos associated with it. As subsequent developments were to demonstrate, the Delors Commission was, in many ways, to serve as the *terminus ad quem* for this early period and for the formula of governance and administrative ethos associated with it.

Two major developments, temporally contiguous but politically and organizationally unrelated to one another, were to clash directly with, and ultimately to undermine, this conceptualization of the role of the Commission in the Union's formula of governance and administrative ethos driven by a top-down logic. Both were linked to what I shall call the 'era of democratization' inaugurated by the adoption of the Maastricht Treaty and by the enhanced significance and salience accorded to accountability and transparency as principles designed to inform and to drive forward a novel *modus operandi* characterized by increased oversight and control over the Union's institutions. Both were very significantly to affect the manner in which the Commission would operate in the future and substantively to reshape its role. The first was the resignation of the Santer Commission in 1999, in the wake of allegations of misconduct and impropriety emanating from an increasingly assertive and combative Parliament (whose role the Maastricht Treaty had significantly enhanced) and involving Commissioner Edith Cresson, which were later to be upheld by the Court of Justice of the European Union. The second was the largest ever enlargement of the Union, which in 2004 increased its membership from 15 to 25 (and shortly thereafter to 27). An important by-product of this development was the enhancement of the powers of the Council and, in combination with the surging influence of the Parliament, a perceptible shift in the logic of decision-making in the Union institutions themselves towards practices more closely adhering to an inter-governmental rather than a 'federalist' logic.

A direct by-product of these developments was a significant, not to say sharp, change in the way the Commission's role came to be conceptualized within the Union. From being the strategic planner for, and locomotive of, the European project, the institution came increasingly to be regarded and gradually to behave more as an executive organ, whose activities were subject to a novel logic of oversight and scrutiny that was very much at odds with the dominant administrative culture that had long been its hallmark. Two illustrative examples of policy initiatives exemplifying this change in the ethos of governance at the EU level will serve to clarify this point. First, the strengthening and re-focusing in 1999, in the wake of the veritable earthquake unleashed by the Santer Commission resignation, of the Union's anti-fraud office, henceforth known by its French acronym as OLAF (office européen de lutte contre la fraude), sought to signal the Union institutions' determination to combat maladministration and corruption through greater transparency and accountability.

The second policy initiative signalling a shift in the Union's approach to citizens that I wish to highlight was Regulation 1049/2001 concerning public access to documents. The new Regulation stood on its head the long-standing practice of regarding all documents in the possession of EU institutions as confidential and subject to release at the discretion of the institution concerned, and made such documents in principle accessible to all, subject only to clearly defined and publicly known exceptions. In so doing, it significantly expanded transparency for the benefit of citizens, in the process empowering them and making it easier all round to combat maladministration. I recall in this context that the accession of Sweden and Finland to the Union in 1995 combined with an already present

Denmark to provide significant political weight to administrative principles and practices of Nordic provenance long attuned to the need to place citizens at the centre of their strategies of governance.[5]

This shift in emphasis neatly reflected a commensurate change in the language employed by the European public administration in its relations with the public. In ideal-typical terms, the top-down paradigm governing such relations in the period before the Treaty of Maastricht had generated a public administration language and discourse exuding a strictly bureaucratic and, therefore, distant logic, which distinguished between members of the public on the basis of their obligations towards the state or simply their functions *vis-à-vis* the administration. Thus, the categories most frequently used for members of the public having dealings with the administration were '*les administrés*', '*les contribuables*' for taxpayers, and '*les usagers*' for users. Such categories astutely confined those members' relations with the state to the strictly administrative realm, in the process accurately capturing their status as subjects – a category implicitly emphasizing obligations rather than rights. In sharp contrast to this state of affairs, the logic governing the new paradigm of relations with the public inaugurated by the Treaty of Maastricht was, as already indicated, marked by a heightened concern with, and sensitivity to, democracy. The result was a commensurate shift in the logic of the language used by the public administration, best exemplified by the adoption of the term 'citizens', who, at the formal level, were henceforth recognized as carriers of rights guaranteed by the Union's Treaties and not just of obligations.

At the time, therefore, of the transition from the first to the second European Ombudsman (2003), the Commission found itself beset by significant uncertainty, disarray and disorientation, as it endeavoured to (re) define its role in a post-Santer age increasingly marked by the bottom-up logic of democratic discourse, and by enhanced external oversight, scrutiny, and control of its activities. In effect, this state of affairs represented a tangible and direct threat to the Commission's administrative culture, ethos, and associated practices shaped over the previous four decades. Its most tangible external manifestation was a remarkably defensive mentality and a visible lack of enthusiasm, reticence, if not aversion, towards novel ways of confronting the challenges emerging from changed circumstances, which gradually but increasingly visibly descended upon the

[5] Regulation (EC) No. 1049/2001 of the European Parliament and of the Council of 30 May 2001 regarding public access to European Parliament, Council and Commission documents, 2001 OJ L 145 p. 43.

Commission. Though at first unspoken and unacknowledged, this mentality pervaded the Commission's actions and approach to the multitude of novel challenges confronting it, and severely complicated its relations with the outside world, including citizens, and external control mechanisms of accountability, such as the Ombudsman.

The 2004 enlargement of the EU coincided with my first year as European Ombudsman. Its impact on the Commission should be understood at two levels. On the one hand, it undoubtedly opened up challenging new opportunities and possibilities for new initiatives designed to create institutional mechanisms and structures capable of responding to the demands, both institutional and political, which unavoidably accompanied the arrival of ten (and soon to be 12) new member states on the European scene. On the other hand, the very creation of these mechanisms and structures inevitably implied the emergence of new pressures and demands, not least from citizens, which confronted the Commission with novel and pressing challenges calling for imaginative and creative policy responses and solutions.

2 THE EUROPEAN OMBUDSMAN IN THE POST-SANTER AND POST-ENLARGEMENT AGE

The conditions just outlined, defined, in many ways, the institutional and political parameters within which the European Ombudsman institution was to operate and proceed in seeking to fulfil its mandate. Seen from my perspective as Ombudsman, these same conditions opened up important and welcome opportunities for moving the institution forward, for implementing a novel strategy, and for fulfilling my vision for it. Two of these stand out. The first sprang from the Commission's decision to set up a number of new agencies, through which to pursue and promote various policy targets. The rapid proliferation of these agencies, which in a space of ten years (2003–2013) grew from fewer than ten to over 40, created a fertile institutional space for the European Ombudsman to exercise his role as an accountability body charged with the task of exercising oversight and control over the Union's institutions and, more generally, of combating maladministration. This particular task was to occupy an increasingly important share of the European Ombudsman's resources and energies and, over the years, was to yield rich results in promoting better administration on the part of European institutions. The high point of this process was the declaration of the agencies, in the 2010 Lisbon meeting of their co-ordinating body, that they would henceforth adopt the European Code of Good Administrative Behaviour and abide by its principles in their relations with citizens – in the process ensuring that the institutional landscape within which they interacted with the public acquired well-defined, transparent and predictable rules. The resulting clarity and enhanced uniformity in administrative practices strengthened the capacity of citizens to engage meaningfully with, and, if need be, hold accountable a set of EU institutions, whose activities, such as *inter alia* the environment, food safety and medicines, affected their daily lives in direct and profound ways.

The second opportunity for the Ombudsman which the 2004 enlargement brought about, was the expansion and deepening of the network of ombudsman institutions in the Member States, formally known as the European Network of Ombudsmen. The purpose of this network, discerningly and far-sightedly set up by Jacob Söderman, was to inform citizens throughout the Union of their rights as European citizens, as enshrined in the Charter. The entry in the Union of ten, soon to be 12, new Member States, all but two of which (Cyprus and Malta) had emerged from decidedly non-democratic political and institutional environments and cultures, effectively presented the European Ombudsman with a unique set of challenges and opportunities. Succinctly put, these entailed reaching out to citizens and systematically familiarizing them with the rights and advantages accruing to them from European, as distinct from national, citizenship, which the Maastricht Treaty had introduced into European legal order.

In pursuit of this goal, I devoted a very large part of my first year in office, the year leading to the 2004 enlargement, to visiting all new Member States and to meeting with as wide an array of actors in the company of the national ombudsman-colleague, who always served as host and co-organizer. As a rule, these actors included the head of state, the prime minister, ministers overseeing the public administration, selected members of the opposition, parliamentarians, political parties, presidents of the courts and senior members of the judiciary, organized interests, civil society organizations, and, to be sure, ordinary citizens. The format of the meetings ranged from face-to-face encounters with principal national figures, to small meetings and lectures to large audiences, usually at universities, and was designed to generate maximum multiplier outcomes from such visits. Two distinct and concrete outcomes of direct benefit to the Ombudsman issued from these developments. To begin with, the number of complaints but also of inquiries, from these states reaching the Office of the European Ombudsman grew significantly, in the process contributing to greater awareness of not only rights but also of redress mechanisms and opportunities available to citizens through European citizenship. The second positive outcome was the growing enhancement of the stature and influence of the European Network of Ombudsmen, which over time emerged as a major instrument of collaboration, through which ombudsmen in the Member States could coordinate their activities for the benefit of their citizens. In addition, through the medium of the European Ombudsman, who served as coordinator of the Network, they could have a voice at the European level.

Taken together, all these developments generated over time a perceptible and powerful dynamic, which almost inexorably set the European Ombudsman on a new policy path, whereby the goal of combating maladministration was gradually, but consciously and deliberately, replaced by the systematic pursuit of good administration as the institution's supreme policy goal. It is important to stress that this shift in focus was not in itself, and neither did it claim to be, entirely novel. The Statute of the institution, adopted as early as 1994, clearly mandated the European Ombudsman to, as far as possible, 'seek a solution' to a complaint designed to eliminate the instance of maladministration and to satisfy the complaint.[6] In addition, the European Code of Good Administrative Behaviour, initially adopted in 2001, sought to advance the same policy goals. What was novel, however, in the new approach adopted by the Ombudsman as of 2004, was the deliberate effort to endow the institution with a more theoretically grounded and coherent approach to addressing instances of maladministration. This new approach was explicitly and systematically based on the fundamental premise that, stripped to its essentials, good administration included two components: first and foremost, respect for the rule of law and, second, the pursuit of fair and equitable solutions, whose logic is not confined to the minimal requirements prescribed by law but goes beyond them. I sought to capture this dimension of good administration by the pithy phrase that 'there is life beyond legality', which, while raising eyebrows in that component of the legal community which remained wedded to a 'strict constructionist' interpretation of the law, was welcomed by those in the same community recognizing the practical utility and added value of such an approach. I hasten to add that such an approach was especially useful and valuable for a legal order, such as the European one, which had historically been constructed on strict adherence to the law, with little attention, if any, being systematically paid to principles of good administration before

[6] See Article 3(5) of Decision of the European Parliament 94/262/ECSC, EC, Euratom of 9 March 1994 on the regulations and general conditions governing the performance of the Ombudsman's duties, 1994 OJ L 113 p. 15, as last amended by Decision of the European Parliament 2008/587/EC, Euratom of 18 June 2008, 2008 OJ L 189 p. 25.

the advent of the Treaty of Maastricht.[7] Under the conceptualization conveyed by the notion of life beyond legality, good administration is delimited by the critical distinction between those actions of institutions that are understood to be *contra legem* and, therefore, by definition constituting acts of maladministration, and those that are just *extra legem.* The conceptual space thus delineated constitutes the *chasse gardée*, the privileged area of good administration and hence of ombudsman activity, where ethical principles and values, in addition to legal rules, can be brought to bear in constructing a dense institutional environment driven by the logic of service to citizens or, as I chose to call it, a service culture.

The essential elements of a service culture are, in turn, rooted in the logic of citizenship and, by extension, of democracy and are driven by the principle that the state (and, hence, the public administration), exists to serve the citizen and not vice versa. Put otherwise, the principles of a service culture imply an expectation that, in carrying out his or her duties, the civil servant should do more than merely not break the law. At a more practical level, service culture, understood in ideal-typical terms, implies the adoption of positive-sum approaches to problem solving, and the pursuit of solutions that privilege fairness and proportionality in decisions affecting citizens. The major advantage of such approaches is that they consciously and deliberately eschew the search for, and assignation of, blame and seek instead to identify solutions that are the least onerous for the complainant/citizen. In so doing, they contribute systematically and substantively to the accumulation of trust – that social capital that is so critical to the construction of a fair society and a fair democracy. Thus, conceptualized, good administration acquires a powerful ethical content that finds its legal grounding in, among others, the Charter, to which the Treaty of Lisbon accorded legal value equal to that of the Treaties, and especially Article 41.

The ethical dimension of good administration, also neatly captured by the European Code of Good Administrative Behaviour, was to inform my vision of the European Ombudsman's mission throughout my ten years in office. To be sure, the *ultimate* beneficiaries of such a vision of good administration were the citizens. For it was they who, in the final analysis, bore the brunt of, and suffered the consequences of, acts of maladministration committed by the European public administration. It was for

---

[7] See P. Nikiforos Diamandouros, 'The Relationship Between the Principle of Good Administration and Legal Obligations', in Carl Baudenbacher, Claus Gulmann, Koen Lenaerts, Emmanuel Coulon and Barbier de La Serre (eds.), *Liber Amicorum en l'honneur de/in honour of Bo Vesterdorf* (Brussels: Bruylant, 2007), 315–41.

this very reason, however, that the *immediate* target of the Ombudsman's efforts to promote good administration, thus defined, were the European institutions themselves.

The challenges confronting the European Ombudsman, as he set out to fulfil this goal and to familiarize the public administration with the principles informing this conceptualization of good administration, were, simply put, formidable. Seized by the defensive atmosphere and mentality that the Santer Commission debacle had generated in the Union institutions, the public administration found itself, on the whole, and with only occasional, if not infrequent, exceptions, ill prepared to respond positively to initiatives adhering to a logic for administrative action that went beyond the 'safe' preserve of what the law prescribed. The frequent initial response of the services, when confronted with a request to take principles of good administration into account when addressing a complaint, was to signal their disinclination to follow the Ombudsman's recommendations, unless they were so mandated by the Court. To be sure, in adopting such an approach, the institutions were acting within their *legal* prerogatives, since the Ombudsman's decisions are not legally binding and cannot force the administration to accept them. From the point of view of good administration, however, such a reaction was not only self-defeating but also profoundly unfair and hostile to the interests of citizens and decidedly dysfunctional as far as the Union's relations with citizens was concerned.

The Ombudsman's response to this situation was to launch a series of 'good will' offensives and actively to reach out to the institutions with the intent of systematically informing them of their obligations, as these were enshrined in their own codes of good administration and the Charter. Over the years, I personally visited all the major institutions and met with both top and, where necessary, middle, management in an effort to familiarize them with the philosophy underlying the notion of a service culture and to disabuse them of the fears associated with the blame culture – so long the rule in the European public administration. These visits included the Commission, which accounted for more than 70 per cent of complaints reaching the Ombudsman, but also the Parliament (over whose administrative affairs I had jurisdiction), the Council, the Court, the Court of Auditors, the European Central Bank, and the European Investment Bank (EIB), etc.

The Ombudsman also put pressure on the agencies, individually and through their co-ordinating body, to adopt the European Code of Good Administrative Behaviour and to abide by its principles. Since many of the agencies dealt with issues, such as the environment, food safety and medicines, which touched citizens in their daily activities and lives, bringing them within the scope of the Code was an important development which significantly enhanced the Ombudsman's stature as the Union's Guardian of Good Administration and as a visible, vocal, and effective defender of citizens' rights.

This, in other words, was a campaign for the long haul, which required persistence, patience, determination and unrelenting commitment to the idea that solutions expressive of a positive-sum logic, embodying fairness and proportionality, based on consensus and compromise, and arrived at through dialogue, suasion and respect of the other, were preferable to conflict, confrontation, blame and zero-sum approaches. This was so, because solutions based on a positive-sum logic better captured the ethical component of good administration and, over time, contributed substantively to the accumulation of trust and ultimately to the quality of democratic life in the Union.

What underlay the institutions' reluctance to accept the Ombudsman's recommendations was the fear, most often articulated by the legal services of the institutions involved, that accepting an Ombudsman recommendation would, whether directly or indirectly, imply admitting to fault. It was above all the fear of the potential legal consequences of such an admission – itself a constitutive element of a blame culture – that drove the institutions to opt for zero-sum solutions, which, from the point of view of both good administrative practice and the citizens concerned, was clearly dysfunctional and suboptimal. Over the years, many battles were fought over this crucial point. Many were the instances, when institutions, while continuing to insist that they had done nothing wrong, proceeded, at some subsequent point in time, quietly to change their rules and to adopt the Ombudsman's recommendations, without acknowledging the circumstances and reasons that had led them to do so. Not infrequent also were instances when institutions, while holding fast to the notion that they had acted properly and had done nothing wrong, proceeded, nevertheless, to accept the Ombudsman's recommendations, explaining their behaviour as an expression of respect for the Ombudsman's moral authority. Classical examples of such a situation were instances when a recalcitrant administration would take the view that it was unable to accept the Ombudsman's recommendation because 'the law did not provide' for it. The Ombudsman's usual response was to ask the institution involved to point to a specific legal provision forbidding it to act as recommended. Since such a provision was very often lacking, the matter was not infrequently settled in line with the Ombudsman's recommendations. But only after long discussion and exchanges, often spanning more than a year or even two, and only after the invocation of the Ombudsman's moral authority by the institution involved had served as a *deus ex machina* in providing a face-saving argument for the administration to comply with the Ombudsman's recommendation. Seen from a long-term perspective, these frequent skirmishes with the administration were, in my view, par for the course. What counted, in the final analysis, was that step by gradual step the Ombudsman's approach managed to make inroads into the public administration's daily practices that inscribed themselves in the logic of a service culture and, in so doing, substantively benefited citizens and good administration.

The Ombudsman's moral authority is a subject often referred to but rarely analysed. French administrative practice speaks of the ombudsman institution, known between 1973 and 2011 as *le Médiateur de la République,* as an '*autorité morale*', in order to underscore the ethical content of the ombudsman's activities and to distinguish it from the law and from the legal authority deriving from it. In a broader context, however, the moral authority of the ombudsman is very much a function of the degree to which an incumbent is able to demonstrate, in tangible, explicit, but also implicit and unspoken, ways, his or her capacity unwaveringly to protect and promote the institution's independence, fairness and impartiality. Such qualities can be detected from the incumbent's actions, decisions, public utterances, and, ultimately, from the ethical content, which s/he manages to impart to his/her institution as a whole, qualities that come to be recognized by the wider institutional settings within which s/he operates, by the public administration, but also by the citizens at large. Put otherwise, moral authority is a form of legitimacy, which is accumulated gradually and with sustained effort and can easily be squandered and lost. It is, therefore, to be carefully nurtured, studiously protected and systematically built upon for the benefit of both the institution involved and, above all, the citizens whom it serves and to whom it is ultimately accountable.

Moral authority, finally, is an important underpinning for another quality that is evanescent and hard to express in concrete terms: influence. Once again, influence is rarely tangible, indirectly felt, and is as often an attribute of an individual as of an institution, which is bestowed from without and is subject to the same vagaries as legitimacy and moral authority. Given these considerations, one of the high moments of my tenure as European Ombudsman occurred in 2010, when, in the context of the impending procedure for the newly elected Parliament to elect a new European Ombudsman, the *Financial Times* recognized the European Ombudsman as one of the 30 most influential individuals in the Brussels-based EU institutional environment.[8] Aside from its obviously positive

---

[8] See Stanley Pignal, Helen Warell, Steve Bernard and Jeremy Lemer, 'Eurostars', *Financial Times*, 3 June 2009, www.ft.com/cms/s/0/3b3aca9a-5022-

implications for the institution, this admittedly rare distinction constituted, above all, a welcome confirmation of the rich, long-term benefits issuing from the determined and unwavering pursuit of a particular vision for the European Ombudsman I had from the very outset adopted. That of the Guardian of Good Administration in the EU charged with ensuring that, in their relations with Union institutions, European citizens would, to recall the late John Rawls, be the happy beneficiaries of both 'justice and fairness'.[9]

3 PROACTIVITY AS A CENTRAL COMPONENT OF GOOD ADMINISTRATION

A final component of this 'second generation' conceptualization of good administration that the European Ombudsman adopted and pursued from 2003 onwards was proactivity. The notion, that is, that principles of good administrative practice expect the public administration as a body and its civil servants as individuals *proactively* to explore ways in which to improve the quality of the services rendered to citizens and the public at large. By its very nature, proactivity is driven by an open-ended logic, whose major intellectual, practical but also ethical advantage is that it encourages initiative, creativity and imagination, as well as promotes the systematic and judicious use of discretion in the handling of problems brought forward by citizens and other interlocutors of the institutions, in this case those of the EU. Whether at the systemic level or at that of the individual civil servant, discretion used as an instrument of proactivity implies an intellectual attitude driven by the logic of anticipating rather than reacting to problems and of *proactively* searching for responses that are least onerous for the citizen. Such an attitude stands on its head the paradigm of a reactive logic of public administration, in which complaints from citizens are perceived as 'a nuisance', which distracts civil servants from what is often referred to as 'core business'. To be sure, such a paradigm, as well as the resulting attitude and approach towards citizens are clearly incompatible with the logic of proactivity and, by extension, of good administration as defined and elaborated over time by the Ombudsman. In fact, as I clearly put it in a number of my public utterances, failure to exercise discretion in seeking

11de-9530-00144feabdc0.html#axzz4DiZK81MU, as well as http://blogs.ft.com/brusselsblog/2009/06/03/, accessed 9 January 2017.

[9] See John Rawls, *Justice as Fairness: A Restatement*, edited by Erin Kelly (Cambridge, MA: Harvard University Press, 2001), and John Rawls, *A Theory of Justice* (Cambridge, MA: Harvard University Press, 1999).

to address a problem could well amount to an act of maladministration and would be examined under such a prism by the Ombudsman and his services.

It is, nevertheless, important to bear in mind that such an attitude was not, as might at first glance appear, the result of deliberate laxity, ill-disposition or sheer negativity towards citizens. It should be regarded rather as an integral part of the lingering but powerful legacy created and left behind by the logic and ethos of the pre-Maastricht era, whose top-down administrative culture stressed efficiency and expertise in dealing with '*les administrés*', '*les usagers*' (users) and '*les contribuables*' (taxpayers), instead of accountability towards citizens, as mandated by the Treaty of Maastricht. According to this earlier and embedded paradigm, 'core business' concerned moving the European project forward. And this was *par excellence* the *raison d'être* of the European public administration during the pre-Maastricht era. Viewed from that systemic perspective, requests or complaints coming from individual citizens that could not readily be subsumed under the systemic and long-range conceptual categories informing the dominant paradigm of the time could well be regarded as distracting the public administration from its 'core business' and, therefore, as 'a nuisance'.

The major advantage issuing from adopting a proactive approach to dealing with one's external environment, institutional or other, is that such a way of proceeding tends, in principle, to yield rich results by creating the conditions for dialogue, improved understanding of the other, and heightened awareness of both one's environment and of the forces shaping it. Beyond this, I would further argue that, properly used as a policy instrument, proactivity entails a powerful self-reflexive dimension, which, as I shall shortly argue, can affect decisively not just the external but also the internal environment of an institution. In the case of the Ombudsman, proactivity is often best expressed by means of own-initiative investigations – a powerful and effective policy instrument explicitly recognized by the Statute of the Ombudsman and used with great effect in promoting proactively inspired Ombudsman initiatives.

In the years after 2003, therefore, the logic of proactivity drove forward an ever-widening number of initiatives, many of them *own*-initiatives, undertaken by the European Ombudsman. Some of these, such as the information campaign launched through the European Network of Ombudsmen, with an eye to informing citizens of the Member States, especially those which entered the Union following the 2004 enlargement, of the rights accruing to them from European citizenship, have already been mentioned. I refer to them again here, just in order to underscore the intellectual and policy coherence which the logic of proactivity imparted to all of them. I will confine myself here to ten salient examples, each of which sought to highlight a particular element of good administrative practice subscribing to a conceptualization of proactivity as a powerful instrument for promoting and embedding a service culture mentality in the EU public administration.

The first of these concerns the 'visits' to the EU agencies, the number of which was expanded rapidly in the early 2000s. The second relates to the decision to sign memoranda of understanding with the EIB and the European Data Protection Supervisor (EDPS), and, as a cautionary tale, the failed attempt to do so with the European Personnel Selection Office (EPSO). The third, regards the decision to prepare and issue what came to be known as the Public Service Principles for EU Civil Servants, which, following extensive public consultation with stakeholders, were formally adopted by the Ombudsman and publicly announced in 2012. The fourth initiative exemplified here was intended to enhance the Ombudsman's monitoring function and, in so doing, to provide the EU institution examined with guidance on how best to follow up on the Ombudsman's recommendations concerning instances of maladministration. The fifth example of a proactive initiative I wish to highlight here concerns the European Network of Ombudsmen. Though established and impeccably led by my predecessor, Jacob Söderman, during its initial years, this institution acquired a major new momentum, as a result of the 2004 enlargement and was, over time, accorded a much larger role in the European Ombudsman's strategy for promoting good administration in the era of the Charter. The rising significance during my years in office of allegations concerning conflicts of interest in the comportment of the EU civil service constitutes the sixth example of a proactive initiative undertaken by the Ombudsman that I wish to focus on. It is an issue which has played a major role in expanding the frontiers of transparency and of providing momentum to efforts to enhance accountability in the EU. The seventh case of proactivity that will be dealt with here will focus on the Ombudsman institution itself and on the efforts undertaken during my term of office to improve its capacity to serve its role as the Union's Guardian of Good Administration in accordance with principles of best administrative practice. The European Ombudsman's decision in 2007 to seek a revision of his Statute in two specific areas affecting his work will be the eighth case of proactive initiative that I wish to highlight. The ninth case concerns the Ombudsman's decision to seek the leave of the Court to intervene before it in cases directly linked to and affecting his work. Finally, the tenth example of proactive ways of contributing to the deepening of a service culture mentality within the EU public administration will focus on the advantages to be derived from the use of plain language in communicating with both citizens and institutions.

(a) Proactivity and the EU Agencies

The visits to the agencies were prompted by two considerations: first, the rapid proliferation of such agencies and the political and administrative realities produced by their decentralized nature. Prior experience with similar practices, including, in particular, the operation of the Commission's delegations around the globe, which of necessity were decentralized and very often geographically distant from their supervising authority in Brussels, had led me to formulate a practical, but, as it turned out, mostly accurate rule of thumb. To wit, that the farther the geographical distance separating a Union body or entity from its administrative centre, most often Brussels for the Commission and Luxembourg for the Parliament, the higher the probability of failure to be fully aware of and to observe the principles of good administration binding on it. Hence the need for enhanced supervision. The second consideration sprang from an insight derived from discussions at a staff retreat (on which, see subsection (g) below), where my colleagues and I learned about the practices and procedures employed by the Swedish Parliamentary Ombudsmen in the process of exercising control over the Swedish public administration. Here, I simply wish to highlight the significance of the comparative learning derived from the Network – a learning which brings into relief the enormous added value that this informal but highly influential structure had both for its members and the European Ombudsman during my time in office.

The visits to the agencies, thus conceived, were accordingly programmed on the basis of a uniform set of criteria designed to ascertain the patterns of good but also suboptimal or bad administrative practices observable in each case. Always led by the Ombudsman himself, these visits consisted of four phases. The first phase entailed a meeting with the management of the relevant agency, in which the Ombudsman initially set out the rationale underpinning the whole undertaking. With the assistance of the team accompanying him, he then proceeded to put forward specific questions designed to ascertain the degree of management's familiarity with principles of good administration, as inscribed in, among others, the European Code of Good Administrative Behaviour and the Charter. At the end of such meetings, the Ombudsman would also raise preliminary areas of concern, if any. The visits customarily ended with a meeting between the Ombudsman and the relevant staff committee, whose purpose was to assist the Ombudsman in identifying potential problems in the agency's knowledge of, and compliance with, principles of good administration as viewed from the staff's perspective. In the second phase of this exercise, the Ombudsman sent the agency a formal letter containing, on the one hand, the questions already posed at the meeting and, on the other, formulating specific recommendations for ways to address problems which the visit had identified. The third phase consisted of the agency's formal written response. In the fourth phase, finally, the Ombudsman assessed the agency's response and proposals for compliance with his recommendations, if any, and, if satisfied by these, formally closed the file and informed the agency's management accordingly. In the very rare cases, where the Ombudsman was not satisfied with the agency's response, he pursued the matter further with management.

Such a case arose, when the management of Frontex, the agency charged with responsibility for monitoring the Union's external borders, proved unwilling to follow the Ombudsman's recommendation to set up an internal body to examine, at a first level, complaints received by the agency. From the point of view of good administrative practice, the advantage of such an arrangement was, in addition to enhancing transparency, that it afforded the agency involved with the opportunity to take ownership of the matter and greatly facilitated *external* review by the Ombudsman, when and if this became necessary. I note here that the issue concerning Frontex extended beyond my time as European Ombudsman into the term of Ms Emily O'Reilly, my successor, who, in late 2013, submitted a special report to Parliament on the matter.

(b) Proactivity and Memoranda of Understanding

During my term as European Ombudsman, the institution signed two memoranda of understanding. The first, concluded with the EDPS and signed in 2007, sprang from the need to provide clarity and coherence in the legal uncertainties created by the adoption of two important Regulations. The first, Regulation 45/2001, sought to regulate matters concerning data protection affecting citizens, residents and legal persons in the EU. Responsibility for its enforcement was assigned to the EDPS, who had not yet been appointed. The second, Regulation 1049/2001, commonly known as the 'transparency Regulation', concerned the right of citizens, residents and legal persons having a registered office in a Member State of the EU to access documents in the possession of EU institutions. It was and continues to be a major, if not the major, instrument of transparency in the EU legal order. Responsibility for its enforcement was assigned to the European Ombudsman and to the courts.[10]

---

[10] See (a) Regulation (EC) No. 45/2001 of 18 December 2000 on the protection of individuals with regard to the processing of personal data by the Community

How best to reconcile the right of access with that for data protection became, from the very start, the subject of both speculation and of intense debate among both practitioners and academics. Many knowledgeable observers foresaw the likelihood of institutional tension, not to say conflict, between the Ombudsman and the EDPS over grey areas where the Regulations overlapped or clashed.

The Memorandum of Understanding (MoU), initiated by the EDPS and, following concerted consultation, fully agreed to by the Ombudsman, provided a well-crafted guide on how wisely and judiciously to navigate the uncharted waters of this potentially contentious issue and on how to avoid overlap and unnecessary friction. I am pleased to say that it worked extremely well and proved the Cassandras who had foreseen troubles ahead for both institutions wrong. A great deal of the credit for this success must go to Peter Hustinx, the first EDPS, who collaborated flawlessly with the European Ombudsman to ensure that the rights of citizens would be respected in a just and fair manner and would not fall victim to inter-institutional turf conflicts.

The MoU with the EIB, signed in 2008, arose from a joint recognition, by the Bank and the Ombudsman, of the need to strengthen the Bank's capacity to address social and environmental concerns about the projects it financed and to ensure a voice for those affected by such projects, whether inside or outside the EU.

The solution to the problem owed much to Philippe Maystadt, EIB President between 2000 and 2011. Under his sagacious leadership, the Bank successfully and imaginatively negotiated a challenging transformation, which allowed it to transit from the more narrowly defined role of a financial institution subject to the logic of the markets to that of a public body conforming to the rules and regulations binding on the EU's public administration.

In close collaboration with Mr Maystadt and his close team of advisors dealing with complaints, the European Ombudsman concluded an MoU with the Bank setting up an *internal* unit ably led by Mr Felismino Alcarpe, a senior EIB official, charged with responsibility to examine complaints against the Bank coming from citizens and legal entities from within or without the EU. This arrangement enhanced the Bank's capacity to engage with its stakeholders, while also providing for *external*

institutions and bodies and on the free movement of such data, OJ 2001 L 8 p. 1, and (b) Regulation (EC) No. 1049/2001 of the European Parliament and of the Council of 30 May 2001 regarding public access to European Parliament, Council and Commission documents, 2001 OJ L 145 p. 43.

control by the Ombudsman. The MoU signed with the EIB proved highly successful and had the potential to serve as a template for similar arrangements with other EU institutions and bodies, most notably the agencies already referred to above. It served also as a strong reminder of the rich benefits to be derived from imaginative and creative proactivity as a mechanism for promoting good administrative practices and of serving citizens better.

The abortive effort to produce an MoU with EPSO is worth recounting as an illustrative example of the rigidities, inertia and, occasionally, resistance to pushing forward the frontiers of good administration, which, notwithstanding notable improvements in his relations with the EU public administration, the Ombudsman continued to encounter from time to time in his relations with the EU institutions.

The specifics of the case are not important for this analysis, other than to say that, because of its critical role in the organization of competitions and selection procedures designed to identify suitable candidates for entering the EU civil service, EPSO constituted a frequent target of complaints to the Ombudsman over allegations of maladministration. Thus, the objective conditions arguing in favour of closer cooperation between the two institutions, with an eye to improving administrative practices relating to this very sensitive area of EU activity, were strong. What is important, however, in this case is the difference in political context and in the resulting political dynamics which distinguish the EDPS and the EIB on the one hand from EPSO on the other. In the former two, the potential 'contracting parties' were, like the Ombudsman, administratively and politically independent, subject only to the Courts. EPSO, however, is an office, that is, an entity over which the Commission exercises considerable administrative control, and which, as things turned out, in practice needed Commission approval in order to enter into an MoU. Thus, while the EPSO leadership at the time sought such an agreement with the Ombudsman, the Commission's legal service expressed strong reservations, in the face of which the EPSO leadership felt unable to proceed. In my mind, this incident constituted confirmation of the lingering persistence of a defensive mentality privileging considerations focusing on real or ostensible risks to the institution over the benefits potentially to be derived from novel initiatives designed to improve the quality of public administration and, in the process, to serve citizens better. The failure to obtain Commission assent for such an initiative was, in the end, an instance of failure, however infrequent, in the Ombudsman's continuing struggle to push forward the frontiers of good administration and to contribute to the substantive improvement of the quality of the Union's civil service. It serves, however, as a cautionary tale highlighting the vagaries surrounding and confronting the Ombudsman's efforts to fulfil his role as Guardian of Good Administration in the Union.

(c) Proactivity and the EU Civil Servants

The third example of a proactive initiative which sought substantively to contribute to the enhancement of a service culture mentality in the EU institutions was the adoption, in 2012, of a set of guidelines addressed to EU civil servants, formally known as Public Service Principles for EU Civil Servants. These principles were not new. They represented, rather, a high-level distillation of the ethical standards which EU civil servants should bear in mind and observe in the daily exercise of their duties and in their dealings with citizens and the public. They thus inscribed themselves in the logic of best practices for the European public administration. The principles formulated in line with this logic were five: (1) commitment to the EU and its citizens; (2) integrity; (3) objectivity; (4) respect for others; and (5) transparency. The adoption of the Public Service Principles in 2012 was preceded by a long period of public consultation with the institutions, the staff unions and the public at large of a draft document initially discussed within the ever-hospitable institutional environment provided by the European Network of Ombudsmen. The final product was published on the Ombudsman's website and incorporated in a new edition of the European Code of Good Administrative Behaviour, published in 2013 in close to 80,000 copies, and widely distributed among the Union's institutions, bodies, offices and agencies, in an effort to reach out to as many civil servants as possible. Overall, this Ombudsman initiative, well received by the relevant stakeholders, served as further convincing demonstration of the substantive benefits to be derived from an imaginative conceptualization of proactivity as an instrument for promoting good administration and of nurturing an administrative culture among civil servants driven by the positive-sum logic of service to citizens.

(d) Proactivity and Follow-up Reports on Ombudsman Recommendations

The fourth initiative embodying the logic of proactivity was the result of the realization that the long-term impact of the Ombudsman's recommendations would greatly benefit from the provision of greater continuity and coherence in the oversight function carried out in the Ombudsman's role as Guardian of Good Administration. With this in mind, the European Ombudsman inaugurated in 2006 a novel monitoring practice, whose aim was to seek to ascertain the extent to, and manner in, which the EU institutions followed-up on his recommendations. The concrete form this initiative took was the production, on an annual basis, of what came to be known as 'Follow-up' reports, in which the Ombudsman recorded the responses of the institutions to his recommendations and the specific actions they undertook in order to implement these recommendations. These 'follow-up' reports imparted additional coherence to the Ombudsman's oversight function, helped strengthen the uniform application of the principles of good administration among the institutions' services, and rendered more efficient the Ombudsman's communications with complainants. In so doing, they proved to be a robust mechanism of effective oversight driven by the logic of proactivity. At the same time, they also served as tangible evidence of the Ombudsman's efforts systematically to promote best practice and to operate in the spirit of positive-sum approaches capable of contributing to the deepening of a service culture and the furtherance of the broader goals of good administration within the EU public administration.

(e) Proactivity and the European Network of Ombudsmen

The fifth Ombudsman initiative exemplifying the logic and advantages of proactivity was the European Network of Ombudsmen. As already mentioned, the 2004 EU enlargement significantly altered the Union's institutional landscape and ushered in a period of dynamic expansion of the Network, not merely in numbers but also in activity. The Network was henceforth to serve as a powerful and precious policy instrument throughout the remaining nine years of my mandate as Ombudsman. With the active and loyal help of highly committed and knowledgeable colleagues from across the EU, it served as a major policy tool through which the European Ombudsman was able to fulfil his strategy of reaching out to citizens of the Member States and of informing them of their rights as European citizens. I add that, quite often but especially in the new Member States, citizens were only dimly aware, if at all, of the rights accruing to them from European as opposed to national citizenship.

The Network proved invaluable to my work as European Ombudsman in yet another way. It served as a vast source of comparative information concerning different conceptualizations of good administration in the EU Member States from which to gain insights that could then be shared with colleagues, with an eye to promoting best practice as widely as possible, at both the national and the European levels. In pursuit of that goal, the European Ombudsman early on set up an electronic service, entitled *Ombudsman Daily News*, whose purpose was to collect, on a daily basis, information reported from national ombudsman colleagues and to disseminate it as widely as possible within the Network. Ideas and practices that percolated to the surface in this manner very often revealed broader concerns which then became the subject of exchanges and debate in the biennial meetings of the Network that were always co-organized by the European Ombudsman and a national colleague who graciously served as host. As such, the Network served as a flexible, and informal institutional setting and forum, a veritable laboratory in which to discuss, debate and try out novel as well as innovative ideas concerning best administrative practices and ways of promoting a service culture mentality in the public administrations of the Network's Member States and, to be sure, the EU. Over time, such a use of the Network contributed to the generation and embeddedness of a firm foundation of trust and of good will that came to be a distinguishing feature and, indeed, hallmark of this common undertaking. Its success owed a great deal to the political commitment and support which the national colleagues, many of whom became good and trusted friends, extended to it and for which I am grateful to this day.

(f) Proactivity and Conflicts of Interest

During my term of office, preoccupation with conflicts of interest viewed as important elements affecting the quality of public administration and seriously impeding its capacity to be efficient, transparent and accountable grew both in numbers and, especially, salience. In turn, this development closely reflected the Ombudsman's decision to accord priority to the ethical dimension of his conceptualization of good administration, as this affected not only the activities of the European public administration but also the public administrations of the Member States when applying EU law. In seeking to develop guidelines for this sensitive area of civil service activity, I, once again, had recourse to one of my favourite rules of thumb, which is to avoid, as a matter of principle, reinventing the wheel. My basic premise in so doing was that good administrative practice can also be advanced through the introduction in the logic governing its operation of insights or ideas developed *extra muros* which have proven successful in promoting good administration and in better serving citizens.

Accordingly, when such matters began to proliferate, during my second mandate (2005–2010), I decided to have recourse to the vast store of experience and knowledge which the Organization for Economic Cooperation and Development (OECD) had accumulated over the years, in trying to formulate guidelines for good administrative practice in the more than 30 developed countries, which constitute its membership.

A very useful insight thus derived concerned the distinction between three types of conflicts of interest: actual, apparent and potential.[11] The purpose of this distinction, I hasten to add, was primarily practical in that its intent was to provide guidance to both individual civil servants and public administrations as bodies on how to identify different types of conflicts of interest and on how best to confront them. At the same time, however, such a distinction contributed substantively to the re-conceptualization of a topic which, in a post-Santer era distinguished by heightened concerns with issues of transparency and accountability, was acquiring increasing salience and political weight in the Union's administrative culture.

The European Ombudsman successfully incorporated this distinction into the institution's daily practice and applied it systematically in dealing with relevant cases. Such an approach was to stand him in good stead in handling the increasing number of complaints involving serious allegations of such conflicts, some of which, however infrequently, implicated civil servants at the very highest levels of the EU administration. Though such cases often generated significant tensions with the institutions involved, they also contributed to the elaboration of criteria which, whether explicitly or implicitly adopted, resulted in notable successes and helped push forward the frontiers of good administration in the EU. Taken together, the Ombudsman's proactive initiatives in the realm of conflicts of interest were to impart a perceptible positive dynamic to the institution's continuing efforts to deepen the foundations of good administrative practice within the Union's institutions.

The common distinguishing characteristic of the six preceding examples of Ombudsman initiatives driven by the logic of proactivity was that they were all driven by considerations and by the search for improvements in administrative practice which were *external* to the Ombudsman institution itself. They were, in other words, *other-directed*, in that they were undertaken with the specific policy intent of alternatively promoting among, or imparting in, EU institutions other than the European Ombudsman a shared administrative culture driven by the open-ended logic of (a) service to citizens and (b) best practice.

(g) Proactivity and the European Ombudsman

The seventh proactive initiative introduced by the Ombudsman with an eye to promoting good administration in the EU institutions which I wish

---

11 See, OECD, Council Recommendation on Guidelines for Managing Conflict of Interest in the Public Service, June 2003. Available at www.oecd.org/governance/ethics/2957360.pdf, accessed 9 January 2017.

to highlight here constituted a logical extension of such an approach. This time, however, the logic of proactivity was directed *inwards* and had the institution of the Ombudsman itself as its object. Put otherwise, the seventh initiative was self-consciously and deliberately self-reflexive in that it sought to apply to the European Ombudsman and its staff the same principles regarding best practice and, above all, a service culture which the Ombudsman sought systematically to promote in his capacity as the Union's Guardian of Good Administration. It was a policy initiative driven by the imperative that, when it came to promoting principles of good administration as enshrined in, among others, the European Code of Good Administrative Behaviour and the Charter, the Ombudsman should systematically practice what he preaches.

If a single term can capture the policy logic driving forward this initiative in proactivity geared to the Ombudsman's staff, this is surely 'ownership.' Put otherwise, this was an initiative designed to generate among the Ombudsman staff a powerful sense of identification with their institution and to endow them with the moral commitment to serve it imaginatively, creatively and enthusiastically. The ultimate beneficiaries of doing so would be both citizens but, more broadly, the democratic element of the wider European project envisaged initially by the Treaty of Maastricht and, as of 2009, by the Treaty of Lisbon. To generate such an intellectual climate and to serve this broader goal, the Ombudsman undertook many intramural activities and initiatives. Organized on a regular basis, with an eye to becoming an integral part of the institution's internal rituals and culture, these activities had both a professional and a social content. They included, but were not confined to, the following. First, annual self-evaluation exercises which were completely anonymous and sought to gauge the level of staff satisfaction with the institution and with their working environment and to identify ways for improving it. Second, bi-annual general meetings designed to be substantive rather than formal and geared to maximizing staff participation in exchanges organized around themes directly linked to the work of the institution and selected with input from staff. Third, an annual *randonné*, or walk in the countryside, initiated by Jacob Söderman and held every summer. Finally, a Christmas party organized by the institution's staff committee.

The crowning event in each annual cycle of Ombudsman activity was arguably a two-and-a-half day 'retreat' of the staff, held away from the office in a carefully selected site, which was devoted to an in-depth examination and discussion of issues likely to contribute to the improvement of the institution and its administrative culture. Conceived and self-consciously carried out as an exercise in institutional self-reflexivity, this was an undertaking organized around both plenary sessions and smaller group meetings designed to encourage active staff participation, free exchange of ideas and institutional introspection built around what I liked to call 'structured brainstorming'. This concept was meant to convey the need for meticulous planning and preparation, as well as for gentle steering of discussions and of debate, with an eye to ensuring the twin goals of inclusion and efficiency. In other words, as broad a participation of staff as possible, as well as tangible and concrete insights and ideas that management could then integrate into its multi-annual planning for the institution. To enhance the efficacy of this policy goal further, external speakers drawn from national ombudsman offices or other institutions likely to provide added value to the European Ombudsman's strategic agenda for promoting good administration in the EU institutions were often invited to join the retreat. Their task was to address topics and to raise issues in innovative and imaginative ways capable of challenging staff, of contributing to the improvement of the Ombudsman's internal administrative culture, and, ultimately, of enhancing the institution's capacity better to serve its mission by improving its internal procedures, mechanisms, *modus operandi* and ways of thinking.

Such, for example, was the rationale underpinning the decision to devote an entire retreat to a systematic review the institution's overall management style and culture and to explore ways of improving both. To that effect, the Ombudsman sought the assistance of the European Foundation for Quality Management (EFQM), which had an established track record of approaching matters concerning administrative reform in a flexible, non-bureaucratic and imaginative manner. The association with the EFQM proved to be a successful experiment that was to occupy the Ombudsman over a number of years. Its single most important achievement in my mind was that it set in motion a continuous process of self-reflexivity, enabling both management but also staff to pursue two policy goals. First, to search creatively and productively for ways to improve the Ombudsman's internal administrative culture. Second, to integrate the insights thus derived into the institution's strategy for promoting good administration for the benefit of both EU institutions and, to be sure, European citizens.

All in all, the retreat, viewed as an annual ritual, graphically captured the logic of a gradually unfolding process geared to generating a sense of ownership among staff with respect to their institution. An eloquent demonstration of such sense of ownership and of the moral commitment that it brought with it was the social event organized with great care and preparation and held annually, on the second and last evening of each retreat. This event involved all staff, management and the Ombudsman himself in a series of musical and theatrical improvisations or skits and served as yet another mechanism for sharing, for bonding, and for generating affective learning, which cumulatively translated into enhanced capacity building and strengthened the dynamic of ownership through continuous moral investment. The very high degree of staff participation in the retreat and the social evening constituted, in my mind, tangible evidence of such investment. In accordance with the logic of self-reflexivity, each retreat was invariably accompanied by an anonymous evaluation exercise conducted after the event which proved very useful in identifying positive aspects in the operation of the institution and in drawing attention to areas that needed improvement in the future. Taken together, the various initiatives linked to this search for institutional self-reflexivity served, in my mind, as a potent reminder that, over the long run, an institution's capacity to succeed owes as much to its leadership as to the degree of loyalty and, ultimately, the sense of ownership it can generate, nurture and retain among its staff.

The final dimension of the seventh proactive initiative, which the Ombudsman undertook with an eye to enhancing the institution's capacity to 'practise what it preached', concerned the decision taken in 2010, at the beginning of my third mandate, thoroughly to review its staff policy, so as to ensure the Ombudsman's long-term capacity to retain its staff's continuing engagement, commitment and loyalty, and to avoid gradual loss of enthusiasm, institutional fatigue, resignation and even apathy. In short, it was an important step to ensure the institution's diachronic capacity to serve as an exemplar of a service culture mentality and of good administration in the Union and as a credible and powerful vehicle for its dissemination and embeddedness.

Over a period of three years, from 2010 to 2013, the staff situation was effectively addressed through the organization of carefully planned and impeccably executed internal competitions conducted in strict conformity with the EU's Staff Regulations. At the end of this long process, the Ombudsman had successfully set up an institutional landscape making it possible for those members of his professional staff who had qualified as permanent civil servants (and most had) to exercise, among others, the right of professional mobility, if they so chose and not to feel constrained by the inability to do so. Viewed from what I would call a narrow, unenlightened and defensive institutional perspective, such an arrangement carried with it the considerable risk that, given the opportunity, staff could henceforth more easily exercise that 'exit option' and look for employment prospects in other EU institutions. My own personal response to this potential dilemma was that the situation created by these new institutional arrangements presented the Ombudsman with a major, long-term challenge. That is, to maintain an internal administrative culture and working conditions of such calibre that the exercise of the exit option would be the result of free choice based on careful weighing of the benefits, as opposed to the costs, of remaining with the institution.

(h) Proactivity and the European Ombudsman's Statute

The eighth proactive Ombudsman initiative that I wish to highlight here concerns the Ombudsman's decision in 2006 to seek a revision of his Statute in two areas which unnecessarily constrained his freedom to investigate cases and, by implication, encroached upon his independence. These concerned, first, the provision in Article 3, paragraph 2 of the Statute, which qualified the Ombudsman's right of access to documents in the possession of EU institutions by excluding those documents where the administration could invoke 'duly substantiated grounds of secrecy'. The second area of concern related to the obligation of EU civil servants, also provided in Article 3, paragraph 2 of the Statute, to testify before the Ombudsman. The same article went on to state that, in testifying, civil servants 'shall speak on behalf of and in accordance with *instructions* from their administrations . . .' (emphasis added).

The Ombudsman's rationale for seeking the elimination of these two provisions reflected the *Zeitgeist* of the times, that is, the heightened sensitivity to issues of transparency, which, in the aftermath of the Treaty of Maastricht, the Santer affair, and the subsequent adoption of, among others, Regulation 1049/2001, had become a salient feature of the European legal order. In putting forth his arguments in favour of such elimination, the Ombudsman took the view that these provisions imposed restrictions on his independence which, in an era of enhanced sensitivity about transparency and accountability, could have detrimental effects on his moral authority and could commensurately diminish his capacity to convince citizens and other interlocutors.

The revision process was in the end successful, as Parliament, with the consent of the Council, eventually approved the changes. On the issue of testimony to be provided by civil servants, Parliament accepted the Ombudsman's main argument that, in conducting his inquiries, his primary concern was to ascertain the truth and not to be given a version of such truth handed down to the civil servant by his/her superiors. Accordingly, the amended Statute did not contain such a restriction on the Ombudsman's powers of investigation.

The matter regarding access to documents in cases where concerns about secrecy could be invoked turned out to be more difficult. The major concern in this case was how to assuage the fears of institutions, and especially the Council, that information contained in sensitive documents would not become public as a result of granting the Ombudsman access to such documents. An astutely constructed compromise was eventually arrived at, with critical support from Sweden, which at the time held the Presidency of the Council and whose long-standing commitment to transparency proved invaluable to the Ombudsman in this as in other instances. According to that compromise, the principle of access to sensitive documents was recognized, subject to the Ombudsman's obligation to negotiate with the institution involved the precise terms governing actual access to such a document. The formula thus arrived at proved successful. Parliament approved the amended Statute in June 2008. Shortly thereafter, a case involving a restricted document fortuitously came up and served as a test case for what had been agreed upon. I was pleased to see that it was handled uneventfully, to the satisfaction of both the Ombudsman and the institution involved.

The successful amendment of the Ombudsman's Statute carried with it important benefits, both tangible and intangible. To begin with, it enhanced the Ombudsman's moral authority by demonstrating his capacity to be persuasive in his relations with the institutions, even in areas of heightened sensitivity. In addition, it served as concrete evidence of the climate of respect and of trust which the Ombudsman had gradually been able to establish in his dealings with the public administration and, more generally, the institutions. Finally, and as a cumulative outcome of the above, it strengthened his position as Guardian of Good Administration in the EU and sent a reassuring message to citizens and stakeholders of his determination vigilantly to defend their rights and actively to push forward the frontiers of good administration.

(i) Proactivity and the Courts

The ninth example of proactive initiative concerns the Ombudsman's decision to seek the Court's leave to intervene in a case before it that was directly related to a decision concerning the same subject matter already taken by the Ombudsman. My rationale in seeking such a leave was dual. To begin with, recognition of the right to intervene, I was convinced, would perceptibly enhance the Ombudsman's moral authority and would strengthen his role as Guardian of Good Administration in the EU. Secondly, I was aware that such a right had already been accorded to the EDPS in cases relating to his realm of activity. Given the complementarity in the missions of the two institutions, I considered that granting a similar treatment to the Ombudsman was both reasonable and less likely to encounter reservations or objections.

For a number of years, I had asked my staff to be on the lookout for suitable cases which could provide a convincing argument for asking the Court's leave to intervene. The case eventually selected emerged in 2013 and concerned the European Medicines Agency and a request for access to data relating to clinical trials the Agency had conducted in relation to a particular medicinal product. When a third party opposing the Agency's initial acceptance of the Ombudsman's recommendation to grant access took the matter to court, it appeared that the strict conditions for seeking the Court's leave to intervene had been met and that a suitable opportunity for so doing had materialized.

Subsequent developments in the case took place after I had left office and Emily O'Reilly had assumed her duties as the EU's third European Ombudsman. Accordingly, a discussion of the substantive aspects of the case chronologically and logically falls beyond the boundaries of this account and will not be pursued here. The major gain deriving from this case is indisputable, however. In granting the Ombudsman leave to intervene before it in this case, the Court confirmed that such a course of action was, under the proper circumstances, indeed open to the Ombudsman. Seen from the institution's perspective, this development constituted solid confirmation of the power of proactivity as an instrument of the Ombudsman's long-term strategy for promoting good administration in the Union and for defending European citizens' rights.

(j) Proactivity and Plain Language

The tenth and final proactive initiative on which I wish to focus was inspired by insights gleaned through the European Network of Ombudsmen and, more specifically, from practices concerning the language to be used in communicating with citizens employed by the British and Swedish Ombudsmen. The goal of this initiative was to combat the use, in both decisions concerning complaints and in general communications with the public, of bureaucratic or excessively technical or arcane language laden with jargon. Such language, often pejoratively referred as 'bureaucratese', is difficult for the average citizen to understand and, in addition, creates a sense of distance and remoteness on the part of the public administration in its dealings with the public which is erosive of the climate of trust that good administration by definition ought to nurture and promote.

The 'plain language' initiative, as this came to be known, assumed notable success in the United Kingdom, where the Ombudsman devoted great efforts and energy in ensuring that her staff would systematically apply the principles of plain language writing in their work and daily communications with citizens. In pursuit of this policy goal, she published and widely distributed elegantly designed and well-written leaflets explaining the rationale underpinning her initiative and its added value for both citizens and the public administration.

Transferring this experiment to the European Ombudsman institution and making plain language a part of the institution's administrative practice and culture was not an easy task. To begin with, a choice had to be made about which specific language to use in this context. In the final analysis, a number of practical considerations tipped the balance in favour of English. One such consideration issued from the inescapable reality that, following the 2004 enlargement of the EU, English was fast becoming the de facto dominant language in the institutions' daily communications with citizens. With this in mind, English had the distinct advantage of serving as the most convenient linguistic medium through which to attain the Ombudsman's strategic goal of formulating and refining his message in clear, direct and unambiguous ways. Such an approach had the additional advantage of facilitating the production of accurate and reader-friendly translations of the Ombudsman's annual reports and of the website in all official languages of the Union which, by the time I left office in October 2013, had reached 24.

This background set the context for the Ombudsman's plain language initiative, whose major goal, I wish to underline, was not linguistic purity or excellence but, rather, *effective* communication with the institutions and, especially, citizens, with an eye to promoting and deepening the major principles of the Ombudsman's service culture.

In many ways, the initiative proved to be a success. The staff responded warmly to the idea and devoted significant energy and effort in the many training sessions which were devoted to explaining the rationale and the mechanics of the whole project. With critical support from senior management and from first-class lawyer-linguists, it produced notable improvements in the language the Ombudsman used in his decisions, his publications and in his communications with the public. It constituted further demonstration of the dynamic inherent in the notion of good administration and of the cumulative benefits of proactivity put to the service of a broader goal and vision.

4 CONCLUDING REFLECTIONS OF A RETROSPECTIVE NATURE

As I approach the end of the retrospective part of my account concerning my ten-and-a-half years in office, the question which almost inevitably comes up is the following: to what extent can one argue that, during the term of the Second European Ombudsman (2003–2013), the Ombudsman institution adequately fulfilled its mission of better serving European citizens by systematically, inventively, proactively and convincingly acting as the Guardian of Good Administration in the EU?

The answer to this question that I would tentatively venture is that, in my view, the proverbial glass was, on the whole, more half-full than half-empty. As I have endeavoured to demonstrate throughout this account, the European Ombudsman was the happy beneficiary of a novel intellectual climate shaped fortuitously by the powerful dynamic for greater transparency and enhanced accountability which the Maastricht Treaty, the 1996 Nordic enlargement, and the 1999 Santer crisis unleashed. In the process, the institution was gradually but steadily to emerge as a credible and increasingly authoritative agent for energetically and systematically reshaping and expanding the institutional space occupied by good administration in the activities and practices of the EU institutions. In this challenging and, in many ways formidable, task, the Ombudsman was enormously aided by the opportunities which the largest ever enlargement of the EU created and brought forward.

To be sure, the process was neither uniform nor linear. Rather, it was marked by a long series of advances, successes and occasional triumphs, coupled by setbacks, disappointments and frustration. Two distinct, diverging, and, in many ways, opposing dynamics drove these developments forward. In ideal-typical terms, the first embodied the vision for change, for reform and for citizen empowerment which was generated by the Treaty of Maastricht, was accelerated by the 1995 addition of Sweden and Finland to the ranks of Member States adhering to such a reformist logic, and brought to its high point with the Treaty of Lisbon (2009). This Treaty, which explicitly enhanced the rights and benefits associated with European citizenship, constituted the natural high point of what I would call the 'reformist' dynamic and, in many ways, served as its *terminus ad quem*. Viewed from the Ombudsman's perspective, the distinguishing feature of this dynamic was the emergence, over time, of a discernible pattern and configuration of improved relations with the EU institutions, of a more transparent and more citizen-friendly administrative culture, and of a greater habituation with, and acceptance of, the principles of a service culture underpinning it. Step by tortuous step, the logic of consensus, of conciliation, of proactivity, of suasion, of open-ended solutions, and of fairness made its way into the daily reality and practices of the EU institutions, managed to secure their cooperation and began to influence decisions affecting citizens – in the process providing the concept of European citizenship with substantive meaning and political content.

The second dynamic characterizing the decade of my tenure as European Ombudsman was informed by a lingering but powerful intellectual temper more inclined to privilege greater continuity with the past and with practices more rooted in the logic of the pre-Maastricht administrative culture. In many ways, this was a defensive intellectual temper, less disposed to deal with the discontinuities and disruptive effects brought forward by the changes which the Treaty of Maastricht had introduced, the Santer affair had accelerated, and the Treaty of Lisbon sought to consolidate. It was a temper diachronically sustained by powerful constituencies within the EU institutions, including the Commission, which held to the view, if not the conviction, that the pendulum had swung too far in the direction of change and that initiatives were needed to stem the tide, and move in the opposite direction, in order to gain greater systemic equilibrium. The inter-governmental rather than 'integrative' logic which, as already noted, the 2004 enlargement gave rise to certainly added to this momentum.

Three illustrative examples of such initiatives will serve to demonstrate this point. The first was the move to reform Regulation 1049/2001 for access to documents held by the EU institutions. I recall that the overarching principle driving this Regulation was that, documents held by the EU institutions were, in principle, accessible to citizens and the public, subject to a very limited number of exceptions explicitly stated in the Regulation itself and with no need to provide reasons for requesting access. The initiative to reform the Regulation generated very considerable acrimony among the EU institutions and pitted the Commission and the Council on the side favouring change and the Parliament on the side opposing it. Though shrouded in the intensity of the resulting controversies, its net effect, if adopted, would be to make the right to access more restrictive by defining more narrowly a number of its provisions which were crucial for citizens in gaining access to documents. The result was political deadlock, as neither side succeeded in having its position prevail. Though the Regulation has so far survived unscathed, it is clear that the dynamic which initially pushed it forward and secured its adoption has petered out and that its protection as opposed to its expansion currently constitutes the preferred strategy of the forces constituting the 'transparency coalition' in the EU.

The same fate has befallen efforts which both the Parliament and the European Ombudsman have strongly endorsed to adopt a regulation governing administrative practice in the EU. In the Ombudsman's view, such a regulation would greatly simplify the institutional landscape governing the operation of the European public administration and would provide clarity and greater certainty likely to benefit both the EU civil service and European citizens in their dealings with the Union's public administration. This initiative enjoys the strong support of academics and experts on EU administrative law and inscribes itself in the logic governing the reform tradition generated by the Treaty of Maastricht. It has, however, been stalled by the profound ambivalence of the Commission towards the need for such a project, which has usually assumed the form of arguing for further examination of the matter before it can be settled. The Council's attitude has ranged from initial opposition to the proposal to a more recent indication, expressed in a hearing on the subject organized in January 2016 by the Parliament's Committee on Legal Affairs, that it would not stand in the way of such an initiative if it were to come forward. Here again, the clash between the reformist and the traditionalist dynamics affecting the fortunes of good administration in the EU has produced a stalemate that awaits solution.

The final example of the clash between the two dynamics concerns the European Court of Justice and its 2010 judgment on the *European Commission v the Bavarian Lager Co. Ltd.* case.[12] This judgment set aside a 2007 decision on the matter by the Union's Court of First Instance strongly endorsing the logic of transparency exemplified by Regulation 1049/2001 on access to documents. In so doing, it explicitly rejected the Commission's argument for a restrictive interpretation of the Regulation that would enable it to withhold the names of participants in a meeting, to which the plaintiff wanted to obtain access.

In rejecting the position of the Court of First Instance, the Court of Justice adopted the view that, when it came to granting access, the Court should endeavour to balance two rights that often stand in opposition to one another. To wit, the right of access guaranteed by Regulation 1049/2001 with the right for the protection of personal data provided for by Regulation 45/2001. The Court's ruling seemed to indicate, in substance, that, in case the rights clash, the need for protection guaranteed by Regulation 45/2001 takes precedence over the right to access set out in Regulation 1049/2001. To be sure, subsequent case law has been more nuanced and the EDPS has subsequently come up with an inventive and convincing strategy which makes it possible for access to be granted in such cases, once the prior consent of those whose private data are affected by the case has been obtained. This notwithstanding, this was clearly a ruling whose logic moved in the direction of restricting rather than expanding access. The future will tell whether this is likely to be a permanent situation or a transitory moment in the swing of the pendulum in the direction of further transparency and the enhancement of a heightened culture of accountability in the EU's institutions. Its eventual outcome will undoubtedly have a perceptible impact on, *inter alia,* the European

---

12 *Commission v Bavarian Lager* C-28/08 P, EU:C:2010:378.

Ombudsman's capacity meaningfully and convincingly to act as a robust Guardian of Good Administration in the EU.

5 CODA: PROSPECTIVE REFLECTIONS ON THE EUROPEAN OMBUDSMAN INSTITUTION

As I indicated in my prefatory remarks, I wish to conclude this personal account containing my retrospective reflections on my ten years as European Ombudsman with a short set of further reflections, this time prospective, on the nature of the European Ombudsman institution and on the systemic challenges and dilemmas confronting it over time, irrespective of particular incumbents.

I will confine myself to two sets of parameters. First, the particular, indeed idiosyncratic, characteristics of the ombudsman institution, in general, and of the European Ombudsman in particular. Second, I wish to focus on the European Ombudsman's privileged relationship with the Parliament, to highlight the exceptional features of that relationship, and to point to the challenges and risks associated with it.

Let me start by clarifying two points: first, my analysis in what follows will, where needed, take into account primarily, if not exclusively, the experiences of ombudsman institutions in the EU, at both the national and the supranational levels. Second, I shall deal exclusively with *public* sector ombudsmen. To turn now to my substantive argument, I will confine myself to saying that, in many ways, the ombudsman is a *sui generis* institution, whose capacity to grow and thrive requires meticulous nurturing, vigilance and care designed to ensure its integrity, independence and efficacy. In turn, such qualities are instrumental in enabling the institution to serve its purpose of acting as the Guardian of Good Administration and, in complement to the courts, of the rule of law and of fundamental rights. Stated more broadly, the capacity of the ombudsman credibly to discharge his or her duties is very much a function of the degree to which democracy and the rule of law are sufficiently embedded in a polity and in a corresponding legal order equipped with stable institutions. Such institutions, in turn, ensure the generation and, over time, the consolidation of a climate of predictability, within which citizens can meaningfully pursue their interests.

Even in these optimal circumstances, the ombudsman is, in principle, a vulnerable institution, in that, with the exception of the Nordic countries, it is an institution of recent vintage and therefore very often unfamiliar even to those with whom it has to co-exist and interact. To the extent that it stands outside the classical division of powers (executive, legislative, judicial) posited by Montesquieu, it is often difficult to understand and to classify in terms of the traditional categories associated with most constitutional orders. Its need, furthermore, to ensure its independence and its moral authority, and to distinguish itself clearly from other, older and more established, institutions and sources of authority, combines with the unease, if not diffidence, with which many of the latter regard this novel arrival to create, very often, an intellectual climate of distance and even isolation around the ombudsman. In this sense, I would argue that the ombudsman is in many ways a lonesome or solitary institution, whose idiosyncratic (and mostly monocratic) nature requires that the individual incumbent possess, in addition to all other qualifications, intellectual, administrative, emotional and experiential, very significant *political* skills. These, I add, are critical in ensuring the ombudsman's capacity to steer the institution through the turbulent and often uncharted waters of the political process. For though, in ideal-typical terms, an ombudsman by definition stands above politics in the *partisan* sense of the term, it is clear that, in discharging his or her daily functions, s/he will have to deal with the realities of the political process, if only to ensure that her/his institution stays clear of dangers associated with partisan politics.

This situation presents the political authorities charged with establishing an ombudsman in a given legal and constitutional order with an intriguing dilemma. To wit, how to ensure independence from all other powers and, at the same time, endow the institution with sufficient power and authority as to enable it meaningfully to carry out its mission of serving as an effective external mechanism of control and accountability for the public administration and, where provided for, other institutions falling within the public sector.

While individual countries' arrangements vary, the classical model employed by most established constitutional orders in order to provide an adequate and convincing response to this policy dilemma opts for a privileged relationship between the Ombudsman and Parliament. Such an arrangement has multiple advantages. Election (or, in certain cases, confirmation) by parliament invests the ombudsman with democratic legitimacy, which commensurately enhances his/her moral authority and capacity to serve her/his mission efficiently. In addition, it makes parliament the ombudsman's ultimate ally, his *ultimum refugium*, in cases where a recalcitrant institution refuses to comply with his/her recommendations and political pressure to persuade it to do so is called for. Finally, in such arrangements, the ombudsman submits an annual report on his activities to parliament, and in so doing reinforces his privileged links with that institution.

To be sure, the whole arrangement hinges on one critical assumption, that is, that parliament will respect and, where necessary, defend the independence of the ombudsman and will not seek to undermine it in any way. In return, and in order to avoid the danger of potential conflicts that would jeopardize the efficacy and utility of this arrangement, ombudsmen are not, as a rule, given authority to control parliament's activities. While not definitively eliminating the potential for conflict, this pattern, clearly observable in most established democracies in the EU, makes it possible for ombudsmen to rely on parliament in seeking to promote good administrative practices in their respective countries.

Surprisingly enough, the logic informing this arrangement was not followed when it came to establishing the European Ombudsman in the Maastricht Treaty. In contrast to the Danish experience, which does not allow the national ombudsman to exercise control over parliament, and which, in many ways, served as the model for setting up the new institution at the EU level, the decision finally taken at the EU level was different.[13] As recorded in what is now Article 228 of the Treaty on the Functioning of the European Union (TFEU), it provided that the Parliament, like all other institutions with the exception of the Court of Justice when acting in its judicial capacity, fell within the remit of the European Ombudsman. Such a decision, whatever its merits, raised from the very start the possibility of conflict between the Ombudsman and Parliament, in cases where complaints against the latter were to be submitted to the former.

To deal with the problem, the first European Ombudsman, Jacob Söderman, decided to draw a clear conceptual distinction between matters administrative and matters political, when it came to handling complaints against the Parliament. He then proceeded to declare that matters political, that is, decisions of Parliament which pertained to its political functions and taken either in plenary or in committee, would fall outside the Ombudsman's remit. By the same decision, the Ombudsman retained authority to investigate the activities of Parliament's administration.

This is not the place to attempt an in-depth examination of how this arrangement has played itself out. Suffice it to say that in at least two cases during my term of office great, if not explosive, tension was generated, when, prompted by complaints submitted by citizens under Regulation 1049/2001, which sought to obtain information concerning Members of the European Parliament's (MEP's) allowances and an auxiliary retire-

---

[13] On the influence of the Danish model on the establishment of the European Ombudsman, see Peter Biering, 'The Danish Proposal to the Intergovernmental Conference on Political Union,' in P. Nikiforos Diamandouros (ed.), *The European Ombudsman: Origins, Establishment, Evolution* (Luxembourg: Office for Official Publications of the European Communities, 2005), 38–51.

ment plan for MEPs, the Ombudsman opened investigations on these. The second case was closed, after the Ombudsman established that a decision relating to the use of the retirement plan had been taken by Parliament in plenary and, therefore, fell clearly within Parliament's political activities and, according to established practice, was outside the Ombudsman's remit.

The first case, however, did produce very significant friction as it put the Ombudsman on a direct collision course with Parliament, which initially refused to accept an Ombudsman recommendation asking it to provide a Maltese citizen with information concerning the allowances received by Maltese MEPs. The Ombudsman rejected the various arguments which Parliament put forward in defence of its refusal, and took the view that the matter at hand concerned administrative accountability, for which he, as Guardian of Good Administration in the Union, had clear authority (and obligation) to act. In the end, a compromise solution was tortuously arrived at, whereby Parliament provided the complainant with aggregate figures, which shed significant light into the matter and, in the process, enhanced transparency in areas heretofore unexplored and relating to how Parliament's administration handled such matters. The case, nevertheless, served as a stark reminder of the dangers for severe conflict arising from the initial decision, included in the Maastricht Treaty, to give the Ombudsman authority to investigate Parliament. Such a provision places the Ombudsman in an extremely delicate position. If he fails to act, when confronted with a legitimate complaint, he runs the clear risk of being suspected of political timidity and, more generally, of behaviour that is incompatible with his obligations. If he does investigate, the prospect of a confrontation with Parliament can certainly not be excluded. Until and unless a solution to this vexed issue materializes, the best way forward is for both Parliament and the Ombudsman to work closely together to reinforce transparency, accountability and trust in their relations. In addition, it behoves them proactively to endeavour to exercise vigilance designed to anticipate such problems and to combat their root causes, in line with the positive-sum logic of good administrative practice.

The second and final reflection I wish to record before concluding concerns the election of the Ombudsman. The problem once again stems from a relevant provision contained in what is now paragraph 2 of Article 228 TFEU. This provides that 'the Ombudsman shall be elected' (prior to 2009, 'appointed') 'after each election of the European Parliament for the duration of its term of office.' In accordance with such a phrasing, the Ombudsman's election coincides temporally with the election of Parliament's leadership, its Committee chairs, and the chairs of its many organs. These elections are subject to political competition, bargaining and resulting agreements among the political groups represented in Parliament designed to ensure some degree of political group representation in Parliament's various organs. The potential, therefore, exists for the election of the Ombudsman to be made part of such an agreement, or 'packaging' as it is commonly known, the inevitable result being the politicization of an institution which stands or falls on its capacity to demonstrate convincingly that it stands above partisan politics.

To date, the election of the Ombudsman has mercifully not been subjected to the partisan logic driving these arrangements. Two factors seem to have contributed to this happy outcome. First, the fact that, in this case, there is only one office to be filled and, therefore, no room for the logic of bargaining and of 'packaging' to insinuate itself into the election process, has effectively served as a mechanism inhibiting the politicization of the election. Second and most importantly, for fortuitous reasons the elections where a *new* ombudsman, as opposed to an incumbent, was elected by Parliament did not, to date, temporally coincide with the procedure to elect new Parliament officers following the election of a new Parliament. Since the election procedure concerned a single post and involved a sitting Parliament with already elected officers, the possibility for political agreements into which the ombudsman could be subsumed mercifully could not materialize. The problem, however, remains, since there is no certainty that the decisions taken by the first two ombudsmen to retire early, thus providing for an *ad hoc* Ombudsman election not subject to the vagaries of 'political packaging', will be repeated in the future. Since any change of the relevant provision linking the election of the Ombudsman to the election of a new Parliament requires a treaty change, a formal solution to the problem seems at present remote. One can only hope that the political groups will exercise restraint and prudence on this matter and will not subject the one institution over the election of which Parliament has exclusive competence to a partisan logic that could irreparably damage it.

The last reflection I wish to record here relates to a different potential threat that could eventually affect the election of a European Ombudsman, by insinuating partisan considerations into the electoral process. The issue most recently arose at the time of the 2013 procedure to elect a new Ombudsman to succeed me. Until then, European Ombudsman elections had been primarily contested by professional ombudsmen, whether national or regional, who were familiar with the nature of the institution and with the need for it to be non-partisan. The two exceptions that I am aware of concern the 1995 and the 2003 elections. In the former, the very first European Ombudsman election, when these unwritten 'rules of the game' were still in a formative stage, a sitting MEP from Germany contested the election and lost to Jacob Söderman in the final round. In the latter, a sitting MEP and Vice President of Parliament's Committee on Petitions presented himself as a candidate. A distinguishing feature of this candidacy was that, by the very nature of their work, both the Committee on Petitions and the candidate himself had long experience in handling citizen complaints and extensive familiarity with ombudsman matters.

In the 2013 election, however, of the six candidates who put themselves forward, only two were professional ombudsmen. A third was a senior official of the Council of Europe with experience in ombudsman matters and the remaining three were sitting MEPs occupying prominent positions in their respective political groups, and serving in committees with little or no direct experience with the Ombudsman. Their candidacies directly raised the question of the potentially adverse impact on the authority of an ombudsman arising from the election to that non-partisan office of individuals active in partisan politics at the time they stood for office. Mercifully, the ombudsman institution was spared the problems inevitably associated with such an eventuality. The convincing victory of Ms O'Reilly, at the time the Irish Ombudsman, ensured that the tradition of electing professional ombudsmen to this important post had been reaffirmed.

The matter, however, remains and requires attention. While it would be improper, unrealistic and unfair to argue that individuals active in politics should never be candidates for this office, it would equally be detrimental to the interests of the European Ombudsman institution to allow for a direct move from active partisan politics to a non-partisan institution such as the ombudsman. A potential solution might be to require a certain temporal hiatus between active involvement in partisan politics and a bid to become European Ombudsman. Let us then add this to the wish list of items which it behoves the Parliament and the European Ombudsman to tackle for the benefit of the ombudsman institution itself, but also of European citizens, of good administration, and ultimately of good governance in the EU.

6 CONCLUDING REFLECTIONS, NEITHER RETROSPECTIVE NOR PROSPECTIVE

To end this long account, I wish to go back to Cavafy's 'Ithaka', with which I started, and to repeat that I consider my ten-and-a-half years as European Ombudsman as one of the high points of my professional life. This was a long, eventful and wonderful journey, which, on the way, made me, as Cavafy puts it, wealthier with experiences and wiser with new knowledge. For that alone, I am grateful, as I am also to all those who, whether physically or mentally, shared this memorable voyage with me: my ombudsman colleagues in the European Network of Ombudsmen, Jacob Söderman who paved the way, and, above all, my staff at the European Ombudsman. Without them, my efforts would certainly have borne lesser and more meagre fruit.

10. Variations around the O-word: the European *Ombudsman* from *Médiateur* to *Garante*? Some concluding remarks[1]

Jacques Ziller

As a co-pilot, with Herwig Hofmann, of the endeavour that brought this book to the public, I had to find some way of catching the readers' attention without repeating too much of the previous chapters and without simply piling up quotations from those chapters. Concluding remarks have to be written both for the reader who starts with the end – as academics are often accustomed to do in order to get a quick idea of the content of a publication, as well as impatient readers of detective novels – and for the (normal?) readers who have scanned all that precedes.

Let me stress, first, that the idea of this book came about during the second part of Nikiforos Diamandouros' term of office, from the perspective of the then-upcoming twentieth anniversary of the creation of the European Ombudsman's office in 1995, and taking into account that the holder of the office did not have an intention to repeat what had been done in 2005 with the publication of a rather institutional type of book taking stock of the office's establishment and development.[2] Looking for another way of celebrating the anniversary – a more academic way, in the good sense of the word (i.e., with a theoretical and critical approach) – our idea was to convene a number of scholars from different disciplines who had not, for the most part, specifically published about the European Ombudsman (EO) (not the 'usual suspects' in ombudsman studies) in a workshop at the time of this twentieth anniversary. The

---

[1] This chapter, as the whole volume, is part of a publication in the framework of PRIN project 2012 (2012SAM3KM) on Codification of EU Administrative Procedures, financed by the Ministero dell'Istruzione, dell'Università e della Ricerca, Italy.

[2] European Ombudsman, *The European Ombudsman: Origins, Establishment, Evolution*, Office for Official Publications of the European Communities, 2005.

workshop took place on 22 June 2015, also in the presence of former EO Jacob Söderman and present EO Emily O'Reilly, as well as a number of members of the staff of the EO and of other institutions, bodies, offices and agencies of the European Union (EU). The future authors had submitted first drafts of what they wanted to write about and a very fruitful discussion ensued, which has had a direct impact on the content of the entire book. The time necessary for editing a collective work being what it is, we cannot call it the book of the twentieth anniversary; but, for my generation, twenty-one was the year of majority and so it is for the Office we are studying.

This book, albeit being a typically interdisciplinary product, does not, alas, include the contribution of linguists – this is entirely due to my fault. The contributions of economists, lawyers, political scientists and sociologists that are included nevertheless show how the diversity of wording in the legal and para-legal instruments relating to the EO's office and its work in the context of a EU with 24 official languages are in fact reflecting the many facets of the EO as an office with many different functions. My own education as lawyer, political scientist and – in a modest way – linguist pushes me ever more to enquire about the power of words in the multilingual context of EU law.[3]

One of the most often cited quotes about 'words' – leaving aside Shakespeare's 'words, words, words' in Hamlet – seems to be the phrase by the Maltese physician, psychologist and management guru Edward de Bono: 'In a sense, words are encyclopaedias of ignorance because they freeze perceptions at one moment in history and then insist we continue to use these frozen perceptions when we should be doing better.'[4] In full conscience of the arrogance of what I am writing, I submit that the notion of 'encyclopaedias of ignorance' applies particularly well to the word 'ombudsman'. Let us thus hope that the book reduces the breadth of this ignorance about the topic to which it is dedicated. This being said, if the first part of the quote seems to be the best way of synthesizing what I am trying to say here, the rest of de Bono's statement does not apply to our case, because far from being frozen, the meaning of 'ombudsman' is a

---

[3] See Jacques Ziller, 'Multilingualism and its Consequences in European Union Law' in Hermann-Josef Blanke, Pedro Cruz Villalón, Tonio Klein and Jacques Ziller (eds.), *Common European Legal Thinking – Essays in Honour of Albrecht Weber*, Springer, 2015, pp. 437–56.

[4] The quote, given by innumerable authors without further indication, apparently comes from: Edward De Bono, *Serious Creativity: Using the Power of Lateral Thinking to Create New Ideas*, HarperBusiness, 1993.

constantly evolving one, as fully demonstrated by the different chapters of this book.

1 OMBUDSMAN, YOU SAID *OMBUD*?

Taking full account of the multilingual nature of the EU and of its law may help understand better the EU's institutions, bodies, offices and agencies; however, it is an exercise that is only too often left aside in legal and political science scholarship, I'm afraid. By the way, it seems that even some seasoned interpreters and translators do forget[5] that the English language version of the EU Treaties is the only one – at least amongst those most in use – which uses four words where other language versions use three: *institutions, organes*, and *organismes* in French; *Organe*, *Einrichtungen*, and *sonstige Stellen* in German, etc. Typically, back when the office of European Ombudsman was introduced in the EU institutional framework by the Maastricht Treaty of 1992, differing choices were made in the different linguistic versions of the Treaty.

As far as one who has not mastered the Swedish language can understand, the original word *ombudsmän* may be best translated literally by the word 'agent' or 'delegate' or 'proxy'[6] – as a person (*män*), not as an office. Indeed, the *Riksdagens ombudsmän*, who was later embedded as an Institution of the Swedish Kingdom in the Constitution of 1809 had been appointed by Parliament (*Riksdag*) in order to investigate the actions of the King's servants and offices at a time when trust was not high between Parliament and King – this being an understatement. Scandinavian languages, which are basically Germanic languages[7] are very similar to each other and they include words that are typically not Germanic, such as, indeed, *ombud*; this means that neither the Dutch, nor the German, nor the English language – the latter being the most Latin of Germanic

---

[5] It suffices to compare different Internet pages of the EU in different languages to see how carelessly some of them are written – an exception being, for the last 20 years, the European Ombudsman's website.

[6] Interestingly, the webpage of the New Zealand Ombudsman says 'the word "Ombudsman" is Swedish and loosely translated means "grievance person", which is true as far as the global use of the word is meant, but linguistically incorrect': www.ombudsman.parliament.nz/about-us/history, consulted on 1 May 2016.

[7] Also called North Germanic languages, group of Germanic languages consisting of modern standard Danish, Swedish, Norwegian (Dano-Norwegian and New Norwegian), Icelandic, and Faroese' *Encyclopaedia Britannica*: www.britannica.com/topic/Scandinavian-languages, retrieved on 1 May 2016.

languages[8] – have a word that sounds alike *ombud*. Therefore, I submit that the ordinary citizen who does not know a Scandinavian language cannot have intuitive access to the word 'ombudsman'. Even where there is a well-established body or function with the word 'ombud' in it,[9] a good understanding of the concept cannot be but hindered by the somewhat mysterious sound of that word. True, in Sweden and Finland, where the institution of the ombudsman has existed for more than two centuries, the ordinary citizen probably has an idea of the functions of the *Justitieombudsmannen* or *Riksdagens ombudsman* that goes beyond the very abstract, and quite neutral, idea of an agent or delegate, and which includes its functions. But, the context is one of a long-established office. In Denmark, also, where it is much younger, the office has reached the age of 62.

As Denmark is at the origin of the treaty provisions of the Maastricht Treaty on the European Ombudsman, it is only logical that the Danish version of the EU Treaties says *Europæiske Ombudsmand* using the word *ombudsmand*, which is the name of the body created in that country in 1954 following the example of its Swedish predecessor. In the case of three of the eleven other Member States of 1992 a more genuine word was used on the basis of the corresponding national institution, the French *Médiateur* of 1973, the Portuguese *Provedor de Justiça* of 1975, and the Spanish *Defensor del Pueblo* of 1982 – words that are close enough to English not to need a literal translation here. There was no such office at the time of the Maastricht Treaty in Belgium, Greece and Luxembourg. In Germany and Italy, there were comparable institutions only at the regional or local level, called *Bürgerbeauftragte* (citizen's authorized representative) or *difensore civico* (citizen's defender); indeed, the same word is used in the German version of the Treaties, but the Italian version uses the word *Mediatore* – corresponding to the French institution of 1973.

In Ireland, an *Ombudsman* was established in 1980 and in the Netherlands a *Nationale Ombudsman* in 1982 – although the word *ombud* does not exist

---

[8] The French linguist Henriette Walter, having written: '*Si l'on veut caractériser la langue française, on peut dire que c'est la plus germanique des langues romanes*', in *L'aventure des langues en occident, Leur origine, leur histoire, leur géographie* (Robert Lafont, 1994, p. 225), further writes '*Grâce à cette double filiation, latine d'un côté – à travers le normand et le français – et germanique, de l'autre, l'anglais peut aujourd'hui s'offrir le luxe d'avoir le plus souvent deux mots là où les autres langues n'en ont qu'un*' (p. 382).

[9] The webpage of the Dutch National ombudsman, is very impressive with respect to *ombudsmannen* and *ombudsfunctie*, see www.nationaleombudsman.nl/, accessed 9 January 2017.

either in Dutch or English – nor does it, by the way, exist in Celtic languages like Frisian and Gaelic – and, hence, the Dutch and English version of the Treaties also use the phrase *europese/European Ombudsman*. It may be stressed, however, that whereas the UK was one of the first European countries to follow the Nordic move by establishing an *ombudsman* with its own 'Parliamentary Commissioner for Administration' of 1967, the English version of the Maastricht Treaty nevertheless used the word *ombudsman*, even though the EO was also to be elected by Parliament like its UK counterpart. Maybe one of the reasons for the choice of translation was simply that a 'European Parliamentary Commissioner for Administration' might have generated confusion amongst members of the European Commission. What would have been more important would have been to understand what kind of impact on the public the choice of words could have at the time of drafting of the relevant provisions, but it is probably too late to make an inquiry, 25 years later, about the public's perception of the word *ombudsman* in the UK – and in the other EU Member States – in the early 1980s.

With the enlargements that followed, some new language versions of the EU Treaties used the same method as the French, Portuguese and Spanish versions, taking over the name of the corresponding Member States' institution. In 1994, the Finnish *Euroopan oikeusasiamies* and the Swedish *Europeiska ombudsmannen* (not astonishingly) and, later, the Polish *Rzecznik Praw Obywatelskich* (literally, intercessor for civil rights), which is also the title of the corresponding Polish institution established in 1987, were taken up for the EO. The same happened in 2003 with the Czech *Evropský veřejný ochránce* (literally, public protector) corresponding to the Czech institution established in 2000, as well as with the Slovenian *Evropski varuh človekovih pravic* (literally, guardian of the human beings' rights) corresponding to the Slovenian institution established in 2000. Differently, however, the Estonian, Hungarian, Latvian, Lithuanian, Maltese, Slovakian, Bulgarian, Romanian and Croatian language versions all use the word *ombudsman* for the EO, albeit the corresponding national institution is not called an *ombudsman*. Thus, the language versions for those new Member States of 2004, 2007, and 2013 use the same method, in a way, that was used by the Italian translators for the Maastricht Treaty in 1991, with one big difference: *mediatore* has exactly the same meaning in common Italian language as *médiateur* in common French language, whereas *ombud* does not exist in any of the Baltic languages or in any of the Slavic languages, let alone in Romanian, which is basically a roman language, or Maltese, which has both Arabic and Italian roots.

It is not my purpose here to discuss whether the use of a somewhat mysterious Scandinavian word in other languages is justified because the concept has long since been taken over worldwide; what I want to point out is, rather, that the focus of the concept is different according to the different language versions of the EU Treaties.

In the Scandinavian wording (as, seemingly, in the Finnish one), the accent is on the idea of an 'agent' (*ombud – asiamies*) in the same way as in the German *Beauftragter* – albeit in *Bürgerbeauftragter,* the principal of that agent being clearly identified as 'the people' (*die Bürger*) and not as the Parliament. The same is true for the UK Parliamentary Commissioner for Administration, but there was a double indication in its title, namely Parliamentary and administration.

The French *Médiateur*, taken over not only in the Italian version of the Treaties, but also in the Greek one, Ευρωπαίος Διαμεσολαβητής, focuses on the function of mediation – whereas the Greek institution's name is Συνηγοροσ Του Πολιτη. In the same way, the Portuguese version focuses on the function of 'provision' – in the latter case, it is 'justice' that is provided, not 'rights' that are protected.

The Spanish version, as well as the Czech, Polish and Slovenian versions of the Treaties focus on the function of protection of rights, as does the Greek National Ombudsman's title Συνηγοροσ Του Πολιτη since its establishment in 1998. It might be noted that the French *Médiateur* was replaced by a *Protecteur des droits* (protector of rights) after a constitutional amendment in 2013; however, it clearly did not come to anybody's mind to call the institution *Ombudsman* or anything like it. Differently, in Belgium, the *Médiateur federal* is being called *Federale Ombudsman* in Dutch – not astonishingly taking into account the Netherlands *Nationale Ombudsman* – and in German *Föderale Ombudsmann*, a very odd combination from a German-language point of view. The website of the Belgian federal ombudsman contains a page dedicated to all the ombudsmen, which in French is called *Tous les ombudsmans,* albeit the French language titles of the relevant offices are all either *médiateur* or *service de médiation*, with the exception of the so called *ombudsfin* and the *Ombudsman communal d'Ixelles*.

Typically, whereas the Italian regional/local ombudsmen are usually called *difensore civico* – citizen's defender – the more recent tendency in Italy for independent administrative bodies that have a somewhat similar kind of function is to call them *Garante* (guarantor), as nowadays used in the name of the 'European Data Protection Supervisor': *Garante europeo della protezione dei dati*. If there is a difference between a protector and a guarantor, warrantor, or guardian (such as exists in the Slovenian version of the EU Treaties and for the Slovenian institution), isn't it that the latter concept extends the function beyond the protection of persons to ensuring the good functioning of the system – and a function of dispute resolution?

As a result of this panorama of language versions of the title of the EO, the question is thus: are we sure there can be a common perception of the EO in all Member States, at least at first sight, by the non-expert citizen, who by definition should be the first one to need the Ombudsman's protection?

2 A FEW QUERIES ABOUT *MALADMINISTRATION* AND *BONNE GOUVERNANCE*, PRINCIPAL–AGENT RELATIONSHIPS AND THE DIFFERENT FUNCTIONS OF THE EUROPEAN OMBUDSMAN

Nikiforos Diamandouros and Ian Harden, who write in this book on the topics 'From maladministration to good administration: retrospective reflections on a ten-year journey' and 'The European Ombudsman's role in promoting good governance', respectively, are both academics but are long-time insiders in the EO's office. They both very much emphasize how the office and function has evolved from resolving maladministration to enhancing good governance. Without repeating what they have said far better than I could ever do, I would like to stress two points here, partly of a linguistic nature.

'Maladministration' is a typically Franco-English way of expressing a phenomenon and its perception, which is not that easy to render in German: *schlechte Verwaltung* is 'bad administration', *mauvaise administration.* This being said, the word 'maladministration' is only being used in the English version of the Treaties and not – alas – in the French version, which contains the words *mauvaise administration,* whereas the word *maladministration* exists without any doubt in the French language – Turgot (1727–1781), the Finance Minister for Louis XVI, wrote '*Le Roi ne peut être coupable de maladministration*'.[10] It is a pity that maladministration is not used in roman language versions for two reasons. First the words 'bad' administration as opposed to 'good' administration generate, according to me, a too-simplistic type of perception, which might be too close to the legal dimension of legal or illegal behaviour, whereas the whole purpose of the ombudsman's way of dealing with administration is to do what judges cannot do and, hence, go beyond a strict binary perception of the phenomenon of maladministration. As demonstrated by Joana Mendes, writing on 'Discretion and law in the EU administration: where the courts

---

[10] Pierre Samuel Dupond de Nemours, *Mémoires sur la vie et les ouvrages de M. Turgot, Ministre d'État*, Philadelphia, 1788, p. 162.

do not enter', the office and functions of the EO are embedded in the legal setting of the Treaties, the Charter, and secondary law, as well as in the jurisprudence of the Court of Justice of the EU, but there is a role of the Ombudsman that goes beyond law, due to the fact that many of the legal limitations that channel the exercise of their powers by courts are not imposed upon the EO.

Second, albeit the sound is due to the combination of two different word forms (i.e., mal- and administration),[11] the dimension of illness 'malady'-*maladie* which comes out in the sound of *malad*-ministration is not so obviously present in *mauvaise administration* and, hence, the idea that not only individual disputes need to be solved, but the illness needs to be cured[12] is more remote. Clearly the Danish experience, which was at the root of the Maastricht Treaty, was very much based upon a way of functioning where the Ombudsman's function had grown well beyond simple dispute resolution to a function of diagnosis and proposals for cure, as it also had in Sweden and Finland.[13] Hence, the fact that the EO has a power of self-referral according to the Treaties themselves, different from courts that are usually limited by the need of a referral being made to them, and by the object and content of that referral, has a double meaning. The self-referral power is clearly a way to avoid the limitations of standing in a procedure (i.e., the limitation of review to the benefit of parties to the procedure) and, thus, to open access to the ombudsman to 'non-parties' – an expression that I deem clearer for non-experts than the saying 'third parties'. However, the self-referral powers go far beyond such a technical tool of opening single case reviews: self-referral is also a power

---

11 It has to be noted, however, that in English 'mal' is not a stand-alone word. It can only be used in combination with another word. Furthermore it has to be acknowledged that both the English and the French combining form 'mal-' is nuanced. It can mean bad or badly, abnormal or abnormally, inadequate or inadequately (www.merriam-webster.com/dictionary/Mal, accessed 9 January 2017) or it can mean 'to an unpleasant degree', 'faulty', 'improper', or simply 'not' (perhaps even so far as 'the opposite of' the other word): www.oxforddictionaries.com/definition/american_english/mal-, accessed 9 January 2017. What I want to underline here is the 'sound' of the word, as it may be perceived by the ordinary citizen.

12 An article in a Belgian newspaper presenting the new Belgian ombudsmen was typically entitled 'Au chevet de la maladministration': Dimitri Tonneau, La Libre Belgique on 6 December 2004. '*Au chevet*' means 'at the bedside'.

13 See Peter G. Bonnor, *The European Ombudsman, a Novel Rule-source in Community Administrative Law*, PhD thesis, Florence, European University Institute, 2001; a short version of the author's main line of research has been published in Peter G. Bonnor, 'The European Ombudsman: A Novel Source of Soft Law in the European Union', *European Law Review*, Vol. 25, No. 1, pp. 39–56, 2000.

of diagnosis and prescription that has been embedded in the functions of the EO since the beginning and has constantly been developed, as analysed not only by Diamandouros and Harden, but also, in a very thorough way, in Herwig Hofmann's introduction to this book 'The developing role of the European Ombudsman'.

The word *gouvernance* has been commonly used in francophone countries for about two decades. It took the Canadians to convince the French to use again a word that had been very much used in their language some centuries ago rather than indulge in an Anglicism, using *governance* in a French context. The fact that the word had acquired a totally new meaning was not a deterrent to its use, as the same evolution had happened in the English language. The Spanish also have their own word *gobernancia*, different from most of the other European languages, which either use the English word or a clumsy equivalent such as the German *Steuerung* (which includes the idea of guidance) in some cases. Clearly, 'governance' goes beyond 'administration', as clearly put in evidence by the same authors, Diamandouros, Harden, and Hofmann in their chapters. Article 15 of the Treaty on the Functioning of European Union (TFEU) explicitly states that '[i]n order to promote good governance and ensure the participation of civil society, the Union's institutions, bodies, offices and agencies shall conduct their work as openly as possible'. The French version uses indeed the word *gouvernance*, but the German version speaks of a *verantwortungsvolle Verwaltung* (literally, a responsible administration). The German text, thus, seems far more limited, as the word 'governance' is commonly used in a much broader sense, which includes the relationship between different institutions, offices, bodies and agencies. This being said, all language versions of Article 15 TFEU throw the spotlight on the link between transparency and good governance and, thus, the legitimacy of the EO's function as a *garante* of access to documents, even though neither the European Convention of 2002–2003 nor the succeeding Intergovernmental conferences of 2004 and 2007 used the opportunity for treaty revision in order to embed into primary law the new function that resulted from Regulation 1049/2001. As a matter of fact, the treaty makers did not either take the opportunity to embed the office of European Data Protection Supervisor resulting from Regulation 45/2001 in primary law, either. The chapter by Roberto Mastroianni, 'New perspectives for the European Ombudsman opened by the Lisbon Treaty', nevertheless demonstrates that the changes in the wording of primary law, the legally binding character of the Charter, and the new provision on the citizens' initiative, although not making fundamental changes in primary law, have a potential that has only started to be used in practice. The link I am speaking of here is even clearer if one takes into account the structure of the Charter of Fundamental Rights, in which Articles 41 on the right to good administration, 42 on access to document and 43 on the European Ombudsman are put together. The succession of those three articles probably has a rather limited significance from a strictly legal point of view. From the point of view of citizens, for whom the Charter has been written, it is, on the contrary, extremely significant. The chapter by Dacian C. Dragos and Bogdana Neamtu on 'Advancing transparency in the EU: the role of the European Ombudsman' is based on empirical evidence that shows how the link between good governance, access to documents and the European Ombudsman's office works in practice, with a number of new insights that are worthwhile to think about.

A somewhat different question is related to the word 'ombud': which principal–agent relationship are we talking of? A number of chapters of this book respond to that question. The chapter by Christine Neuhold on '"Monitoring the law and independent from politics?" The relationship between the European Ombudsman and the European Parliament' is mainly devoted to exploring the different dimensions of said question, as does the chapter by George and Takis Tridimas, even though its title does not make such a dimension immediately apparent: 'Public awareness of EU rights and the functions of the European Ombudsman: some unpleasant findings.' The assumption that I am tempted to draw from many of the empirical findings that these authors discuss is that, beyond the legal/formal relationship deriving from the EO's appointment by the European Parliament, there is another, broader, principal–agent relationship at stake, namely that of 'the public'. Certainly, reading the chapters by Harden and Diamandouros confirms this view in the most clearly possible way. The chapter by Jarle Trondal and Anchrit Wille on 'The European Ombudsman: a resilient institution in a turbulent, evolving administrative order' might, at first sight, be much further away from the issue of the principal–agent relationship, but on balance, the many facets of accountability explored by the authors could even help to develop a third type of very specific principal–agent relationship, namely that between the EO and its corresponding institutions in Member States.

There is no chapter in this book specially dedicated to the Network of Ombudsmen that was set up by EO Jacob Söderman and further developed by his successor. It suffices to look at the titles of the corresponding offices in the Member States of Central and Eastern Europe to see that their remit is less linked to maladministration than to the protection of fundamental rights as a whole. It is worthwhile to stress that not only the combination of the official titles of the EO and its counterparts in the Member States in the different languages, but more simply the text of the relevant EU primary and secondary law provisions, have been, since the beginning, the basis for a role of *médiateur* (i.e., dispute resolution as a major original function, the importance of which should not be underestimated) as well as a role of *defensor* (i.e., protection and redress). The many ways in which the European Ombudsman and its Member States' counterparts interact are an important feature of the 'Turbulent, Evolving Administrative Order' and, more generally, of the 'Turbulent, Evolving' institutional/political systems in which those institutions live, especially in times where there are questions about a common understanding of the rule of law. Such questions have, alas, gained momentum since the workshop organized for the twentieth anniversary of the European Ombudsman, especially after the elections in Poland and the assaults on some of the major institutions that are guardians of the rule of law, which have been unprecedented in recent times, even in the case of Hungary. Far beyond principal–agent relationships, the Network of Ombudsmen is based upon a peer-to-peer relationship through which offices can and should reinforce one another. The question of how best to do that is also one of the challenges that the European Ombudsman will have to face at the age of 21.

Index